Lazuri

An Endangered Language from the Black Sea

Edited by

Züleyha Ünlü
Tokat Gaziosmanpasa University, Turkey

Brian George Hewitt
*Emeritus Professor of Caucasian Languages (SOAS, London);
Fellow of the British Academy;
International Circassian Academy of Sciences, Jordan;
Abkhazian Academy of Sciences*

Series in Language and Linguistics

Copyright © 2023 by the Authors.

All rights reserved. No part of this publication may be reproduced, stored in a retrieval system, or transmitted in any form or by any means, electronic, mechanical, photocopying, recording, or otherwise, without the prior permission of Vernon Art and Science Inc.

www.vernonpress.com

In the Americas:
Vernon Press
1000 N West Street, Suite 1200
Wilmington, Delaware, 19801
United States

In the rest of the world:
Vernon Press
C/Sancti Espiritu 17,
Malaga, 29006
Spain

Series in Language and Linguistics

Library of Congress Control Number: 2022947698

ISBN: 978-1-64889-776-4

Also available: 978-1-64889-221-9 [Hardback]; 978-1-64889-664-4 [PDF, E-Book]

Product and company names mentioned in this work are the trademarks of their respective owners. While every care has been taken in preparing this work, neither the authors nor Vernon Art and Science Inc. may be held responsible for any loss or damage caused or alleged to be caused directly or indirectly by the information contained in it.

Cover design by Vernon Press. Cover image by 愚木混株 Cdd20 from Pixabay.

Every effort has been made to trace all copyright holders, but if any have been inadvertently overlooked the publisher will be pleased to include any necessary credits in any subsequent reprint or edition.

To all endangered languages
And to those who contribute to vitalise them, the treasures of the world.

Contents

List of Tables	vii
List of Figures	ix
Acknowledgements	xi
Contributors	xiii
Introduction	xix

[B.] George Hewitt
Emeritus Professor of Caucasian Languages (SOAS, London); Fellow of the British Academy; International Circassian Academy of Sciences, Jordan; Abkhazian Academy of Sciences

PREFACE Laz words, Laz worlds	xxxv

K. David Harrison
Vin University, Hanoi, Vietnam

Chapter 1	The Current Status of Laz in Turkey	1

Belma Haznedar
Boğaziçi University, Turkey

İsmail Avcı-Bucaklişi
Istanbul Laz Institute, Turkey

Chapter 2	On the Significance of Laz for Theoretical Research in Linguistics	33

Ömer Demirok
Boğaziçi University, Turkey

Balkız Öztürk
Boğaziçi University, Turkey

Chapter 3	A Spotlight on the 'Lazian' Lexis: Evidence from a 19th-Century Lexicographic Resource	63

Zaal Kikvidze
Tbilisi State University, Georgia

Levan Pachulia
Sokhumi State University, Georgia

Chapter 4	**Linguistic Variation and Complexity in Laz**	85
	Ömer Eren
University of Chicago	
Chapter 5	**Stories of Perseverance: Using the Lazuri Alboni for the Emergence of Literary Genres in a South Caucasian Endangered Language**	113
	Peri Yuksel
New Jersey City University, New Jersey, USA	
	Irfan Cağatay Aleksiva
Laz Cultural Association, Istanbul, Turkey	
Chapter 6	**Principles of Designing a New Dictionary Model for Endangered Languages: The Case of Laz**	143
	Fahrettin Şirin
Bielefeld University, Germany	
	Hanife Yaman
Tokat Gaziosmanpaşa University, Turkey	
Chapter 7	**Speaking Lazuri Beautifully: Discourses on Lazuri as an Endangered Language**	177
	Gülşah Türk-Yiğitalp
Universitat Autònoma de Barcelona, Spain	
Chapter 8	**An Applied Linguistics Perspective on the Preservation of the Laz Language**	201
	Züleyha Ünlü
Tokat Gaziosmanpaşa University, Turkey	
	Index	217

List of Tables

Table 1.1 - Gender	7
Table 1.2 - Age	7
Table 1.3 - Occupation	7
Table 1.4 - Educational background	8
Table 1.5 - Place of residence	8
Table 1.6 - Language-skills in Laz and Turkish	10
Table 2.1 - Spatial Prefixes in PL	52
Table 2.2 - The Simplex and Complex Prefixes of PL	53
Table 3.1 - English head-words and their "Lazian" translations	69
Table 3.2 - "Lazian" lexis in D. R. Peacock's collection	75
Table 3.3 - D. R. Peacock's transliteration conventions	78
Table 4.1 - Reflexivization in Laz	97
Table 4.2 - Distribution of case-markers based on semantic roles in Laz (Öztürk 2008, p. 4)	101
Table 4.3 - Partial paradigm of Comparative Case Forms (Common Kartvelian kac 'man') (Harris, 1985, p. 388)	101
Table 5.1 - Different Laz Alphabets with Equivalent IPA	123
Table 5.2 - Morphological and Lexical Differences between two Lazuri Dialects (Viçe, Ardeşen) and their Equivalent IPA transcription	126
Table 5.3 - *Regional Lazuri Dialect-affiliation of the Literary Book Authors/Translators (N=29)*	127
Table 5.4 - Lazuri Writing Rubric with Scoring Outcomes (N=56)	129
Table 5.5 - Lazuri Books by Genre Printed in Turkey from 1997 to 2021 (N=58)	130
Table 5.6 - Lazuri Poetry	130
Table 5.7 - Translations, References, Political Fiction, and Wisdom-literature in Lazuri	133
Table 5.8 - Novels, Essays, Short Stories, and Theatre in Lazuri	134
Table 5.9 - Memoirs, Autobiographies, and Interviews in Lazuri	136
Table 5.10 - Lazuri Fairy Tales and Folk Tales	137
Table 6.1 - Lexican Object Elements	166
Table 6.2 - Lexicon-entry Elements	169
Table 8.1 - Inclusion- and Exclusion-criteria	205
Table 8.2 - List of existing studies on Laz	206

List of Figures

Figure 0.1 - Laz words as documented by Hervás y Panduro (1787), with Italian and Turkish equivalents. xxxviii
Figure 0.2 - Laz words–as compared with Georgian and Mingrelian– from Peacock (1887). xxxviii
Figure 2.1 - Underlying structure of unergative verbs derived from nouns 39
Figure 2.2 - The AxPart affixes of PL 53
Figure 8.1 - Kuryakov, Y. (2002). Kartvelian: Overview [Map]. In Y. Kuryakov, *Atlas of the Caucasian Languages with Language Guide*. Moscow: Institute of Linguistics. 214
Figure 8.2 - Kuryakov, Y. (2002). Kartvelian: South-West [Map]. In Y. Kuryakov, *Atlas of the Caucasian Languages with Language Guide*. Moscow: Institute of Linguistics. 215
Figure 8.3 - Kuryakov, Y. (2002). Caucasian Languages in Turkey [Map]. In Y. Kuryakov, *Atlas of the Caucasian Languages with Language Guide*. Moscow: Institute of Linguistics. 216

Acknowledgements

The contributors of this book are the first I want to thank for working on this project despite all the difficulties life has presented to them while developing this book. I also want to thank the following people who have been of an immense help to me: Dr. Erkan Külekçi, Dr. Didem Erdel and Research Assistant Okaycan Dürükoğlu. I thank them for their continuous appreciation and for their support and encouragement in completing this project.

Contributors

Balkız Öztürk is a Professor of Linguistics at Boğaziçi University, Istanbul. She received her PhD from Harvard University in 2004. Her research interests include the interface between syntax, morphology, and the lexicon. She focuses on Altaic and South Caucasian languages. She is the author of the monograph "Case, Referentiality and Phrase Structure" and has co-edited the volumes "Exploring the Turkish Linguistic Landscape," "Morphological Complexity Within and Across Boundaries," and "Pazar Laz." Her research on Laz covers a wide range of phenomena, such as thematic suffixes and the verb classification system, valency markers, spatial markers, indexical shift and the complementizer system.

Belma Haznedar holds a PhD in Linguistics from Durham University, UK. She is currently a full Professor of Applied Linguistics at Boğaziçi University, Istanbul-Turkey. Prof. Haznedar's expertise area focuses on early childhood bilingualism, with special reference to the acquisition of morphosyntactic properties of successive and simultaneous language acquisition in children. In her recent work, she also investigates (i) literacy development in monolingual and bilingual children; (iii) adult and child immigrants with low literacy skills; (iii) heritage language maintenance, language loss and language vitality in endangered languages.

[Brian] George Hewitt was born in Doncaster (Yorkshire) in 1949 and educated at Doncaster Grammar School for Boys, from where he won a scholarship in Classics at St. John's College (Cambridge). After the Cambridge Diploma in Linguistics, he registered for a Ph.D. comparing the syntax of subordination in Ancient Greek and Old Armenian. However, after visiting a Circassian and a Ubykh village in Turkey in 1974 and then after spending the academic year 1975-76 learning Georgian in Tbilisi, where he also had theoretical instruction in Abkhaz, Avar, and Chechen, he returned to Cambridge with an Abkhazian wife and changed his thesis-topic to a comparison of subordination in Abkhaz and Georgian. He was a lecturer in Linguistics at Hull University (1981-88), securing his Cambridge doctorate in 1982, and was then transferred to SOAS (London University), where he remained until his retirement in 2015, having become Professor of Caucasian Languages in 1996. He was elected to the British Academy in 1997. First President of the (now defunct) Societas Caucasologica Europaea (1986-88 & 1988-90), he is an Honorary Member of the

International Circassian Academy of Sciences (1997-) and of the Abkhazian Academy of Sciences (1997-). His publications include: Lingua Descriptive Studies 2: Abkhaz (1979); Typology of Subordination in Georgian and Abkhaz (1987); Indigenous Languages of the Caucasus 2: North West Caucasus (1989 as editor & contributor); Georgian: a Learner's Grammar (1995); Georgian: a Structural Reference Grammar (1995); A Georgian Reader (1996); (with his wife Zaira Khiba) Abkhaz Newspaper Reader, with Supplements (1998); The Abkhazians: A Handbook (1998 as editor & contributor); Introduction to the Study of the Languages of the Caucasus (2004); Abkhaz: a Comprehensive Self-tutor (2010); Discordant Neighbours. A Reassessment of the Georgian-Abkhazian and Georgian-South Ossetian Conflicts (2013).

Fahrettin Şirin took his BA in English Language Teaching in the Department of Foreign Language Education, Faculty of Education, Middle East Technical University (METU), Ankara, Turkey. He then took his MA in Linguistics in the Department of Linguistics, Faculty of Letters, Ankara University, Ankara, Turkey. Currently, he is a PhD candidate in Germany. He worked as an English teacher in different high schools and as an instructor of English, lecturer in computer classes and as a research assistant at several universities. He also worked as a web admin editor, translator, and technical coordinator for many different projects in different institutions. Currently, he is working as a dictionary database developer and making and compiling a Turkish monolingual and a Turkish-English-Turkish bilingual dictionary.

Hanife Yaman was born in 1989 in Ardeşen. In 2011, she completed her undergraduate education at Ordu University, Faculty of Arts and Sciences, Department of Turkish Language and Literature. In the same year, she started her graduate studies at Ordu University, Institute of Social Sciences, Department of Turkish Language and Literature. She defended her master's thesis entitled *Verb valence in Azerbaijani Turkish* in 2013. Currently, she is studying for a doctorate in education at Ondokuz Mayıs University, Institute of Social Sciences, Department of Turkish Language and Literature. She has also been working as a lecturer in the Department of Turkish Language and Literature at Tokat Gaziosmanpaşa University since 2014.

İrfan Çağatay Aleksiva was born in Ardeşen/Rize in 1981. He studied Turkish Language and Literature at Marmara University, Faculty of Letters, between 2002 and 2006. He has taken active roles in the movement of protecting Laz culture since 2002. Also, he has been active in fieldwork for lexicographic collections since he was twelve years old. In 2007, he co-authored the expanded version of the Laz-Turkish dictionary (Uzunhasanoğlu, Bucaklişi & Cağatay Aleksiva, 2007). Cağatay published his toponymic collection under the title Svacoxo, Laz Toponymic Dictionary (Bucaklisi & Cagatay, 2009) to spread awareness about one of the most salient elements of the vanishing Laz heritage- the loss of original Laz place names. He worked as a writer and editor for various Laz magazines and periodicals (e.g., Skani Nena, Tanura, Ağani Murutsxi, Ogni, Uncire).

İsmail Bucaklişi was born in 1970 in Noxlapsu in the Pazar town of the province of Rize in Turkey. He established the first-ever Laz youth group at the university in 1989 and started conducting research on the Laz people. In 1993, he became one of the founders of OGNİ, the first Laz culture periodical in Turkey, in which he wrote articles. In 1993 he started working on collecting words and writing the first Laz dictionary in Turkey. The dictionary was published in 1999 with the inclusion of a co-author. He is the co-author of the Laz Grammar Book, which was published in 2003 (Kojima & Bucaklişi, 2003). He is the first author of the Great Laz Dictionary, published in 2007 (Bucaklişi, Uzunhasanoğlu & Aleksiva, 2007), which is the most extensive dictionary of the Laz language to date. In 2003, he started his collection work for Svacoxo – Laz Toponymic Dictionary, which listed the original Laz names of villages and places and was published in 2009 (Aleksiva & Bucaklişi, 2009). He wrote and published a Laz study book in 2014 in order to facilitate the learning of Laz. He shot online Laz learning videos composed of 14 units, which are available on YouTube. In addition, Bucaklişi is the author of a book on the life and poems of the Laz poet Hasan Helimişi (Mu Pat E Skiri, 2006) and the Laz Alphabet-Lazuri Alboni (2013). He established and became the editor-in-chief of the Laz periodicals named Mjora (2000), Skani Nena (2008), and Tanura (2011). İsmail Avcı Bucaklişi is the author of four Laz study books prepared for the Turkish Ministry of Education, which are currently used for the elective Laz lessons in the years 6-8 of secondary schools (Lazuri 5; 2014, Lazuri 6, 2015; Lazuri 7, 2017; Lazuri 8, 2018). In 2018, he initiated the "Training of Instructors of the Laz language" and organised a number of pieces of training, by which he has created the foundations for the Laz language education in Turkey. He led the establishment of the Lazika Yayın Kollektifi (Lazika Publishing Collective) in 2011, which to date published more than 80 books, the majority of which are in the Laz language. Additionally, he is the editor of more than 100 books. Bucaklişi led the establishment of Laz Kültür Derneği (Laz Cultural Association) in 2008 and the Laz Enstitüsü (Laz Institute) in 2013 and became a board member in both. He is currently the chairman of the Laz Institute. He initiated the EU-funded projects titled "Mother-tongue based Multilingual

Education" (2016) and "Network of Laz and Circassian Civil Societies" (2020) within the Laz Institute. He led the establishment of TADNET- Tehlike Altındaki Diller Ağı (Endangered Languages Network) in 2020, in which the NGOs and activists of 12 different endangered languages in Turkey came together for the first time ever. He is working towards finalising a study on the Intangible Laz Cultural Heritage, which he started in 1990. To date, he has collected and recorded a large pool of materials on the Laz music, dance, tales, epics, craft, customs, and other materials related to the Laz folklore. He has acted as an informant and consultant to academics working on the Laz language. Bucaklişi, who has devoted his life to the survival of the Laz language, has opened courses to teach Laz on different platforms. He has been teaching the Laz language as an elective lesson at Boğaziçi University since 2011 and at İstanbul Bilgi University since 2015.

Gülşah Türk-Yiğitalp is a second-year PhD candidate in English Studies at Universitat Autònoma de Barcelona. Her PhD project deals with issues of mobility, temporality, and belonging through a critical sociolinguistic ethnography of language-in-education policies for Syrian refugee students in Turkish public schools. Her main research interests include minoritized languages in Turkey, language ideologies, and language policy. She holds a BA in English Language and Literature from Hacettepe University and MA in Humanities and Social Sciences from Yıldız Technical University, where she wrote her thesis on the language ideologies of Lazuri speakers. She has another MA in Nationalism Studies from the Central European University, where she worked on the discourse of education policies for Syrian refugee students in Turkey.

K. David Harrison is an anthropologist, linguist, and National Geographic Explorer documenting endangered languages and cultures around the world. He has done collaborative fieldwork with indigenous communities in Siberia, Mongolia, India, and Vanuatu. He was featured in the acclaimed documentary film *The Linguists*, and his work has been covered by The New York Times, The Economist, USA Today, and Science. David is Professor and Vice Provost of Academic Affairs at VinUniversity in Hanoi, Vietnam, and is a fellow of the Explorers Club.

Levan Pachulia is Associate Professor at the Faculty of Humanities, Sokhumi State University, where his scholarship and courses concentrate on the Kartvelian languages. He has published books on methods in linguistics research and comparative linguistics and papers on various aspects of the structures of the Kartvelian languages, with particular reference to Megrelian and Laz. For years, he has been a visiting professor at Akaki Tesereteli State University, Georgia.

Ömer Demirok is an Assistant Professor in the Department of Linguistics at Boğaziçi University, Istanbul. He received his PhD in Linguistics from the Massachusetts Institute of Technology in 2019. His primary research interests include syntax, formal semantics, morphology, and their interfaces. He has done fieldwork on the Pazar (At'ina) dialect of Laz and on Georgian heritage varieties spoken in Turkey. His research on Laz covers various topics such as case marking, agreement, valency marking, root allomorphy, indexical shift, complementizers, logophoricity, and modality.

Ömer Eren is a PhD candidate in the Linguistics Department at The University of Chicago. He holds an MA from Boğaziçi University in Turkey (2017). The primary focus of his work is on morphology, syntax, and their interface in Turkic and Caucasian languages. He is mainly interested in the structure of nominals and spatial constructions. He is also currently working on language contact, endangerment and linguistic variation, specifically focusing on Laz. His dissertation project aims to investigate the current state of the Laz grammar as spoken by different generations in terms of their morphosyntactic properties, which involve valency-changing operations and the distribution of case & agreement as well as imperfective aspect markers.

Peri Yüksel earned her Ph.D. in Human Development from The Graduate School and University Center of the City University of New York. She received the Isenberg Award in recognition of her language documentation, which helped in the publication and distribution of two children's books in the endangered Laz language. As a tenured Associate Professor in the Psychology Department at New Jersey City University (NJCU), she teaches undergraduate courses (cross-cultural psychology, psychopathology, lifespan), graduate courses (research methods, developmental psychology), and designs and assesses faculty-led trips abroad. Dr. Yüksel's research concerns bilingual language development and effective teaching and learning environments that facilitate student success and engagement in psychological literacy and global citizenship. Dr. Yüksel published in the field of psycholinguistics, scholarship of teaching and learning, and international education, and always encourages her students to conduct research for peer review. Dr. Yüksel chairs the Annual NJCU Pedagogy Day, serves in the NJCU's Honors Program, and the

Institutional Review Board, and is part of the advisory board for the Frank Guarini Institute for International Studies.

Zaal Kikvidze, *Professor Dr.hab.,* is a senior research fellow at the Arnold Chikobava Institute of Linguistics, Ivane Javakhishvili Tbilisi State University. His research interests include Kartvelian languages, sociolinguistics, language and gender, cognitive linguistics, lexicography and so forth. His latest publication is *A Glossary of Sociolinguistics Terms* (2021). He has taught linguistics at various universities both in Georgia and abroad (Germany, Italy, Sweden and so forth).

Züleyha Ünlü currently works as an Assistant Professor at the English Language and Literature Department of Tokat Gaziosmanpasa University in Turkey. Following her MS. Ed in TESOL at the University of Pennsylvania, USA, with full funding from the Ministry of Turkish National Education, Dr. Ünlü has specialised in classroom feedback practices on academic writing as well as qualitative research, with a particular focus on Grounded Theory, during her PhD at the University of Warwick in the UK. Her main research interests are Reflective Practice, Classroom Discourse in EAP and ELT settings, Professional and Academic Discourse, and Grounded Theory Methodology. However, her learning background at the University of Pennsylvania, particularly through the Sociolinguistics and Classroom Discourse courses, focused on diversity, heritage languages, and minority languages in mainstream education, which led her to work on endangered languages as well. She has taught linguistics, applied linguistics, language skills, and language teaching methods courses since she began her teaching career at Tokat Gaziosmanpaşa University.

Introduction

[B.] George Hewitt[1]

Emeritus Professor of Caucasian Languages (SOAS, London); Fellow of the British Academy; International Circassian Academy of Sciences, Jordan; Abkhazian Academy of Sciences

In an Introduction to a monograph or, as here, a collection of individually authored chapters around a broad theme, readers might expect to be presented with some form of a summary of the contents and/or the context behind, or the reasons for, the composition of the work. However, as the eight chapters are summarised in exemplary fashion by K. David Harrison in his *Preface* under the sub-headings: Laz-endangerment and recovery; Laz linguistics and lexicography; Laz linguistic ecology; Laz environmental linguistics; and Valuing Laz, I shall not address the single contributions but shall rather take this opportunity to talk somewhat more generally about Laz studies in the context of research on the language-family to which it belongs, touching upon a relevant issue in this or that article where it is appropriate to do so – I hope that any anticipatory reduplication of material later presented in the body of the work will be forgiven. I would just stress at the outset how valuable it is to have the results of the surveys which (a) lay out the current situation in which Laz finds itself (Haznedar & Bucaklişi) and (b) indicate both how speakers assess their own and others' competence in the language and when they feel it appropriate to speak it (Türk-Yiğitalp). Editor Ünlü's discussion of the need to co-opt the expertise of applied linguists when it comes to framing methods of teaching Laz is instructive and was much appreciated by this non-applied linguist.

So, the South Caucasian[2] language-family, which has not been demonstrated to be genetically related to any other, is comprised of Georgian, Mingrelian, Laz and Svan. At least this is the accepted opinion outside Georgia, where a widespread view holds that Mingrelian and Laz should rather be regarded as

---

[1] I thank Eylem Bostancı of the Laz Institute for reading this Introduction and supplying supplementary material, now incorporated.

[2] Otherwise widely known among caucasologists as 'Kartvelian' (from Georgian *kartvel-i* 'Georgian (person),' an association which results in the Laz preferring the term 'South Caucasian.'

co-dialects of the so-called Zan[3] language. Generally speaking, the family's areal distribution has always been confined to western Transcaucasia (or the South Caucasus, as the politically correct would have it), mostly concentrated in today's Georgia, and north-eastern Turkey. A Laz-Mingrelian dialect-continuum along the Black Sea littoral is assumed to have been fractured as christian Georgian speakers moved westwards during the five centuries of the Arab presence in, and indeed domination of, central Georgia from the mid-7th to the early 12th century.[4] This left the Mingrelian language (*margal-ur-i nina* in Mingrelian)[5] spoken in the lowlands of western Georgia, bounded by Abkhazia (located in N.W. Transcaucasia) to the north-west, Svaneti(a) to the north, Georgian-speaking Lechkhum-Imereti(a) to the (north-)east, and, more pertinently for the topic of the present volume, divided from the Laz homeland (along the coast and in hinterland-regions from Sarpi to Rize) by the Georgian-speaking provinces of Guria and Ach'ara (*aka* Adzharia) to the south. A further divide was introduced on 13 October 1921 when by the Treaty of Kars, which established the frontier between Turkey and the Transcaucasian republics of what became the Soviet Union (most relevantly, Soviet Georgia), the majority of Laz speakers found themselves on the Turkish side of the border, cut off from the small number of fellow speakers mostly located in/around the split village of Sarpi on the Soviet side[6] – a few Laz also resided in Abkhazia.

Since Laz and Mingrelian are the only two South Caucasian tongues between which there exists a degree of mutual intelligibility, the question always arises as to the extent to which any statement about the one might also be applicable to the other. And this is surely a thought that is likely to be in the mind of at least some readers as they wend their way through this work, just as it certainly was in mine, though one cannot but wonder how much awareness/knowledge of, or (dare one say?) interest in, each other actually exists in the two speech-communities based in Lazistan/Turkey, on the one hand, and Mingrelia/Georgia, on the other. Therefore, I have judged it to be a reasonable (and

---

[3] Cf. Svan *zän* 'Mingrelia' and *zan-är* 'Mingrelians.'
[4] An Emirate existed in Tbilisi from 736 to 853.
[5] Some commentators prefer the form 'Megrelian' (from the Georgian [sic] *megrel-i* 'Mingrelian (person)'), though, oddly, none has thus far chosen to create an English calque 'Margalian' from the Mingrelians' self-designation, viz. *margal-i* 'Mingrelian (person).'
[6] Also assigned to Turkey were the ancient Georgian-speaking provinces of T'ao, K'lardzheti and Shavsheti, though the number of Georgians (in particular speakers of Georgian) in Turkey today is unknown but not thought to be large.

Introduction xxi

hopefully acceptable) approach to adopt to refer in these introductory remarks to relevant parallels in the light of issues raised in the contributions below.

The obvious starting-point is to observe that, whilst Georgian has a writing-tradition that stretches back over a millennium and a half, the three remaining South Caucasian languages have essentially been unwritten, and all three have the dubious status of being labelled by UNESCO as endangered. Though there are estimates of how many speakers each can boast, there are no official figures, because within Georgia Mingrelians and the few Laz (plus the Svans) are classified as 'Georgians,' whereas in Turkey the Laz are categorised as 'Turks.' Furthermore, in Georgia there has been no official teaching of Mingrelian, Laz or Svan,[7] whilst in Turkey minority-languages have, until relatively recently, been ignored/actively discouraged, especially since the founding of the Republic, with the result that the majoritarian languages (Georgian and Turkish) have naturally gained ground at the expense of those spoken by the various minorities. This state of affairs, of course, lies at the very heart of this book and indeed motivated its composition. One of those whose work is referenced here is the indefatigable champion of the rights of the Laz and Mingrelian peoples and their languages, the German Wolfgang Feurstein. And his 1992 article *Mingrelisch, Lazisch, Swanisch. Alte Sprachen und Kulturen der Kolchis vor dem baldigen Untergang* can serve as a useful introduction to the parallel destinies that have been played out on each side of the Turko-(Soviet) Georgian border. Moreover, it may be pertinent to add at this point that neither Georgia nor Turkey has signed (much less ratified) the *European Charter for Regional or Minority Languages*, adopted in 1992 under the auspices of the Council of Europe.

Colchis was the name assigned by the Greeks and Romans to a geographically amorphous area of the western Transcaucasus and is popularly best known from fable as the destination of Jason and the Argonauts' voyage in search of the legendary Golden Fleece. From the beginning of the 1st millennium of the christian era the toponym Lazica came to be associated with (parts of) the Black

---

[7] An anonymous reviewer has stated that there is apparently teaching of Mingrelian at high-school level in both Tbilisi and Kutaisi. As for Laz tuition in Turkey, İsmail Bucaklişi (Director of the Laz Institute) has reported that Laz has the status of an elective course and can be taught for two hours per week in schools. Course-materials exist, and Laz teacher-training sessions have been conducted twice thus far in accordance with the protocol signed with the Ministry of National Education. Also, there are 15 teachers who can teach Laz. Compared to previous years, the number of Laz learners at schools has recently fallen.

Sea's eastern littoral and features in the writings of the 6th-century historians Procopius of Cæsarea and Agathias Scholasticus.[8] This, then, provides two thousand years of testimony for linking the root *laz-* to this general area, the people being then known in Greek as *Lazoí*.

But what of the language itself? In Laz we have the name *laz-ur-i nena* 'Laz language.'[9] However, in Georgia at least there is an alternative designation, seen in the phrase *ch'an-ur-i ena* 'Laz language', the term being avoided in Turkey because of another unfortunate meaning of the root *ch'an-*, namely 'impotent' (Kadzhaia 2001-2). As for the dominant root *laz-*, its origins, despite much speculation, are unknown – for a discussion see Hewitt (2014).

Despite some earlier collections of words and phrases, it was really only in the 19th century that philologists started to pay serious attention to the linguistic treasure-store that is the Caucasus, and Laz was actually one of the first to become on object of scholarly study[10] when the German Georg Rosen published a 38-page description in 1844 entitled *Über die Sprache der Lazen*.[11] The vocabulary-gathering tradition of such early visitors to the Caucasus as the Germans Johann Güldenstädt (1787) and Julius von Klaproth (1814; 1823) was carried on by the Russian-born British diplomat Demetrius Peacock, whose lexical study of five West Caucasian languages (Georgian, Mingrelian, Laz, Svan, and Abkhaz) in 1887 provides the only contribution to this book to come from scholars based in Georgia, Zaal Kikvidze and Levan Pachulia, who discuss the author together with his treatment of his Laz material in chapter III.

But it was 1910 which could be said to be the year that saw the grammatical study of Laz really take off when the St. Petersburg-based, Scottish-Georgian scholar Nikolaj (Nik'o) Marr published his *Grammatika Chanskago (Lazskago)*

---

[8] For a short description of the Lazic War see Bury (1958, vol. II, 113-123).

[9] For the sake of comparison and completeness, note that Georgian for 'Georgian language' is *kart-ul-i ena*, whilst Svan has *lu-shn-u nin* for 'Svan language.'

[10] French orientalist Marie Félicité Brosset Jeune (1802-1880), member of the St. Petersburg Academy from 1836 and resident in Russia from 1837, had produced a grammar of Georgian (*L'art libéral ou Grammaire géorgien*) in 1834, in which he expressed the (mistaken) view that Georgian belonged to the Indo-Iranian branch of the Indo-European family – because of the large number of Persian loans, precisely the same misinterpretation was applied to Armenian until Heinrich Hübschmann finally demonstrated that Armenian, though Indo-European, formed a separate branch within the family.

[11] Rosen followed this in 1846 with 84 pages on (Iranian) Ossetic (43 pages), Mingrelian (9 pages), Svan (13 pages) and Abkhaz (12 pages), all studied *in situ* in his *Ossetische Sprachlehre nebst einer Abhandlung über das Mingrelische, Suanische und Abchasische*.

Jazyka s Xrestomatieju i Slovarem 'Grammar of the Ch'an (Laz) Language with Chrestomathy and Dictionary' – this same year also saw the appearance of Marr's article *Iz poezdki v Turetskij Lazistan* 'From a Journey to Turkish Lazistan,' the Turkish translation of which, namely *Lazistan'a Yolculuk*, came out in 2016.[12] Georgian graduate of Marr's Oriental Faculty, Ioseb Q'ipshidze, published in the year of his graduation (1911) a supplement to his professor's grammar in his *Dopolnitel'nyja Svedenija O Chanskom" Jazyke (Iz" Lingvisticheskoj Èkskursii v" Russkij Lazistan"* 'Supplementary Reports on the Ch'an Language (From a Linguistic Excursion to Russian Lazistan).' He went on to produce his impressive *Grammatika Mingrel'skago (Iverskago) Jazyka s" Xrestomatieju i Slovarem"* 'Grammar of the Mingrelian (Iberian) Language with Chrestomathy and Dictionary' in 1914 – both of these important works were reprinted in one volume in 1994. Given what was to follow, it is ironic to note that, with the publication of these works by Marr and his pupil, Laz and Mingrelian were the best described (sc. according to contemporary philological/linguistic standards) of the four South Caucasian languages. Q'ipshidze also put together a selection of Laz texts, but the resulting book (*ch'anuri t'ekst'ebi*) only saw the light of day in Tbilisi in 1939, twenty years after the compiler's death in 1919 from Spotted Typhus at the tragically early age of circa 35.[13] One early beneficiary of this output from Marr and Q'ipshidze was the distinguished German kartvelologist, Gerhard Deeters, who mined their works for the Laz and Mingrelian materials he included in his seminal comparison of the verbal systems across all four South Caucasian languages *Das kharthwelische Verbum* (1930).

What then needs to be highlighted about developments following the fixing of the Turkish-(Soviet) Georgian border in 1921? I believe it is fair to say (though I stand to be corrected) that, until the stirrings of the revivalist-movement in Turkey in the 1980s, there were only two substantial works to appear as a result of study carried out in Turkey, and both emanated from the pen of the indomitable investigator of Caucasian languages spoken in Turkey, namely the French scholar Georges Dumézil, being published in Paris. First came his *Contes Lazes* in 1937, representing the Arhavi dialect spoken by informant Niazi

---

[12] 1910 also saw the publication of Ivane Nizharadze's substantial *Russko-Svanskij Slovar'* 'Russian-Svan Dictionary,' which had been preceded in 1902 by Nizharadze's collection of Svan texts. Marr's original Russian text was re-published in Tbilisi by Artanuji Press in 2021 in a volume which first presents the work's translation into Georgian. The book is entitled *Nik'o Mari: Lazeti; Nikolaj Marr: Lazistan.*

[13] There was some doubt about the precise year of his birth.

Ban and recorded in Istanbul in 1930-31. Dumézil's *Récits Lazes (en dialecte d'Arhavi (parler de Şenköy))* appeared in 1967. In addition to the tales, registered in Istanbul between 1960 and 1964, this volume also contains a short grammar, as was Dumézil's wont.

Across the border in Georgia the collection and publication of texts continued. Arnold Chikobava (1898-1985), a Mingrelian, who founded and headed until his death the Caucasian Languages' Department at the Georgian Academy of Sciences, first produced his *Ch'anuri T'ekst'ebi. Nak'veti P'irveli. Xopuri K'ilok'avi* 'Ch'an Texts. First Part. Khopa Dialect' in 1929. This was followed in 1936 by his *Ch'anuris Gramat'ik'uli Analizi (T'ekst'ebiturt)* 'Grammatical Analysis of Ch'an (with Texts)' in 1936, whilst his third major contribution was the *Ch'anur-Megrul-Kartuli Shedarebiti Leksik'oni* 'Ch'an-Mingrelian-Georgian Comparative Dictionary' in 1938. This same year Sergi Zhghent'i published his *Ch'anuri T'ekst'ebi. Arkabuli K'ilok'avi* 'Ch'an Texts. Arkabe Dialect.'[14] He then delved into the phonetics with his study *Ch'anur-Megrulis Ponet'ik'a* 'Phonetics of Ch'an-Mingrelian' in 1953.

The business of collecting and publishing Laz materials was then taken up by younger researchers. To the pen of Irine Asatiani, who recently died just short of her 100th birthday, belongs *Ch'anuri (Lazuri) T'ekst'ebi. I. Xopuri K'ilok'avi* 'Ch'an (Laz) Texts. I. Khopa Dialect' (1974). Her Laz dictionary, which I have yet to see, appeared in 2012. Guram K'art'ozia (b. 1934) has compiled two collections: *Lazuri T'ekst'ebi* 'Laz Texts' (1972) and *Lazuri T'ekst'ebi II* 'Laz Texts II' (1993). One might also add Zurab Tandilava's *Lazuri Xalxuri P'oezia* 'Laz Folk-poetry' of 1972. Worth noting too, in my opinion, is Irine Asatiani's Candidate's Dissertation (1953) as outlined in the accompanying *avtoreferat* (or dissertation-summary), for the topic was *Preverby v Zanskom (Megrel'sko-Chanskom) Jazyke* 'Preverbs in the Zan (Mingrelo-Ch'an) Language'.

These works happen to be relevant to themes aired in this book for the following reasons. Eren in chapter IV examines a case of dialect-variation, advancing the interesting argument that simplification in one area of grammar can lead to greater complexity elsewhere, whilst Yüksel & Aleksiva in chapter V *inter alia* very helpfully list and describe the 58 publications in Laz that have been composed since the start of publishing in Turkey in 1997 as part of the

---

[14] This tragic decade also witnessed the publication of a volume of Svan poetry (*Svanuri P'oezia*) in 1939 and the first volume (of four) of Svan prose-texts in the Upper Bal dialect (*Svanuri P'rozauli T'ekst'ebi, I. Balszemouri K'ilo*), also in 1939. Two years earlier Mak'ar Khubua's *Megruli T'ekst'ebi* 'Mingrelian Texts' had also come out.

Introduction

revitalisation-movement[15]. But as is clear from what has been said, there exists in print a wealth of texts garnered over the course of more than a century such that burrowing into them might well provide researchers with a wide range of source-material for potentially turning up many more examples of both language-change and dialectal variation.

As part of their argument that the structure of Laz is of importance for the general linguist, Demirok & Öztürk in chapter II highlight the spatial markers seen in the preverbal system. It would be interesting at some point in the future to learn the authors' opinions about the Laz preverbal system in comparison with that of Mingrelian once they take into consideration not only the observations of Asatiani (assuming her oeuvre could be made available to them) and others who have worked on Mingrelian[16] but also the opinion that both these languages were most probably once influenced by the well-known extensive system of spatio-directional preverbs in the neighbouring North-West Caucasian languages (with special reference to Abkhaz). Demirok & Öztürk also raise the issue of ergativity/activity during their discussion of the case-system of Laz. Here again there might be fruitful possibilities of widening the significance of the Laz patterns by looking at Mingrelian (and Georgian, with reference to which ergativity vs activity has been a topic of debate).[17]

Şirin & Yaman present a template for the production of an idealised dictionary (not exclusively for Laz) suitable for the digital age, noting near the start of chapter VI: 'The Laz dictionaries produced so far are unsatisfactory for many reasons: for their usability and reliability, their lexicographic standards,

---

[15] Indeed, the Laz Institute confirms that, with the establishment of the Lazika Publication Collective in 2011, at least 100 Laz books have been published in Turkey to date, half of which are in the Laz language, and there are at least 10 more books in Laz awaiting publication by the Lazika Publication Collective and the Laz Institute.

[16] Might I mention in this regard the appendix on 'Kartvelian Preverbs' that I appended to my *Introduction to the Study of the Languages of the Caucasus* (Lincom 2004, pp. 284-315)?

[17] See relevant sections in my articles: *Georgian - Ergative or Active?*, in *Lingua Studies in Ergativity* (special edition edited by R M W Dixon), 1987, pp. 319-340; *Review-article of Syntax and Semantics 18: A. C. Harris 'Diachronic Syntax: The Kartvelian Case,'* in *Revue des Etudes Géorgiennes et Caucasiennes, 3,* 1989, pp. 173-213; *Georgian: Ergative, Active, or What?*, in *Subject, Voice and Ergativity* (ed. D. C. Bennett, T. Bynon, B.G. Hewitt), 1995, SOAS, pp. 202-217; *Similarities and Differences: some verbal contrasts between Georgian and Mingrelian,* in *Chomolangma, Demawend und Kasbek. Festschrift for R. Bielmeier,* 2008, pp. 657-676).

structural organization, content, design and corpus-usage, while also failing to provide many lexicographic requirements and industry-standards.' One imagines that much time and many resources will be necessary if one is to satisfy the standards set by the authors. Were an aspiring lexicographer to aim at improving existing models but at a more modest level, one wonders if any of the approaches adopted for the sister-languages would meet the needs of everyday-users. I have in mind the following templates: (a) for Georgian, Kita Tschenkéli's root-dictionary (*Georgisch-Deutsches Wörterbuch*, Zürich, 1965-74), where all relevant verb-parts are given beneath the root, or the Georgian Academy's 8-volume 'Explanatory Dictionary of the Georgian Language' (*Kartuli Enis Ganmart'ebiti Leksik'oni*, Tbilisi, 1950-64), where a verb is entered in either the 3rd person Present or 3rd person Future singular accompanied by its, as it were, 'principal parts,' viz. (Future), Aorist and Perfect – the 'masdar' (= verbal noun) and participles are assigned their own entries, a pattern largely followed by Donald Rayfield's 2-volume *A Comprehensive Georgian-English Dictionary* (London, 2006), though alongside the verbal noun he repeats the principal finite tense-forms, and (b) for Mingrelian, whose verbs were entered by Q'ipshidze (1914) as a root, accompanied by a selection of finite and derived forms, whilst Otar Kadzhaia in his *Megruli Enis Leksik'oni* 'Dictionary of the Mingrelian Language' (in 3 volumes, 2001-2002) basically did the same as Q'ipshidze but used the verbal noun as the basic entry-form. Despite the unavoidable reduplication inherent in the approach, my own preference lies with the practice adopted by the Georgian Academy and Rayfield.

There is a host of material on, or related to, Laz(-Mingrelian) written in Georgian in the form of books or articles too numerous to be listed here, though perhaps I could single out two volumes by Iuri Sikharulidze, namely *Ch'aneti (Lazeti). Saist'orio Geograpiis Masalebi* 'Lazistan. Historical Geography Materials' (Batumi, vol. 1 1977; vol. 2 1979), as well as the monumental *Lazur-Megruli Gramat'ik'a. I. Morpologia* 'Grammar of Laz-Mingrelian. I. Morpholoy' (2015) by Ch'abuk'i Kiria, Lali Ezugbaia, Omar Memishishi, and Merab Chukhua. Other useful information on Laz(-Mingrelian) can be located scattered in such series dedicated to language-research as *Iberiul-k'avk'asiuri Enatmetsniereba* 'Ibero-Caucasian Linguistics' (from 1946-), the sadly defunct *Ts'elits'deuli Iberiul-K'avk'asiuri Enatmetsnierebisa* 'Annual of Ibero-Caucasian Linguistics' (1974-1994), and the language-series of the once-quarterly *Matsne* 'Reporter', the resurrection of which is apparently planned from the spring of 2022. Some specific references are given in the bibliographies of the following works, which are of course indispensible contributions to Laz/South Caucasian studies in their own right: Holisky (1991), Feurstein (1992), and Boeder (2005). The various studies of Laz produced by the Westerners Ralph D. Anderson,

Ulrich Lüders and René Lacroix will, no doubt, be too well known to all interested in the language to need specific mention at this point in the book.

Of course, it is only natural that Laz together with the other two minority South Caucasian languages (Mingrelian and Svan) should have been studied by linguists, folklorists and lexicographers based at the Georgian Academy of Sciences' Department of Caucasian Languages or at Tbilisi State University over the decades since these institutions were founded, leading to grammatical studies of various kinds, collections of folk-tales, and lexicological investigations. Nor is it surprising that Laz, as one of the 'exotic' languages of the Caucasus, should have attracted the attention of Western linguists from the very start of philological interest in languages outside the well-known members of the Indo-European family. But more extraordinary is the creation of scripts for previously unwritten tongues, and so we have to examine what happened in the early years of the Soviet Union, with particular focus on Laz, part of the topic of Yüksel & Aleksiva's contribution in chapter VI, to which I now turn.

One major task (among many) for the young Soviet state was to eradicate the high level of illiteracy inherited from tsarist times. In order to help with this, several languages were selected for the award of literary status and became collectively known as the 'Young Written Languages', these literary forms to be used for teaching in schools in their associated autonomous regions. Where there was a history (at some level at least) of a tradition of writing, the relevant orthography tended initially to be adopted, being used for both teaching and the production of printed materials.[18] Where no such tradition existed, scripts were devised. And Laz was one of the languages to be so treated despite the paucity of speakers living within the USSR. As to why poorly represented languages should have been supported at all, there are conflicting views –it may have been simple altruism endowing these languages with a crucial role in the drive to eradicate illiterary. Wixman (1980: 126ff.), on the other hand, with reference to the Caucasus as a whole, sees here a desire on Moscow's part to win approval for Communism's generosity to these peoples from the often large numbers of representatives of these same ethnic groups living abroad (for instance, in Turkey). Here is what Wixman writes: 'One of the groups obviously supported for this reason was the Laz, the bulk of whose population was in eastern Turkey. Although in 1926 the Laz population of the entire Soviet Union was only 645 individuals, a Laz literary language was established in 1927 (using

---

[18] This, for example, was the case with the Arabic-based script for Circassian in the North Caucasus, and A. Ch'och'ua's Cyrillic-based script for Abkhaz in Georgia.

the Latin[19] alphabet) and they were declared a narodnost. By 1938 this folly was dropped, and the Laz were reclassified as an ethnographic group of Georgians.' Feurstein (1992: 299ff.), who numbered the Soviet Laz population at that time as 'no more than 2,000,' then takes the story on, first to the appearance of Iskender Citaši's daily-paper *Mčita Murucxi*[20] 'Red Star', which was born on 1 November 1929 but which ceased publication after only two issues, as well as to the publication in 1935 of Citaši's Laz school-primer for the 1st class *Alboni* 'Alphabet', whose significance is highlighted in chapter VI. The year 1938 saw not only the end of the Soviets' Laz experiment but also the demise of its champion Citaši, who perished in Stalin's 'purges.'

Wixman drew a comparison with the Mingrelians, writing as follows: 'A prime example of a people that did not receive support as a distinct ethnic group are the Mingrelians. The case of the Mingrelians should be compared with that of the other Caucasian peoples (Circassians, Abaza, Abkhaz, and Kurds) that receive 'ethnic support.' Although (1) the population of the Mingrelians in 1926 was almost one quarter million; (2) they had a distinct language, history, and culture; and (3) lived in a compact territory (satisfying all criteria under Salin's definition of a nation), they received no ethnic territory nor ethnic institutions in their own language. This can be explained by: (1) they posed no threat to the regime, given their small population and location away from any sensitive zones; (2) there was no need to create a separate Mingrelian literary language as virtually all Mingrelians were fluent in Georgian; and (3) there are no Mingrelian communities living outside the USSR. There simply was no reason to support the Mingrelians' (*ibid.*). In fact, it was not true to say of Mingrelians of that period that they were all fluent in Georgian. Also a leading Mingrelian at the time, Ishak' Zhvania, was in favour of their being gifted cultural autonomy, and there were publications, employing the Georgian script (plus two extra characters needed representing non-Georgian sounds). Take the example of the daily newspaper – from 1 March 1930 to 20 December 1935 the *Q'azaxiši Gazeti* 'Peasant's Paper,' was published in Zugdidi. This was continued from 1 January 1936 to 22 July 1938 by *K'omunari* 'Man of the Commune,' which was half in Mingrelian, half in Georgian. This development from wholly Mingrelian, through joint Mingrelian and Georgian, to the wholly Georgian *Mebrdzoli* 'Warrior,' which remained as the only local paper for Zugdidi, would seem to suggest that knowledge of Georgian amongst the population of Mingrelia's capital was not as secure or as widespread as was perhaps popularly believed

---

[19] *Recte* roman – BGH.
[20] [mtʃ'ita murutsxi].

Introduction xxix

(and argued?), and that at least a temporary aid was required in the daily dissemination of Party propaganda amongst (presumably) the working class around the capital until Georgian became thoroughly established there. Whatever the truth of the matter, as of 1938 the Soviet Laz and Mingrelian populations found themselves with no teaching of, or publications in, their languages (other, that is, than works produced by folklorists and linguists for the benefit of their professional colleagues rather than the native speakers themselves).[21]

I first met Wolfgang Feurstein when he introduced himself at the 2nd colloquium of the European Caucasological Society that was held in Vienna in 1984, when he spoke to us about his work on Laz. Nine years later he met in his home-town of Schopfloch the famous journalist and writer Neal Ascherson, who penned an article about him and his work in the newspaper for which he then worked, the sadly now defunct *Independent on Sunday*. Here is part of what he wrote (1 November 1993): 'In the village of Schopfloch lives Wolfgang Feurstein, a German intellectual who has devoted his existence to the rescue of the Lazi from "assimilation." From this remote village, almost single-handed and quite unrewarded, Feurstein has set about nothing less than the foundation of a national culture. He has given the Lazi an alphabet, and prepared schoolbooks which are now beginning to circulate – clandestinely – in their villages. He and the small group of expatriates who form the "Katchkar Working Group" (named after a mountain range) are working on the first dictionary and the first volumes of what is to be a source-book and bibliography of Lazi history.'[22] Feurstein illustrates in his 1992 article the three scripts that have been employed for Laz, viz. that of the 1936 *Alboni*, then the *Lazuri Alfabe* devised by him and colleagues for use in the materials infiltrated into Turkey from 1984, plus the Georgian-based equivalent.

Ascherson went on to write the following in his 1993 article: 'For myself, I support Feurstein. A scientist is not just a camera. A scientist's duty to a vanishing culture is not just to record but to offer wisdom and say: "This end is

---

[21] For more on Mingrelian see Hewitt (1995; 1995a).

[22] After reading this article and noticing that Ascherson was a fellow-guest one evening at St. Antony's College (Oxford), I introduced myself to him and gave him something I had written on Mingrelian. Yüksel & Aleksiva write about Ascherson's comments on Feurstein's activities on behalf of the Laz in his books *Black Sea* (1995) and *Black Sea: The birthplace of civilization and barbarism* (2007). These books were written after the author's first visit to Georgia, including Abkhazia, in 1994, and, unsurprisingly, allusion is also made to the parallel between Mingrelian and Laz.

not inevitable. There is a way to survive, and I can point you towards it!" And, anyway, it is too late to stop the journey. The Turkish ban on spoken Lazuri was lifted two years ago. The little books from the Black Forest are passing from family to family. More letters and poems in Lazuri are reaching Schopfloch. Young men working in Germany appear and ask: "Who are we really? Where did we come from?" All that is certain is that the Lazi have eaten the forbidden fruit of an alphabet, and are beginning to see themselves with new eyes.'

The path to full recognition of the right to publish in Laz has not, however, been entirely smooth. To quote again from Ascherson (1995.209): 'In 1992 Feurstein's alphabet was seen for the first time on student placards, in an Istanbul demonstration. Early in 1994, a journal named *Ogni*,[23] written in Turkish and Lazuri, was published in Istanbul by a group of young Lazi. The editor was arrested after the first number, and now faces charges of "separatism." A second issue of the journal appeared a few weeks later. It called, more clearly than before, for an end to the assimilation of Lazi culture. One of the publishers said: "A new age has dawned!".' In fact, a more detailed (and accurate) account of the interesting fate of *Ogni* has been provided by the Laz Institute, which I reproduce here: '*Ogni* was published in Istanbul in November 1993. A Laz from Ardeşen, the lawyer Ahmet Kirim was the person who started the process. His office was being used and he was legally the leading figure in the matter. Mehmedali Baris Besli was chosen as the editor-in-chief. Mehmedali was tried in the DGM (State Security Court) for three separate articles in the magazine and was acquitted in the first trial, but there was no case of an arrest being made. One of the articles in the first issue of the magazine that led to the lawsuit belonged to Ismail Avci Bucaklişi, whilst the other two articles belonged to Ahmet Kirim and Mehmedali Baris Besli. Ali İhsan Aksamaz also wrote articles for the magazine. Ismail and Mehmedali were the only ones who could speak Laz, and the content in Laz belonged to them.'

With specific reference to the history of publishing Laz material(s) in Turkey and Ascherson's representation of Feurstein's role, the Laz Institute respectfully points out that, whilst his primer reached many readers, it would be something of a romantic hyperbole to claim that the availability of this alphabet at the time caused, accelerated, and influenced the Laz cultural movement in Turkey. They stress that: 'It should not be forgotten that the 1990s was a period of significant changes in the world and in Turkey when the consciousness and awareness towards ethnic identities had begun to increase and movements

---

[23] The Laz sentence *Ogni skani nena* means 'Know your language' – BGH.

Introduction xxxi

were established, including the Laz cultural movement. Also, with reference to the statement about the circulation of Laz school-books, although Feurstein may have prepared Laz school-books, it is unclear that he has ever published or circulated them to the Laz people since we have not come across any such in Turkey. As to Laz study-books prepared so far, we can say the following. The first Laz language-courses in Turkey started in 1998 at the offices of an NGO in Istanbul. However, there were no Laz study-books or information on how to teach Laz available at the time. On the other hand, although Iskender Citaši's books were known, these books could not be used as course-material since they were prepared to teach literacy to those who already knew Laz. The first Laz language-learning materials were prepared at Boğaziçi University in 2011, following the introduction of elective Laz lessons at secondary schools affiliated to the Ministry of National Education. The first Laz language study-book is the one entitled "Laz Textbook," published in 2014 by *Lazika Yayın Kollektifi* (Lazika Publication Collective), which was established in Istanbul in 2011 to publish in the Laz language. Afterwards, a donation-protocol was signed between the Laz Institute and the Turkish Ministry of National Education, and four Laz textbooks (for levels A1, A2, B1, B2) for the 5th, 6th, 7th, and 8th grades in secondary schools were delivered to the Ministry by the Laz Institute. The author of these books was İsmail Avcı Bucaklişi, together with two academics, namely Ömer Demirok, now Vice-president of Linguistics at Boğaziçi, and Ömer Eren, now a Ph.D. student in linguistics at Chicago University, who both participated in the preparation of the books as authors. In addition, another 250-page Laz textbook for adults, entitled 'Lazuri Doviguram' ('I am Learning Laz'), was published in 2018 as a Laz Institute publication (supported by the EU). Apart from these, we have no information on the availability of a textbook written for the purpose of teaching Laz. The collective volume of all these books is around 1,400 pages.'

As for Feurstein himself, as a result of his 'clandestine' operations in Turkey, he personally fell foul of the authorities[24] – for encouraging minorities and their languages, which was prohibited at the time – but such pressure never diminished his enthusiasm and determination. His and his collaborators' efforts are, of course, rightly lauded in what follows, but it cannot be denied

---

[24] When I first visited Turkey in the summer of 1974 to collect materials on Circassian (and, as it turned out, Ubykh) in Anatolia, those who arranged my trip warned me that, if asked upon entry into the country to explain the purpose of my visit, under no circumstances should I mention I was travelling to work with a minority. In the event, I was not asked, and my sojourn passed off in entirely pleasurable tranquillity.

that there is no time to rest on one's laurels, given that much remains to be done. Indeed, the essential *raison d'être* of this collection of essays is to address the question of how to build on the successes already achieved by reaching a stage when the tag 'endangered' is removed from Laz and its future is guaranteed. Hopefully all readers will agree that such is a noble goal and wish everyone engaged in the enterprise to attain its complete success.

Postscript

I have then not confined myself exclusively to the case of Laz but have discussed topics in parallel with the closely-related sister-language Mingrelian. Additionally, I have tried to draw attention to works published in Georgia (largely in Georgian) that either contain Laz materials or deal with aspects of Laz grammar. The reasons are: (i) I would like to encourage interested parties on the Laz side to make every effort to acquaint themselves with valuable materials that are probably not readily accessible to them in Turkey (or elsewhere wherever their studies happen to have taken them), and (ii) I dare to hope that the time might come when dedicated individuals from both the (mainly Turkish) Laz and (Georgian) Mingrelian communities will be willing and in a position to collaborate for the mutual benefit of both their mother-tongues. Naturally, any such moves for cross-border co-operation will need to be handled sensitively. For one thing, the Laz have taken exception to moves from Georgia to persuade political and/or educational authorities in Turkey to describe them as 'Georgians' and their language as a 'Georgian dialect.'[25] On

---

[25] In 2014 there were suggestions that Düzce University might build on its instituting of courses on Circassian and Georgian language and literature, with collaboration from both Circassia (North Caucasus) and Tbilisi, by introducing parallel teaching for Laz. In a statement *My Visit to Düzce University*, circulated in 2015, İrfan Çağatay writes about a meeting he had on 19 December 2014 with the chancellor of the University. I quote from the translation by Kadir Erdi Öge: 'The lady Chancellor explained that they have been considering creating such a programme for the past few years but had been unable to realise their intention. [...] The organisation with which they were connected in Tbilisi was საქართველოს საპატრიარქოს წმიდა ანდრია პირველწოდებულის სახელობის ქართული უნივერსიტეტი in other words the "The Georgian University Named After St. Andrew the First-Called of the Patriarchate of Georgia". As can be understood from the name, the University is affiliated with the Patriarchate of Georgia. During our meeting, a Turkish woman of Georgian descent, Nigar Demircan-Çakır, also joined us. According to what was explained by the Chancellor, a delegation, including Nigar Demircan-Çakır and the Dean of the Science-Literature Faculty, Prof. İlhan Genç, had a few days earlier on the 17th December attended a meeting in Tbilisi with the intention of forming a

Introduction xxxiii

the other hand, the mere raising of the question of status for Mingrelian tends immediately to give rise to suspicions among Georgians of an ulterior motive of political separatism, and, it must be acknowledged, Mingrelians do seem to be content with their ethnic categorisation as 'Georgians.'[26] Though once (at best) discouraged or (at worst) prohibited, works on Mingrelian are now appearing – for example, publisher Artanuji has published (2021) Natia Poniava's *Vists'avlot Megruli* 'Let's Learn Mingrelian'; Nargiza Basaria brought out *Chkyni Nina* 'Our Language' in Abkhazia in 2013; Givi Karchava's translation of 'The Little Prince' into Mingrelian *Ch'ich'e Mapaskiri* also came out in 2013, but, interestingly, it was published in Istanbul by the Laz [sic] Cultural Association (*Laz Kültür Derneği*) two years after the Laz translation *Ch'ita Mapaskiri* under the imprint of the Lazika Publication Collective (*Lazika Yayın Kollektifi*);[27] and a journal in Mingrelian/Laz *Skani* 'Your(s)' has also

---

partnership with two Georgian Universities, and at this meeting their intention of creating a Laz Language and Literature programme was also on the agenda of the topics discussed. At the meeting in Tbilisi the attendees from the Georgian side were as follows: Chancellor of the University, Sergo Vardosanidze, Tariel Putkaradze, Teimuraz Gvantseladze, Mikheil Labadze, Sopo Kekua and Nana Kaçarava. I am sure our interested readers will have heard of the names Tariel Putkaradze and Mikheil Labadze before. During their meeting madame Chancellor also mentioned to me a dialogue which she found quite peculiar. The above-mentioned individuals had apparently said the following: "Whether it be in allocating teaching staff for the Georgian classes or in creating the Turkology programmes in Georgia, we have provided every form of assistance. However, we have a polite request. We have heard that you intend to create a Laz Language and Literature programme. Do not go ahead in creating this programme. Or if you do intend to do so please do not bypass us; create the Laz language classes as a subject taught under the aegis of the Georgian Language and Literature programme. We do not accept Laz as a free-standing language but deem it to be a dialect of the Georgian language. If a university in Tbilisi were to have created a programme accepting a dialect of the Turkish language as a language of its own, would you find this to be pleasing? So, therefore, for us the creation of a Laz programme is equally displeasing".'

[26] At the height of Georgian chauvinism in the late 1980s, Mingrelians who spoke out in defence of their Mingrelianness came in for harsh criticism, pressure and in some cases actual physical abuse – for an example see the English translation of an unpublished 'Open Letter' by Nugzar Dzhodzhua, a Mingrelian resident in Abkhazia, which I incorporated as Appendix III in my 1993 article.

[27] The *Lazika Publication Collective* published the first-ever Laz novel "Daçxuri" (Fire, by M. Murğulişi), followed by other novels, poem books, tale books, study books, dictionaries, and translations of world classics, such as Dostoyevsky's *Crime and*

reportedly begun life in Georgia. There is also activity on the internet – one can mention at least two sites: *Megrul-Lazur-Svanuri Enis Sagandzuri* 'Treasury of the Mingrelian-Laz-Svan Language(s)' and *Megrel'skaja Natsija* 'Mingrelian Nation.' From such shoots maybe something substantial will grow to bridge the two language-communities on either side of the geo-political divide to secure the survival of two important Caucasian languages that for too long have suffered neglect. This would be my fervent wish, to the realisation of which this volume might make a meaningful contribution.

REFERENCES

Ascherson, N. (1995). *Black Sea*, London.
Boeder, W. (2005). The South Caucasian Languages. In *Lingua 115*, 5-89.
Bury, J. B. (1958). *History of the Later Roman Empire*. 2 vols. USA.
Feurstein, W. (1992). Mingrelisch, Lazisch, Swanisch. Alte Sprachen und Kulturen der Kolchis vor dem baldigen Untergang. In George Hewitt (ed.) *Caucasian Perspectives*, 285-328.
Güldenstädt, J. A. (1787). *Reisen durch Russland und im Caucasischen Gebürge: auf Befehl der Russisch-Kayserlichen Akademie der Wissenschaftlichen herausgegeben von P. S. Pallas*. 2 vols. St. Petersburg.
Hewitt, [B.] G. (1993). Abkhazia: a problem of identity and ownership. *Central Asian Survey, 12*(3), 267-323.
Hewitt, [B.] G. (1995a). Demographic Manipulation in the Caucasus. *The Journal of Refugee Studies, 8*(1), 48-74.
Hewitt, [B.] G. (1995b). Yet a third consideration of Völker, Sprachen und Kulturen des südlichen Kaukasus. *Central Asian Survey, 14*(2), 285-310.
Hewitt, [B.] G. (2014). History in the context of the Georgian-Abkhazian conflict, *Iran and the Caucasus 18*, pp. 153-179.
Holisky, D. A. (1991). Laz. In Alice C. Harris (ed.) *The Indigenous Languages of the Caucasus. Volume I. Kartvelian Languages*, 395-472. Delmar/New York, Caravan Books.
Peacock D.R. (1887). Original Vocabularies of Five West Caucasian Languages (Georgian, Mingrelian, Lazian, Swanetian, and Abkhazian). *Journal of the Royal Asiatic Society of Great Britain and Ireland, 19*(1), 145-156
von Klaproth, J. (1814). *Kaukasischen Sprachen. Anhang zur Reise in den Kaukasus und nach Georgien*. Halle und Berlin. Reprinted 2018 (Intank Publishing).
von Klaproth, J. (1823). *Asia polyglotta*. Paris: J. M. Eberhart.
Wixman, R. (1980). *Language Aspects of Ethnic Patterns & Processes in the North Caucasus*. Chicago.

Punishment, all representing important developments that have greatly contributed to the development of literature in Laz.

PREFACE
Laz words, Laz worlds

K. David Harrison
Vin University, Hanoi, Vietnam

"*Nananena var goindinen.*"
The mother-tongue must not be lost.

"*Nananena gondinina, ti skaniti gondineri giğun.*"
If you lose your mother-tongue, you lose yourself also.[1]

What can the Laz language–spoken by a shrinking number of people in Turkey and Georgia, and in diaspora–teach us about linguistic diversity, spatial cognition, healing plants, and cultural resilience? The remarkable papers in *Lazuri: An Endangered Language from the Black Sea* (Ünlü & Hewitt, 2023), along with other recent work authored by scholars deeply devoted to the language, show that Laz has much to teach us. With its grammatical complexities, its resilience under socio-political pressure, its poetic aesthetics, and the value speakers invest in it, Laz speaks from its Black Sea homeland to all of humanity.

1. Laz endangerment and recovery

The dynamics of Turkish-Laz co-existence are resulting in speakers shifting from Laz to Turkish. To personalize this process, Haznedar and Avcı-Bucaklişi (2022) invite four Laz speakers–named Zeki, Aslı, Halil and Volkan–to narrate their language experiences in their own words, sharing this perspective with the reader. They note that "official records of the current number of Laz speakers in Turkey are largely unknown." This problem is common to many endangered and diasporic languages, which may be intentionally undercounted or neglected in censuses. The authors then apply quantitative survey methods to a sample population of nearly 500. They establish that Laz is primarily oral, with limited domains of use, and "a definitely endangered language." In their sample population they find that "use of Laz is primarily

---

[1] Chenel (n.d.)

associated with informal personal contexts such as home, neighbourhood, funerals and weddings."

The generational shift away from Laz results from pressure exerted by state policies, the educational system, social prejudice, language contact, and discrimination. But there is reason for hope. As a news article "Turkey's Laz awakening" notes: "The Lazika Publishing Collective has printed 35 bilingual Turkish-Laz books since its founding in 2010" (Tastekin, 2013). The journalist quotes Professor Mehmet Bekaroğlu, who was at that time head of the Laz Institute (Laz Enstitüsü) as saying: "We are recovering the lost Laz words."[2] Of the many different terms that can be applied to any language endangerment situation, the choice of "lost" and "recovering" aptly describes Laz. On November 7, 2021, the first "Laz Language Day" was declared and celebrated in an online event attended by Laz artists, writers, poets and activists. Both the Laz Institute in Istanbul and Lazuri TV have a robust YouTube presence, with popular videos on those channels garnering over 10,000 views each. Choral music, oral histories, foodways, and children's programming are among the video highlights, all domains for the recovering of Laz. The language is increasingly used in publishing, as Yuksel and Aleksiva (2023) report: "since 1997 fifty-eight literary books were published in Turkey by fourteen different publishers and written by a broad range of writers in their native dialects within the contact-induced linguistic community in Lazona and beyond. The work proves a collective effort to document and preserve Lazuri thoughts and expressions in the digital era."

It is important that the endangered status of Laz be established, even though speaker numbers are unclear, because it provides a strong motivation for scholars and activists of all kinds. Language survival benefits the Laz community itself, and also contributes to global linguistic diversity. Laz survival also benefits the Turkish polity, and the authors rightly assert that "language preservation (or at least documentation) is necessary to create more democratic and peaceful societies." Haznedar and Avcı-Bucaklişi (2022) issue a call to action, affirming that "we need to embrace linguistic diversity as a resource and potential for both individuals and societies."

2. Laz linguistics and lexicography

Laz is a primarily oral language (though more recently also written) with significant dialect diversity that exists under intense language contact

---

[2] See also www.lazenstitu.com.

(Kutcher, 2008; Yuksel & Aleksiva, 2023). These qualities may be seen as detrimental, but also contribute to Laz's vitality. First, Laz orality is a cognitive asset, in that speakers must commit to memory large bodies of knowledge, thus exercising their brains as speakers of written languages do not. Second, Laz dialect diversity is used by speakers to identify place of origin of other speakers. The diversity also contributes to linguistic theory, as a kind of natural experiment in language evolution. Thirdly, Laz-Turkish language contact may lead, with effort from the community, to a state of stable bilingualism, which can help sustain Laz in particular domains such as the home. As for contact, which is often framed as degrading a language's complexity, Kutcher (2008, 95) has shown that while Laz indeed borrows from Turkish, it uses borrowings to innovate and increase its own grammatical complexity. For example, Laz adopted the Turkish locational marker *yeri*, but uses it in a novel way to increase expressive precision.

Laz both challenges and complements linguistic theory with its grammatical complexity, including typologically rare features such an active-ergative case system (Demirok & Öztürk, 2023). The morphological encoding of spatial relations in Laz–an elaborated system that deploys 27 verbal prefixes–fills a predicted gap in the spatial encoding typology (Acedo Matellán, 2016). This demonstrates the value of Laz to our understanding of how languages encode spatial relations via elaborate morphological affixation, as is well attested elsewhere in the Caucasus (Comrie & Polinsky, 1998). It is exciting to think how much more Laz will contribute to the linguistic and cognitive sciences theory as its dialect varieties are documented.

Legacy sources, even if flawed, help fill gaps in language documentation. Kikvidze and Pachulia (2023) describe the lexicographic explorations of 19th century British diplomat and amateur linguist Demetrius Peacock (1887). While Laz was historically under-documented in comparison to nearby Caucasus languages, it has a colorful history of amateurs and scholars dating as far back as Spanish philologist Lorenzo Hervás y Panduro (1735-1809), who diligently collected Laz words, creating a continuity of written sources.

Laz lexicography is thus elevated as an essential activity in language documentation, and a valued historical record. The vital tradition collecting Laz words continues to the present day with works such as Çağatay's (2020) *The Dictionary of Laz Plant Names*, summarized below, and other Laz dictionaries (e.g., Aleksiva & Avcı-Bucaklişl, 2009). As Şirin and Yaman (2023) report, Laz lexicography has now entered the digital age, with a range of different lexicographic models being applied.

Figure 0.1 - Laz words as documented by Hervás y Panduro (1787), with Italian and Turkish equivalents.

	Primo dialetto Lesgo.	*Lingua Turca.*
Calzoni.	scalvan.	scalvan.
Capelli.	toma	tui.
Donna.	okurza	koint.
Forno.	furun	furün.
Montagna.	daghi	dägh.
Nuvola.	pula.	bulut.
Sole.	giara	gyunes.
Uccello.	kinczi	kus (144).

Figure 0.2 - Laz words–as compared with Georgian and Mingrelian–from Peacock (1887).

ENGLISH.	GEORGIAN.	MINGRELIAN.	LAZ.	SWANETIAN.	ABKHAZIAN.
Woman	Rali	Ossuri	Okhordja	Zural	Abhüs
Wife	Tsoli	Tchili	Tchili	Yekhv	Abhüs
Child	Bofshi	Tchkhitchkha	Berre	Bebshv	Atchkue
Son	Vaji	Skwa	Bidji	Ghezal-Tchkint	Apá
Daughter	Rali	Dzgabi	Bozo	Dina	Aphá
Slave	Rma	Rotchi	Rële	Glekh	Akhashala=Apü
Cultivator	Tokhneli	Makhatchkali	Makhatchkali	Mukhni	Adghï-khopshi
Shepherd	Mtskessi	Tchkwishi	Tchkeshi	Muldegh	Akhtchi
God	Ghmerti	Ghoronti	Tanghrï	Ghermet	Antcha
Devil	Eskmaki	Mazakwali	Sheitan	Ashma	Aüsta
Sun	Mze	Bja	Mjora	Mlok	Amre
Moon	Mtvari	Tuta	Tuta	Doshdul	Amze
Star	Varsklavi	Muritskhi	Muritskhi	Amtgvaek	Eyetsua

3. Laz linguistic ecology

Laz endangerment and vitality arises from many contributing factors, across time, space, and populations. As the state having the largest Laz population, Turkey's political ideology has played a crucial role. Summarizing the plight of Laz since the 1923 founding of the Turkish Republic, Öner (2015) writes: "as...the history of Republican Turkey suggests, one of the key aims of the state was to control education and to endorse Turkish as a tool for asserting the national identity. In that sense, multilingualism has also been perceived as a threat to national unity."

Applying a language ecology framework to Laz, Eren (2023) shows that forces as diverse as topography, tea plantations, roads, and water sources also come into play. He concludes that "the shift and loss of Laz can be interpreted as simply a strategy that Laz speakers employ to adapt to the changing socio-economic structure" (p. 23). While this is true of almost any endangered language, Laz proves that generalizations should be avoided in looking at any endangerment scenario. Local history, nuances of geography, state policy, land inheritance patterns, customary law, the forced Turkicization of Laz personal names, and other local factors all exerted specific pressures on Laz, constituting its unique linguistic ecology. These factors may also hold the key to Laz survival, which requires a unique strategy.

One approach is evident in the careful positioning of Laz as unthreatening to Turkish language hegemony, and not a separatist movement. Laz activists take care to affirm the unity of the Turkish nation, while still asking if there is a place for Laz within a plurilingual Turkey. In 2012, thanks to these efforts at Laz visibility, Laz was recognized by the Ministry of Education as being among Turkey's "Living Languages and Dialects (LLDs)" eligible to receive government support for pedagogy (Bilmez & Çağatay, 2021). This resulted in government supported Laz elective language courses, beginning in 2012. Despite their high political-symbolic value, the courses had low enrollments, and the authors assess the program to have been a failure. But many parallel efforts to sustain Laz continue, and some hopeful signs are apparent.

If Laz is to survive, it will be due to the efforts of its speakers, and so their attitudes, beliefs and practices are consequential. How do Laz speakers and heritage speakers think and talk about the current state of their language? In her participatory ethnographic study, Türk-Yiğitalp (2023) explores the question of "what it means for its speakers that Lazuri is an endangered language and how they make sense of the process of language 'loss' or 'endangerment'." She cautions that idealized and valuative notions of who is a native speaker obscure the messier, more complex practices that characterize the extended Laz speech community. Speakers' own explanations about the current state of Laz referenced the generational and urban/rural divide. They used metaphors of forgetting and loss, and described spatial dislocation from isolated highlands to more urban lowlands to explain the state of Laz. Ideas of naturalness and purity are also common in these speakers' narratives, describing rural Laz children said to speak "beautifully" and "like a nightingale." Heritage speakers expressed negative views towards borrowing and code-mixing, as indicating the decline of an idealized pure form of Laz to an impure, mixed form. Internalized attitudes about the dominance of Turkish, and the subordinate position of Laz–hardly ever spoken in a 'pure' form–may discourage younger speakers from using Laz in their multilingual repertoires. If Laz is to be revitalized, the author concludes, "acknowledging the more diverse uses of Lazuri along with other languages in one's repertoire would be a more productive path forward."

4. Laz environmental linguistics

Laz dialect diversity is set against a backdrop of the extreme linguistic and biological diversity of the Caucasus region and is a key component of it. Laz thus makes a significant contribution to both biodiversity studies and environmental linguistics. Laz belongs to the Caucasus language hotspot, home to 52 languages belonging to 13 genetic units (language families). Laz also lies within the Caucasus biodiversity hotspot, "one of the most biologically rich regions on Earth…among the planet's 25 most diverse and endangered hotspots" (Critical Ecosystem Partnership Fund, 2003, p. 4). The region has 6,500 species of vascular plants, a quarter of which are found nowhere else– "the highest level of endemism in the temperate world" (CEPF, 2003, p. 7). In terms of animals, the West Lesser Caucasus Corridor–the subregion where Laz is spoken–has been identified as a large herbivore hotspot and may still host rare carnivores such as the Caucasian leopard (*Panthera pardus tulliana*) (Gokturk et al., 2011). Thus situated, Laz contains a wealth of environmental knowledge about plants, landscapes, and traditional lifeways.

But Laz ethnobotanical knowledge is vanishing, perhaps even faster than the language itself. As Çağatay (2020) notes: "Factors such as the end of the traditional agricultural economy, urbanization, migration and the gradual withdrawal of Laz language from modern life has led to the endangering of plant names in particular. This knowledge, which is preserved only in people who have a relationship with agriculture and animal husbandry over a certain age, will be forgotten with this generation." Çağatay's Dictionary of Laz Plant Names lists 1,064 vernacular plant names belonging to 335 taxa, a truly impressive inventory of botanical knowledge. The author notes that it is mostly Laz women who are the bearers of this tradition, and that plant names differ from village to village, thus hinting at an even greater underlying diversity.

As ethnobotanists Kazancı et al. (2020, p. 1) explain: "The Mountains of the Western Lesser Caucasus with its rich plant diversity, multicultural and multilingual nature host diverse ethnobotanical knowledge related to medicinal plants. However, cross-cultural medicinal ethnobotany and patterns of plant knowledge have not yet been investigated in the region." In their ethnobotanical study, the researchers identified 152 native wild plant species and 817 species-use combinations, representing a rich but previously undocumented knowledge base. In comparing findings from Georgia and Turkey, they found that: "Participants in both countries use a significant number of shared species for different purposes. This lack of shared ethnomedicinal knowledge might be a sign of different epidemiology of certain ailments in communities studied as well as various medicinal knowledge systems in ethnolinguistically diverse communities on both sites of the border." The authors found that of the 817 documented species-use combinations, only 9% were shared across the Georgia-Turkey border, even though the communities are in close proximity, inhabit the same mountain landscapes and practice similar semi-nomadic agro-pastoralist lifeways. This study also provides an example of Laz's contributions to scientific knowledge on two fronts. First, the lead author is of Laz origin and is working to document the traditional ethnobotanical wisdom of her community, the Laz people (Kazancı et al., 2021). Second, although the botanical interviews were conducted mostly in Turkish, some sites are on Laz territory. The researchers consulted two Laz families who contributed a total of 28 Laz plant names, with uses ranging from basketry to medicine, to musical instruments (C. Kazancı & S. Oruç, personal communication). Some of the botanical knowledge may thus be understood as belonging to Laz culture, even though narrated in Turkish. A similar ethnobotanical study (Bussmann et al., 2020) was carried out at multiple sites in Georgia, including the Adjara region where the Laz people live. For this study, Laz-speaking participants were interviewed in the Laz language in their homes and gardens. The resulting data set of 276 plant species–although showing a predominance of Georgian names–includes 30 Laz plant names, identified by consultants as useful for nutritional, medicinal, veterinary, and ritual purposes.

5. Valuing Laz

The Laz language should be treasured for many reasons. For the intrinsic value Laz holds for its speakers and heritage speakers, as part of their identity. For Laz grammatical complexity that advances scientific understanding. For Laz's resurgent presence that affirms the multilingual and multicultural nature of the Turkish polity. Laz activists and artists are expanding their Nananena (i.e., mother tongue) into new domains of inquiry and creativity. Laz musicians and performers are winning over a national and global audience with their talent (Taşkın, 2011; Solomon, 2017). Laz journalists, politicians, and scientists are reaffirming its presence and value, most visibly in Turkey but also in Georgia and internationally. Linguists and philologists creating new scholarship on Laz are to be commended for their care and advocacy, and for bringing Laz language matters to a wide audience. May these collective efforts to sustain Laz in the 21st century meet with great success.

REFERENCES

Acedo Matellán, V. (2016). *The morphosyntax of transitions: A case study in Latin and other languages.* Oxford: Oxford University Press.

Aleksiva, İ., & Avcı-Bucaklişi, İ. (2009). *Svacoxo: Laz yer adları sözlüğü.* Kadıköy, İstanbul: Kolkhis Laz Kültür Derneği.

Bilmez, Bülent & Çağatay, İ. (2021). *Elective Language Courses on Living Languages and Dialects in the Context of Language Rights. LAZ LANGUAGE EXAMPLE (2012-2021). SUMMARY.* https://www.academia.edu/48803964/A_RIGHT_UNCLAIMED_Elective_Language_Courses_on_Living_Languages_and_Dialects_in_the_Context_of_Language_Rights_LAZ_LANGUAGE_EXAMPLE_2012_2021_SUMMARY. Accessed January 2022.

Bussmann, R. W., Paniagua Zambrana, N. Y., Sikharulidze, S., Kikvidze, Z., Darchidze, M., Manvelidze, Z., Ekhvaia, J., Kikodze, D., Khutsishvili, M., Batsatsashvili, K., & Hart, R. E. (2020). From the Sea to the Mountains – Plant Use in Adjara, Samegrelo and Kvemo Svaneti, Sakartvelo (Republic of Georgia), Caucasus. *Ethnobotany Research and Applications*, vol. 20, June 2020, pp. 1-34.

Çağatay, I. (2020). *Dictionary of Laz Plant Names.* LINCOM Scientific Dictionaries 03. München: Lincom-Europa.

Chenel, L. (n. d.). *500 Laz Proverbs.* https://lynnchenel.com/500-laz-proverbs/. Accessed January 2021.

Comrie, B., & Polinsky, M. (1998). The Great Dagestanian Case Hoax. In A. Siewierska and J. J. Song (eds.) *Case, Typology, and Grammar.* Amsterdam: John Benjamins. pp. 95-114.

Critical Ecosystem Partnership Fund. (2003). CEPF Ecosystem Profile for the Caucasus Biodiversity Hotspot.

Demirok, Ö., & Öztürk, B. (2023). On the Significance of Laz for Theoretical Research in Linguistics. In Züleyha Ünlü and B. George Hewitt (eds.) *Lazuri: An Endangered Language from Black Sea.* Vernon Press.

Eren, Ö. (2023). Linguistic Variation and Complexity in Laz. In Züleyha Ünlü and B. George Hewitt (eds.) *Lazuri: An Endangered Language from the Black Sea.* Vernon Press.

Gokturk, T., Bucak, F., & Artvinli, T. (2011). Mammalian fauna of Artvin. *African Journal of Agricultural Research* 6, no. 6: 1418–1425.

Haznedar, B., & Avcı-Bucaklişi, İ. (2023). Current Status of Laz. In Züleyha Ünlü and B. George Hewitt (eds.) *Lazuri: An Endangered Language from the Black Sea.* Vernon Press..

Hervás y Panduro, L. (1787). *Vocabolario poligloto con prolegomeni sopra piu' di 150 lingue dove sono delle scoperte nuove, ed utili all'antica storia dell'uman genere, ed alla cognizione del meccanismo delle parole. Opera dell'abate don Lorenzo Hervas socio della Reale Accademia delle Scienze, ed Antichita di Dublino, e dell'Etrusca di Cortona.* Cesena: Per Gregorio Biasini all'insegna di Pallade.

Kazancı, C., Oruç, S. & Mosulishvili, M. (2020). Medicinal ethnobotany of wild plants: a cross-cultural comparison around Georgia-Turkey border, the

Western Lesser Caucasus. *J Ethnobiology Ethnomedicine* 16, 71 (2020). https://doi.org/10.1186/s13002-020-00415-y.

Kikvidze, Z. & Pachulia, L. (2023). A spotlight on the 'Lazian' Lexis: Evidence from a 19th-century lexicographic resource. In Züleyha Ünlü and B. George Hewitt (eds.) *Lazuri: An Endangered Language from the Black Sea*. Vernon Press.

Kazancı, C., Oruç, S., Mosulishvili, M., & Wall, J. (2021). Cultural Keystone Species without Boundaries: A Case Study on Wild Woody Plants of Transhumant People around the Georgia-Turkey Border (Western Lesser Caucasus). *Journal of Ethnobiology*, 41(4), 447-464, (21 December 2021).

Kutscher, S. (2008). The language of the Laz in Turkey: Contact-induced change or gradual language loss? *Turkic Languages* 12, pp. 82-102.

Şirin, F. & Yaman, H. (2023). Principles of Designing a New Dictionary Model for Endangered Languages: The Case of Laz. In Züleyha Ünlü and B. George Hewitt (eds.) *Lazuri: An Endangered Language from the Black Sea*. Vernon Press.

Solomon, T. (2017). Who Are the Laz? Cultural Identity and the Musical Public Sphere on the Turkish Black Sea Coast. *The World of Music*, vol. 6, no. 2, pp. 83–113. Florian Noetzel GmbH Verlag, VWB - Verlag für Wissenschaft und Bildung, Schott Music GmbH & Co. KG, Bärenreiter. http://www.jstor.org/stable/44841947.

Taşkın, N. (2011). *Representing and Performing Laz Identity: 'This is Not a Rebel Song!'* MA Thesis, Boğaziçi University.

Tastekin, F. (2013). Turkey's Laz awakening. *Al-Monitor.* December 1, 2013. https://www.al-monitor.com/originals/2013/12/laz-people-of-turkey-awaken.html#ixzz7GnkUzr3M. Accessed January 2022.

Türk-Yiğitalp, G. (2023). Speaking Lazuri Beautifully: Discourses on Lazuri as an Endangered Language. In Züleyha Ünlü and B. George Hewitt (eds.) *Lazuri: An Endangered Language from the Black Sea*. Vernon Press.

Yuksel, P. & Aleksiva, İ. Ç., (2023). Stories of Perseverance: Using the Lazuri Alboni for the Emergence of Literary Genres in a South Caucasian Endangered Language. In Züleyha Ünlü and B. George Hewitt (eds.) *Lazuri: An Endangered Language from the Black Sea*. Vernon Press.

Chapter 1

The Current Status of Laz in Turkey

Belma Haznedar
Boğaziçi University, Turkey

İsmail Avcı-Bucaklişi
Istanbul Laz Institute, Turkey

Abstract

This study presents the results of a large-scale survey on the Laz language, one of the endangered heritage languages of Turkey. Based on data from 450 Laz-speaking participants, we aim to address (i) the language competence of the participants; (ii) the use of Laz at home and in the wider community; (iii) its intergenerational transmission to the next generations. The results of the study show a severe decrease in the use of Laz in Laz-speaking communities. Overall, the results are compatible with UNESCO's classification of Laz being one of the 'definitely endangered' languages.

Keywords: *Bilingualism-multilingualism, heritage language speakers, endangered language, language maintenance*

* * *

1. Introduction

Bilingual-multilingual communities generally face challenges in supporting the transmission of ethnic or minority languages to younger generations. If you talk to people living in Arhavi, a province in the Black Sea region of Turkey, for instance, and ask them whether or not Laz is disappearing, most will answer 'yes' and add that young people do not speak the language anymore. Indeed, the following quotes from the participants of the current study reveal this explicitly:

Zeki, a young man in his mid-twenties, lives in Pazar, one of the Laz-speaking communities in the Black Sea region, Turkey. When asked what his mother tongue is, he says, 'In my opinion, it is Laz, but if you ask which language I speak, it is Turkish.'

Aslı, a 26-year-old young woman, is also from Pazar. She says, 'Of course, my mother tongue is Laz. I know Laz, but I cannot speak it. If you have a job, people pay attention to your accent.'

Halil, one of the oldest respondents in the study, is 91. He lives in Hopa. On the one hand, he says that his mother tongue is Turkish; on the other hand, he stresses that his mother tongue changed after he started school. 'My mother tongue is Turkish. I also know Laz. I learned it from my family. When I was born, we first grew up speaking Laz only. When we started school, even before going to school, we were able to speak some Turkish. But our mother tongue was initially Laz by then.'

Volkan is 22. He lives in Arhavi: 'I cannot speak Laz fluently, but I can understand it.'

These people are some of the participants of the current study. They all share some knowledge of Laz, ranging from the ability to understand it a little to some decent level of competence in Laz. For almost all of them, Laz co-exists with Turkish, the language with which the majority of them are generally more comfortable speaking. They all completed their schooling in Turkish and had no formal education in Laz. Perhaps, 40 years ago, the label used for these people was semi-bilinguals (Dorian, 1981), or incomplete acquirers (Montrul, 2008; Polinsky, 2007), or unbalanced and pseudo-bilinguals (Baker & Jones, 1998). The lack of a unified definition for these people may be partially a reflection of the general lack of consensus among researchers about what these speakers know of their home language and how best we can define their language competence. Today, millions of people like *Zeki, Aslı, Halil* and *Volkan* with similar or different life stories are known as heritage speakers, a term which has gained popularity among linguists since the mid-1990s (Cummins, 2005).

From a linguistic perspective, heritage speakers refer to individuals raised in a home environment where they are exposed to a non-dominant language spoken in society. This situation generally occurs in first-generation migrants or ethnic groups as well as in second and later generations whose members are exposed to family language but may not necessarily be active users of the language (Valdés, 2000). As highlighted in the above quotes from *Zeki, Aslı, Halil* and *Volkan*, these people are bilingual, but their knowledge of the mother tongue, Laz, appears to be limited, despite the fact that this is the first language they have access to, at least to some degree by hearing it from their parents, grandparents or members of the Laz community (Polinsky, 2018). In most cases, these speakers begin learning their heritage language concurrently with the dominant language, which eventually becomes their stronger language during childhood or later years. Based on data from Laz speakers in Turkey, this is the kind of bilingual and heritage language group examined in this study.

2. Laz and Laz-speaking Communities in Turkey

The Laz people are an ethnic group who live mainly in the Black Sea region of Turkey and Georgia. Their language, Laz, is one of the South Caucasian languages spoken in Sarpi and Batumi in Georgia and in some provinces in Turkey's Eastern Black Sea Region (Benninghaus, 1989; Karimova & Deverell, 2001). Although all the other South Caucasian languages (namely Megrelian, Svan and Georgian) are spoken in Georgia, Laz is the only South Caucasian language spoken in Turkey (Kutscher, 2008), along with the Imerkhevi dialect of Georgia used in Şavşat, a province close to the border with Georgia.

According to UNESCO's *Atlas of the World's Languages in Danger*, Laz has been categorized as one of the 'definitely endangered' languages in the world (Moseley, 2012; UNESCO, 2003). The aim of this study is to present the findings of a large-scale survey/study conducted on the Laz language and Laz-speaking communities in Turkey. On the basis of data collected within the scope of the Living Laz project supported by the European Union, we hope to show the current status of Laz in Turkey, with a focus on the use of Laz at home and in the wider community and its intergenerational transmission to next generations in Turkey. A unique feature of this study is the analysis of the most recent systematic data concerning Laz-speaking communities both in the Black Sea region (Eastern Black Sea) with its highly-populated Laz speakers and those who live in urban areas in the Marmara Region. Given that little to date has been reported in terms of the use of Laz in detailed terms, this is perhaps the first study that examines the use of Laz in a designed large-scale study. The paper will begin with a review of relevant studies of language-shift and language-endangerment in bilingual/multilingual communities, followed by a presentation of the study and its findings. The last section discusses the findings and presents suggestions for the preservation of the Laz language.

3. Language-transmission across Generations, Language-shift and Maintenance

Language-transmission across generations has long been one of the hotly debated issues in sociolinguistic studies, in particular regarding the notion of language-vitality and language-shift in migrant and non-migrant communities.

Much work has addressed the central role of the family as the key element for the transmission of the home-language to the next generations (e.g. Fishman, 1991; Lopez, 1996; Portes & Hao, 1998; Arriagada, 2005). For Fishman (1991, 2013), for instance, intergenerational transmission of minority or ethnic languages needs to be safeguarded at home and in the local community. For other researchers, however, family language-use needs to be supported by other sources precisely because, in most cases, parents and children are influenced by the status and prestige of the majority language widely used in education and administration (e.g., Polinsky, 2018; García, 2009). While various work has examined parental language-practices in children (Alba et al., 2002), others paid attention to social factors such as neighbourhood, workplace, and marriages, which are considered to play key roles in societal bilingualism (García, 2009), emphasizing the dynamic nature of the functions and relationships between languages in bilingual communities.

There is no doubt that the dynamic use of two languages can only be achieved if both languages are acquired and used by children in additive contexts (García, 2009). This way, children will have a chance to acquire the language used both in the family and the outside context, which in turn makes language-transmission possible. If language is not transmitted across generations, however, language shift becomes unavoidable. Language shift refers to the process by which people in a bilingual speech community stop using one of the languages in favour of the other (Fishman, 1991). In his influential work, Fishman (1991) specifies the following conditions for language shift to occur: (i) When more than one language/variety co-exists in the same society; (ii) When there are differences in power, value and status conferred on one of the languages that lead people to maintain or abandon the home language; (iii) When there is pressure in political, economic or social forms on one of the two languages used in the society (e.g. Batibo, 2005; Paulston, Chen & Connerty, 1993).

One major question raised in numerous studies on language shift concerns whether language contact leads to the maintenance of two (or more) languages in the community or language shift, through which the community eventually prefers to use one of them over the other. While most work has focused on the structural effects of language contact, others have emphasized the sociocultural factors of language shift, including attitudes minority speakers have towards their language and linguistic community (Dorian, 1981; Gal, 1979). The connection between the attitudes of bilingual communities toward each language and the use of their heritage languages has been the subject of intense discussion in the literature for many years, often in connection with the notion of ethnolinguistic vitality (EV hereafter). In their EV model, Giles, Bourhis and Taylor (1977) underline factors such as status, demographic and institutional support given to heritage languages, all of which contribute to the vitality of an ethnolinguistic group (p. 308). On similar grounds, other work also makes explicit reference to certain factors that play a significant role in language shift, including absolute numbers of speakers, intergenerational language-transmission, the proportion of speakers within the total population, availability of materials for language-education and literacy, shifts in domains of language-use, response to new domains and media, type and quality of documentation, and governmental and institutional language-attitudes and policies, including official status and use (Edwards, 1992; Moseley, 2012).

All these studies are in line with UNESCO's (2003) 'Language Vitality and Endangerment' framework, which was originally based on Fishman's (1991) Graded Intergenerational Disruption Scale (GIDS) according to which six degrees of language endangerment are specified to show how ethnolinguistic groups can assess the threatened nature of their languages on a continuum from stability to extinction. Under this formulation, a language is considered *safe* if it is spoken by all generations but *unsafe* if its use is limited to specific social domains such as home-environments. Languages are taken to be definitely endangered if they are no longer learned by young generations as a mother-tongue. In the '*definitely endangered*' stage, parents might still address their children in the language, but their children may not necessarily speak the language either while addressing their parents or their siblings. The following two stages right before the extinction of the language are the so-called *severely endangered* and *critically endangered* stages, during which the language is mostly spoken by grandparents or great-grandparent generations (The UNESCO document, 2003, p. 8). In much work, language-transmission from one generation to the next has been the most commonly used factor in evaluating the maintenance or the loss of language (Fishman, 1991). Clearly, the use of the language in various domains, including official (e.g., educational institutions) and public places (e.g., local places where members of the community socialize with each other), has a direct impact on the nature of intergenerational language-transmission (Li, 1995; Holmes, 2013).

As can be seen in the discussion so far, much previous and current work on heritage-languages emphasizes the potential value of preserving ethnic and minority languages. Most linguists and teachers agree that language-preservation (or at least documentation) is necessary to create more democratic and peaceful societies. Among others, Hale (1992) for instance, suggests that the protection of linguistic diversity is of paramount importance to humankind, similar to the preservation of biological diversity. For him, the loss of local languages and 'the cultural systems they represent' refers to the loss of intellectual and cultural wealth and the 'products of human mental industry' (p. 36). On similar grounds, Fishman (2013) explicitly states that 'It is just as scandalous and injurious to waste "native" language resources as to waste our air, water, mineral, animal and various nonlinguistic human resources' (p. 476).

This study is an attempt to document the current status of Laz, one of the definitely endangered languages in Turkey. Before we proceed, it is essential to note from the outset that one unique feature of this study is that it attempts to provide the analysis of the most recent systematic data concerning Laz-speaking communities both in the Black Sea region (Eastern Anatolia) with its highly-populated Laz speakers and those who live in urban areas in the Marmara region, a primary destination for migration flows from rural areas due to the level and growth of industrialization and urbanization in the area.

4. The Current Study

The objective of this study is to present data on the current status of the Laz language and Laz communities in the Black Sea and Marmara regions in Turkey. The specific aims of the study are (i) to form a picture of competence in Laz; (ii) to document its current use in different domains (e.g. family, work and education) (iii) to examine the degree of language-transmission to younger generations. Prior to moving on to the specifics of the methodology used in this study, it is important to note that due to the rise in rural migration from villages and small towns into large cities like Istanbul for employment and educational opportunities, official records of the current number of Laz speakers in Turkey are largely unknown. In some work, it has been estimated that the Laz-speaking population in Turkey is around 250.000 (Kutscher, 2008; Holisky, 1991).

5. Methodology

5.1. Participants

Data in this study were collected via a questionnaire from 450 Laz speakers who volunteered to participate in the survey. Our aim was to seek information relating to their language-use, competence, and transmission of Laz to young people. The distribution of the questionnaires took place in the Black Sea and Marmara regions in July 2017. It should be noted that in the Black Sea region, the Laz people primarily live in two cities: (i) Rize and its provinces of Pazar

(Atina), Ardeşen (Arûaşeni), Çamlıhemşin (Vica) and Fındıklı (Vitze), and (ii) Artvin and its provinces of Arhavi (Arkabi), Borçka (Boçxa), Kemalpaşa (Noğedi / Makriyali) and Hopa (Xopa). Therefore, data gathered in the Black Sea region come from these provinces where Laz is spoken widely. The second portion of the data were collected from the participants living in the Marmara region, including Sapanca, Düzce and İstanbul. Tables 1-5 present demographic information about the participants of the study in terms of gender, age, occupation, educational background, and place of residence.

Table 1.1 - Gender

	Participants	Percentage %
Female	229	50.9 %
Male	221	49.1 %
Total	450	

The numbers of female and male participants were almost equal.

Table 1.2 - Age

< 25	102	22.7 %
26-45	125	27.8 %
> 45	223	49.6 %

Age is divided into three categories in this study: (i) 'young' – aged 25 and below, (ii) 'middle' – aged 26-45, (iii) 'senior/old' – aged 45 and above.

Table 1.3 - Occupation

Blue-collar	243	54 %
White-collar	129	28.7 %
Student	78	17.3 %

The participants' occupations were also examined in three categories: (i) blue-collar jobholders, (ii) white-collar jobholders with high school or university diplomas (iii) students.

Table 1.4 - Educational background

Primary school - below	132	29.3 %
Middle school - high school	189	42 %
University degree- above	129	28.7 %

Around one-third of the participants had a primary school or a university diploma. The largest group in the data consists of graduates of middle school and high school.

Table 1.5 - Place of residence

City	220	48.9 %
Village	28	6.2 %
Dual residence (city-village)	202	44.9%
Total	450	100%

As can be seen in Table 5, while the majority of the participants live in cities, around 45% of them had a dual residence, some spending summer in the village and winter in towns and cities.

5.2. The Questionnaire

The questionnaire devised for this study draws on a number of issues, with special reference to (i) competence in Laz, (ii) the use of Laz, (iii) transmission of Laz to younger generations. It consists of the following sections:

(1) Demographic information (i.e., personal details, age, gender, mother-tongue, educational level, date of birth and place).

(2) Competence in Laz and Turkish (questions about the participants' language-use and language-skills such as speaking, listening, reading and writing in both languages (e.g., How well do you think you speak Laz/Turkish? In which language do you feel more comfortable? – Laz; Turkish; no difference between the two)

(3) The use of Laz and Turkish (questions addressing the use of Laz in the family and the wider community: What language do you speak with (e.g., mother, father, siblings, spouses, children, grandparents, Laz friends, Laz neighbours?) – Only Laz; mainly Laz; Laz-Turkish equally, primarily Turkish, only Turkish. What language do you speak in the following contexts: home, community, shopping places, weddings, funerals, local

community centres such as hospital, municipality and official buildings).

(4) Transmission of Laz to younger people (questions relating to the frequency of exposure to Laz and its use with close family-members and other social networks (e.g., Which language did your parents use to address each other? – Laz, Turkish, Laz-Turkish. How often do you speak Laz with your children? – Always; Sometimes; Rarely; Never).

6. Results

6.1. Language-preference

The language-competence of the participants was examined both in terms of oral language skills (i.e., speaking and comprehension) and literacy-skills (i.e., reading and writing) in Laz and Turkish. First, the participants were asked how comfortable they were in using Laz and Turkish. As shown in Appendix 1, according to the composite scores obtained from all the participants' self-evaluation responses, nearly one-third of them (32.9%) reported no difference in their preference while using Laz and Turkish, their responses being close to each other (32% in Laz and 35.1% in Turkish). One notable finding is that those who live in the Black Sea region report that they feel more comfortable using Laz than Turkish in comparison to those who live in the Marmara region, where the respondents feel better using the majority language, Turkish.

Language-preference of the participants was also analyzed in terms of the socio-demographic factors of the study, which included age, educational background, occupation and place of residence. As can be seen in Appendix 1: (i) only 5.9 % of the young generation (aged 25 or below) reported that they feel comfortable in using Laz; the vast majority of the middle group (aged 26-45) expressed a higher preference for the use of Turkish (39.2%) as opposed to Laz (26.4%); (iii) in the final group with older participants (aged 46 and above), the preference for the use of Laz (47.1%) is robust in comparison to Turkish (30.9%). When education is considered, 68.9% of those with limited formal schooling (primary school or none) expressed that they feel more comfortable using Laz.

Those with middle-school or high-school education have relatively comparable proportions regarding language-preference (Laz 23.8%, Turkish 42.9%). The occupational background of the participants also revealed a similar picture, almost half of the blue-collar participants (49%) indicated that their more preferred language was Laz. In those who perform white-collar jobs, however, this percentage was 15.5%. Finally, differences among the participants existed in terms of urban and rural areas. While those who live in small provinces and villages (71.4%) expressed greater preference for Laz over Turkish, people living in urban areas tend to prefer Laz considerably less at 20.9%.

6.2. Oral and Literacy Skills in Laz and Turkish

Language-competence of the participants in both regions was also examined in terms of four major language-skills: reading, writing, speaking and listening comprehension on a self-rated scale of 'none, little, average, good and very good,' where 1 was the lowest, 5 was the highest. Table 6. presents the language-skills of the participants in both regions in terms of four language-skills.

Table 1.6 - Language-skills in Laz and Turkish

Comprehension	Laz	82%	78%	80%
	Turkish	60%	66%	62%
Speaking	Laz	78%	66%	72%
	Turkish	62%	66%	64%
Reading	Laz	44%	38%	42%
	Turkish	78%	88%	82%
Writing	Laz	38%	36%	36%
	Turkish	76%	88%	80%

First, a comparison between oral and literacy skills reveals that oral skills surpass the latter. While oral skills (listening and speaking) in Laz occurs at 80%-72%, close to 'good', literacy skills (reading and writing, 41% and 36%, respectively) constitute the lower band in their proficiency. These figures reveal that, while the participants have good speaking and comprehension skills in Laz, their literacy skills are rather low. By contrast, the participants' language-proficiency in Turkish was extremely high with regard to reading and writing skills, 82% and 80%, respectively. More detailed information concerning the proportion of Laz competence is presented in Appendices 2 and 3, where percentages are provided according to the socio-demographic variables of gender, age, education, occupation and place of residence.

As Appendix 2 shows, when responses of 'good' and 'very good' are combined, those with the lowest education had the highest percentage in oral skills (87.9% in comprehension, 83.3% in speaking). Those who had middle-high school education or university degrees had lower levels of oral skills in Laz. While the intermediate group's percentages were 68.2% and 55.1%, the most educated participants had the lowest proportions (48.1% and 28.7%, respectively). A similar picture emerged when the participants' occupation was taken into consideration. Those with blue-collar jobs expressed higher proficiency both in comprehension and speaking skills (80%, 72% respectively) of Laz than those with white-collar jobs (63%, 44%), the lowest rates appearing with students whose comprehension and speaking skills occurred around (31% and 23%). On similar grounds, moving from rural areas to urban areas leads to lower levels of proficiency in Laz competence. While those living in the rural areas (villages) reported the highest percentage in oral skills (96.4%), others from somewhat smaller but urban provinces rated their proficiency skills much lower, percentages decreasing down to 60% and 46.8%, respectively.

Overall, it is clear that while the participants have good speaking and comprehension skills, their literacy skills are extremely low. This is mainly due to Laz being mainly limited to oral contexts. On the other hand, language-skills in Turkish are at the opposite end, Turkish being the dominant language in literacy skills for both groups of participants in the two regions.

7. The use of Laz and Turkish at home and in the wider community

The use of Laz and Turkish both at home and in the wider community is examined in various social domains: (i) Language-use at home (Which language is used when speaking to different interlocutors, e.g., parents, grandparents?); (ii) Language-use in the workplace and education; (iii) Language-use in other domains.

7.1. Language-use at Home and in the Wider Community

The scores given in Appendix 4 show the degree of use of Laz with different interlocutors at home and in the wider community. These percentages are based on the following scales: *Only Laz, Mostly Laz, Laz-Turkish equally, Mostly Turkish and Only Turkish*. The greatest amount of Laz is used among the old generation such as grandparents, the rating occurring around 51.8%. This is followed by parents and relatives as well as Laz-speaking neighbours (around 40.3%, 38.5% and 37.9%, respectively). The lowest exchange-levels in Laz occur among siblings, spouses, and children (32.7%, 32.9%, 21.3%).

Similar to the findings in the previous section, when the data are examined in terms of language use in the two regions, it is seen that those who live in the Black Sea region tend to use more Laz than those in the Marmara region. The bilingual use of Laz and Turkish, on the other hand, is systematically higher in the Marmara region (see Appendix 4 for detailed figures). In statistical terms, an independent-samples t-test shows that the average of the use of Laz according to the interlocutors is significantly higher among the participants from the Black Sea region than among those from the Marmara region, $t(428) = 7.68$, $p < .05$, *two-tailed* (degrees of freedom were adjusted from 447 to 428).

A much more striking difference was found in child-directed speech. The rate of speaking Laz with children is 31.7% in the Black Sea region and 5.8% in Marmara. Similarly, the use of Laz with spouses is 46.3% in the region, while in Marmara, this goes down to 12.2%. In contrast, while the rate of speaking in Turkish with parents, siblings, children and spouses was 44%, 53%, 63% -81% - 70% respectively in Marmara, and 29%, 29%, 36%, 45% and 36% in the Black Sea region. It should be noted that despite the questionnaire being devised in Turkish, during data-collection more than half of the conversations were held in Laz in the Black Sea region, which was certainly not the case with the participants living in the Marmara region, even with the grandparents, who formed the group of people who typically preferred to speak in Laz.

As can be seen in Appendices 4 and 5, the data-analysis in terms of socio-demographic factors yields interesting findings. (i) *Age*: appeared to be one of the strong factors in determining which language to use with whom. There appear to be clear differences among the three groups of participants with different age-ranges (<25, 26-45, >45). The youngest group had the lowest proportion of Laz use, their speech-rate decreasing among family-members. The oldest group (>45), on the other hand, had the highest rate of the use of Laz with close friends and family-members, the rate occurring around 54%-70%. (ii) *Education* was found to be another factor determining which language to use with whom. Indeed, many of the participants with the lowest level of education had the highest share of using Laz with all the interlocutors in the environment, the percentages ranging between (88% and 64%). With the increase in years of schooling and education, there was a decline in Laz use among the participants, the rates being (50%-32%). While the participants with a primary school degree consistently reported to speak Laz with the elderly and their peers in the same generation (82-88%), the degree of Laz use decreased when they communicated with the younger family-members. Overall, the results suggest a considerable amount of Turkish used in the family. (iii) *Occupation*: Recall from Table 3 that more than half of the participants (54%) were blue-collar workers. Despite varying proportions with different interlocutors, the use of Laz in this population appears to occur around 50% (with mothers at 56.8%, fathers at 57.3%, siblings at 49.8%, spouses at 49.8%, children at 31.2%); this rate, however, drops radically in those with white-collar jobs (with mothers at 31%, fathers at 25.8%, siblings at 19%, spouses at 10.2%, children at 4.5%) or students (with mothers at 7.7%, fathers at 7.7%, siblings at 2.6%, children at 5%). These percentages get relatively higher while addressing grandparents, percentages occurring around 40% with university graduates and 19% with students (iv) *The place of residence*: In small towns and villages the proportion of communication with people is at least two times higher in Laz than in Turkish.

7.2. The Use of Laz in the Workplace and Education

One should note from the outset that Laz has had almost no official status in the educational or official domains in Turkey. This was clearly found in the data, which revealed that 97% of the participants did not take any courses on Laz in an educational context. The remaining 3% of the participants (12 people out of 450) were the participants who either attended a Laz course in a Laz Cultural Institute or took it as an elective course in a local school[1]. One should note that these 12 people are mostly young people. No participants from the old generation had a chance to take any courses on Laz.

7.3. Language-use in Other Domains

Appendix 6 presents data on the use of Laz and Turkish in various social domains. Our aim was to find out which language was used with whom in what contexts. These data show that in addition to its use at home and in the neighbourhood with percentages of 24.9 and 28.4, respectively, Laz is most frequently used in certain cultural rituals such as funerals (19.8%) and weddings (19.3%), which was followed by other social settings with more complex networks like the bazaar (16.4%). What is striking is that in almost all local and official institutions, Turkish is the dominant language, Laz being limited to certain informal contexts. On average, Turkish is used 87.8% of the time in schools, 86.4% in workplaces, 90.7% in local public places and 92.7% in governmental institutions.

---

[1] Following the decree issued by the Ministry of Education in 2013, Laz has been offered as an elective course in the Laz-speaking provinces of the Black Sea Region. There need to be at least 10 registered students for the course to be officially opened. The content of the Laz courses and the methodology used in teaching remain to be examined in further research.

8. Transmission of Laz into Younger Generations

8.1. Language-use in the Family

Appendix 7 presents data on the language of communication between parents and their language while addressing their children. On average, 46.2% of the participants reported that their parents addressed each other in Laz, 16% in Turkish, and 38% in Laz and Turkish equally. As in previous sections, a robust difference was observed between the Black Sea and Marmara regions, suggesting the more use of Laz as a family language in the Black Sea region. While 52.9% of the parents addressed each other in Laz in the Black Sea region, only 37.2% used Laz in the Marmara. A reverse relationship was found in the use of Turkish in both regions. The proportion of the use of Turkish between the parents was 20.9% in the Marmara and 12.4% in the Black Sea region.

A similar result was found in the language addressed to the participants prior to the start of formal education. Those who live in the Black Sea region addressed their children only in Laz with a percentage of 41.7%, but people from the Marmara region used Laz less, with a percentage of 23.6%. The Turkish-only context in family-communication in the Marmara and the Black Sea region is as follows: 35.6% and 17.8%, respectively. In statistical terms, the results show that the use of Laz both as the language of communication between parents ($t(448) = 3.54$, $p < .05$, two-tailed) and as the language addressed to the participants prior to the start of formal schooling ($t(448) = 5.06$, $p < .05$, two-tailed) is significantly higher among the participants from the Black Sea region than those living in the Marmara region.

Overall, the use of Turkish was found to be higher both in parents' communications and child-directed speech, particularly in the speech of those who are more educated and younger. It was observed that even though couples with a university degree consistently addressed each other in Laz 25.6% of the time, they used Laz only 7.8% of the time in communicating with their children. Overall, these results show that parents tend to use Turkish more with children, which makes Laz even more vulnerable in a society where there is limited recognition and daily use of the language in the community.

8.2. Children's Knowledge of Laz

Appendix 8 presents data on children's knowledge of Laz. While 27.9% of the participants indicated that their children do not know Laz at all, 49.1% reported some knowledge of Laz. It was only 23% of the children whose competence in Laz was reported to be advanced. What this means is that, while close to one-fourth of the participants were able to transfer Laz to their children, almost half of the children could only develop passive competence in Laz. The remaining one in four did not transmit their mother-tongue, Laz, to their children.

A comparison of the two regions reveals that the proportion of the participants who reported that their children did not know Laz was almost four times higher in the Marmara (50%) than in the Black Sea (13%). An independent-samples t-test also shows that the children from the Black Sea region know Laz better than those from the Marmara region, $t(281) = 8.43$, $p <$ .05, *two-tailed*. As can be seen in Appendix 9, when parents were asked how often they addressed their children in Laz, more than one in four (22.3%) said 'never'. Another quarter rarely used Laz when communicating with children. It is only 17.7% of the parents who report that they used Laz systematically.

9. Discussion

On the basis of a large-scale survey, the present study sought to provide data on the current status of Laz in two different regions of Turkey. It examined three main areas: (i) language-competence of the participants, with reference to their oral and literacy skills in Laz and Turkish, (ii) the use of Laz at home and in the wider community; (iii) the degree of intergenerational language-transmission to younger generations.

First of all, the findings of this study are fully compatible with UNESCO's classification (Moseley, 2012) in that Laz is a definitely endangered language. There is robust evidence of a shift from Laz to Turkish in Laz-speaking communities, and Turkish is used as the dominant language in every sphere of life. While older generations appear to use more Laz, the language is in decline in both regions where the study was conducted. The use of Laz between parents and immediate family-members decreased in all age-ranges. The young group under the age of 25, in particular, speaks dominantly Turkish. The middle age-group between 26-45 years speaks Laz with the older generation (i.e., parents, grandparents) and Turkish with their siblings and other family-members. The oldest group, aged 46 and above, uses more Laz and less Turkish in their conversations with other people. This radical and clear decrease suggests that the transmission of Laz across generations is rather alarming. The fact that these core family-members, who are among the most important components of the socialization of the individual, mainly use Turkish in daily life can be taken as a sign of language-shift towards Turkish in the community. The linguistic behaviour of the participants observed here appears to be compatible with the notion of generational language shift proposed by Fishman in his pioneering studies (e.g., Fishman, 1965, 1966, 1972).

The results also show that the use of Laz is primarily associated with informal personal contexts such as home, neighbourhood, funerals and weddings and that Turkish as the majority language dominates in almost 90% of the time in formal and educational contexts. In almost all social domains, except for the neighbourhood-context in the elderly group, and in all age-groups, Turkish was used more than Laz. These limited domains of use, together with the lack of institutional support, have brought about a process of language-shift away from Laz, which might eventually lead to language-loss across generations. The results in this sense are consistent with previous work on migrant-communities and their heritage-languages (Bettoni, 1989; Li, 1994; Yağmur et al., 1999).

Today we know that the continuous use of language across generations is largely shaped by how often it is used as a medium of communication among individuals or within the community in everyday life. The maintenance and sustainability of language depend on many socio-political factors as well as the perceptions and attitudes developed within the community in relation to the language itself (Fishman, 2001). The more the language is used by individuals not only in daily life within the community and but also in formal settings and education, the more possible it is to prevent its loss (Baker & Wright, 2017; Polinsky, 2018). The findings in this study, however, do not show bilingual use of Laz and Turkish as part of daily life not only in the more industrialized provinces of the Marmara region, but even in the Black Sea region where Laz is spoken relatively more widely.

The findings also reveal that, while the participants have good speaking and comprehension skills in Laz, their literacy skills are extremely low. This is mainly due to Laz being limited only to oral contexts in Turkey. By contrast, language-skills in Turkish are at the opposite end, Turkish being the dominant language in literacy-skills for both groups of participants in the two regions. Once again, these results are in line with previous work on heritage-languages that suggests that consistent use of the heritage-language not only at home but also in the educational contexts has a direct impact on literacy development (August & Shanahan, 2006), which in turn reinforces oral language-skills as well as vocabulary-knowledge, decoding and fluency skills in reading-acquisition (Bialystok, 2007).

Regarding the intergenerational transmission of Laz to younger generations, it was found that one in four families do not address their children in Laz at all. Another 25 per-cent of the parents rarely use Laz when conversing with children. Around 30% of the families use Laz relatively more frequently. Only 18% of the parents systematically use Laz in their child-directed speech. What this suggests is that, while close to a quarter of the participants were able to transfer Laz to their children, almost half of the children could only acquire passive competence in Laz. In technical terms, this is referred to as receptive bilingualism in the relevant literature, where speakers can understand the language but have limited proficiency in using it (Li, 2007). Indeed, as previously quoted in the introductory section, this was what the participants of this study *Aslı* and *Volkan* said in specific terms. They stated that they could understand Laz but could not speak it. When parents were asked to provide reasons for not speaking Laz with their children, some replied that they did not want their children to develop accented Turkish. Most believe that their children need standard Turkish for access to social and economic benefits in Turkish society. In a way, the findings of this study confirm the language power-relations in language contact-situations that increase the use of Turkish (Fairclough, 1989; Holmes et al., 1993; Pai et al., 2015). Undoubtedly, the majority of the participants consider Turkish as an essential tool for their careers and status in society. Turkish is also the means of communication in official settings, including the educational system where Laz-speaking children continue their studies. In order to reverse this situation and prevent Laz from losing ground against Turkish, much work that aims at promoting its use in the wider community, including official settings, is needed.

10. Concluding remarks

In line with UNESCO's classification, the results presented in this study demonstrate that with respect to language-proficiency and competence in Laz language-use is seriously decreasing in Laz-speaking communities, becoming mostly restricted to daily communication at home or in the neighbourhood. These findings underline the need to reflect critically on the status of Laz in Turkey. We believe that there is an urgent need for supportive efforts towards Laz as well as other ethnic or minority languages in the country. Given the widespread nature of bilingual and multilingual populations across the world (Bhatia & Ritchie, 2013; Rothman, González-Alonso & Puig-Mayenco, 2019), a new paradigm appears to be needed for the preservation of heritage-languages like Laz. In Fishman's words (2013, 481), 'demographically, economically, symbolically and functionally minoritized languages need preventive and proactive measures before they reach a stage of disappearance' (p. 481). Clearly, there are many linguistic, cultural, political, social and demographic factors, which need to be taken into consideration in the preservation of heritage-languages like Laz. The use of Laz not only at home but also in different domains will have a great impact on its intergenerational transmission. In its current form, because there is limited reinforcement at home and almost none in the wider community, Laz will not survive in the years to come. It needs to be supported in official domains, educational institutions and the media. As stated previously in Section 5.2. in recent years we have witnessed small steps taken in the recognition of Laz as an elective course in primary schools in the Black Sea region. Following the decree issued by the Ministry of Education in 2013, Laz is officially offered as an elective course once a week for small groups of children in the Black Sea region. While it is beyond the scope of this paper, it remains to be seen how effective these courses are, given the restrictions and the limited number of hours allocated to Laz in the region. In order to further advance the vitality of Laz, not only Laz language-courses but also Laz medium-courses and schools are essential. We would like to close by stating that we need to embrace linguistic diversity as a resource and potential for both individuals and societies.

Acknowledgements

We would like to thank all the participants of the study both in the Black Sea and Marmara Regions for providing us with the data that shed light on the current status of Laz in Turkey. We also acknowledge the contributions of the assistants who collected the data in different cities and provinces. Many thanks to the audience at The United Nations at 75: Listening, Talking and Taking Action in a Multilingual World Symposium, New York, May 9-10, 2019 for their helpful comments and suggestions on an earlier version of this paper. This research was funded by the European Instrument for Democracy and Human Rights (EIDHR) (Reference: EuropeAid/136297/DD/ ACT/TR), for which we are extremely grateful.

References

Alba, R., Logan, J. R., Lutz, A. & Stults, B. J. (2002).'Only English by the third generation? Loss and preservation of the mother tongue among the grandchildren of contemporary immigrants. *Demography, 39*, 467-484.

Arriagada, P. A. (2005). Family context and Spanish-language use: A Study of Latino children in the United States. *Social Science Quarterly, 86* (3), 599-619.

August, D., & Shanahan, T. (2006). *Developing literacy in second-language learners: Report of the national literacy panel on language minority children and youth.* Mahwah, NJ: Lawrence Erlbaum Associates.

Baker, C. & Jones, S. P. (1998). *Encyclopedia of bilingualism and bilingual education.* Clevedon: Multilingual Matters.

Baker, C. & Wright, W. E. (2017). *Foundations of bilingual education and bilingualism.* Bristol: Multilingual Matters.

Batibo, H. M. (2005). *Language decline and death in Africa: Causes, consequences and challenges.* Clevedon: Multilingual Matters.

Benninghaus, R. (1989). The Laz: An example of multiple identification. In P. A. Andrews (Ed.), *Ethnic groups in the Republic of Turkey* (pp.497–502). Göttingen: Hubert and Co.

Bettoni, C. (1989). Language loss among Italians in Australia: A summary of current research. *I.T.L. Review of Applied Linguistics, 83,* 37-50.

Bhatia, Tej K. & W. C. Ritchie. (Ed.). (2013). *The handbook of bilingualism and multilingualism.* West Sussex: Wiley-Blackwell.

Bialystok, E. (2007). 'Acquisition of literacy in bilingual children: A framework for research.' *Language Learning, 57*(1), 45-77.

Cummins, J. (2005). 'A proposal for action: Strategies for recognizing heritage language competence as a learning resource within the mainstream classroom.' *The Modern Language Journal, 89*(4), 585-592.

Dorian, N. C. (1981). *Language death: The life cycle of a Scottish Gaelic dialect.* Philadelphia, PA: University of Pennsylvania Press.

Edwards, J. (1992). 'Sociopolitical aspects of language maintenance and loss: Towards a typology of minority language situations.' In W. Fase, K. Jaspaert, and S. Kroon (Eds.), *Maintenance and loss of minority languages* (pp. 37-54). Amsterdam: John Benjamins.

Fairclough, N. (1989). *Language and power.* London: Longman.

Fishman, J. A. (1965). 'Language maintenance and language shift: The American immigrant case within a general theoretical perspective.' *Sociologus, 16*(1), 19-39.

Fishman, J. A. (1966). Language maintenance and language shift as a field of inquiry. In J. A. Fishman (Ed.), *Language loyalty in the United States* (pp. 32-70). The Hague: Mouton.

Fishman, J. A. (1972). *The sociology of language; An interdisciplinary social science approach to language in society.* Rowley, Mass. Newbury House.

Fishman, J. A. (2013). Language maintenance, language shift and reversing language shift. In T. K. Bhatia & W. C. Ritchie (Eds.), *Handbook of bilingualism and multilingualism* (pp. 466-494). Malden, M. A: Blackwell Publishing.

Fishman, J. A. (1991). *Reversing language shift: Theoretical and empirical foundations of assistance to threatened languages.* Clevedon: Multilingual Matters.

Gal, S. (1979). *Language shift: Social determinants of linguistic change in bilingual Austria.* New York, NY: Academic Press.

García, O. (2009). *Bilingual education in the 21st century: A global perspective.* Malden, MA: Wiley-Blackwell.

Giles, H., Bourhis, R. Y., & Taylor, D. M. (1977). Towards a theory of language in ethnic group relations. H. Giles (Ed.), *Language, ethnicity and intergroup relations* (pp. 307-348). London: Academic Press.

Hale, K. (1992). Special issue on 'Endangered languages'. *Language, 68,* 1- 42.

Holisky, D. A. (1991). Laz. In A. C. Harris (Ed.), *The indigenous languages of the Caucasus: The Kartvelian languages* (Vol. 1, pp. 395-472). Delmar/New York: Caravan.

Holmes, J. (2013). *An introduction to sociolinguistics.* 4th ed. New York: Pearson.

Holmes, J., Roberts, M., Verivaki, M. & Aipolo, A. (1993). Language Maintenance and Shift in Three New Zealand Speech Communities. *Applied Linguistics, 14*(1), 1-24.

Karimova, N. & Deverell, E. (2001). *Minorities in Turkey. Occasional Papers.* No. 19. Stockholm: The Swedish Institute of International Affairs.

Kutscher, S. (2008). The language of the Laz in Turkey: Contact-induced change or gradual language loss? *Turkic Languages, 12*(1), 82-102.

Li, W. (2007). *The bilingualism reader.* New York, NY: Routledge.

Li, W. (1995). Variations in patterns of language choice and code-switching by three groups of Chinese/English speakers in Newcastle upon Tyne. *Multilingua—Journal of Cross-Cultural and Interlanguage Communication, 14*(3). 297-322.

Li, W. (1994). *Three generations, two Languages, one family.* Clevedon: Multilingual Matters.

Lopez, D. E. (1996). Language: Diversity and assimilation. In R. D. Waldinger & M. Bozorgmehr (Eds.), *Ethnic Los Angeles* (pp. 139-163). New York: Russell Sage Foundation.

McCarty, T. I. (2013). *Language planning and policy in native America: History, theory, praxis.* Bristol, UK: Multilingual Matters.

Montrul, S. (2008). *Incomplete acquisition in bilingualism: Re-examining the age factor.* Amsterdam: John Benjamins.

Moseley, C. (2012). *The UNESCO Atlas of the world's languages in danger: Context and process.* World Oral Literature Project. Cambridge: University of Cambridge. https://aspace.repository.cam.ac.uk/bitstream/handle/1810/243434/WOLP_OP_05_highres.pdf?sequence=1&isAllowed=y

Pai, M., Cummins, J., Nocus, I., Salaün, M., & Vernaudon, J. (2015). Intersections of language ideology, power and identity: Bilingual education and indigenous language revitalization in French Polynesia. In W.E. Wright, S. Bun & O. Garcia (Eds.), *Handbook of bilingual and multilingual education* (pp. 145-163). Malden, MA: John Wiley and Sons.

Paulston, C. B., Chen, P. C. & Connerty, M. C. (1993). Language regenesis: A conceptual overview of language revival, revitalization and reversal. *Journal of Multilingual and Multicultural Development, 14* (4), 275-286.

Polinsky, M. (2018). *Heritage languages and their speakers.* Cambridge: Cambridge University Press.

Polinsky, M. (2007). Incomplete acquisition: American Russian. *Journal of Slavic Linguistics, 14*(2), 161-219.

Portes, A., & Hao, L. (1998). E pluribus unum: Bilingualism and loss of language in the second generation. *Sociology of Education, 71,* 269-294.

Rothman, J., González-Alonso, J. & Puig-Mayenco. (2019). *Third language acquisition and linguistic transfer.* Cambridge: Cambridge University Press.

UNESCO (2003). http://www.unesco.org/new/fileadmin/MULTIMEDIA/HQ/CLT/pdf/Language_vitality_and_endangerment_EN.pdf

Valdés, G. (2001). Heritage language students: Profiles and possibilities. In J. K. Peyton, D. A. Ranard & S. McGinnis (Ed.), *Heritage languages in America: Preserving a national resource* (pp. 37-77). Washington, DC ve McHenry, IL: Center for Applied Linguistics ve Delta Systems.

Yağmur, K., de Bot, K., & Korzilius, H. (1999). Language attrition, language shift and ethnolinguistic vitality of Turkish in Australia. *Journal of Multilingual and Multicultural Development, 20* (1), 51-69.

Appendices

Appendix 1. How comfortable participants feel while speaking in Laz and Turkish (%)

		Laz	Turkish	Both
Gender	Female	29.3	34.5	36.2
	Male	34.8	31.2	33.9
Age	<25 age	**5.9**	29.4	64.7
	26-45 age	26.4	39.2	34.4
	> 46 age	47.1	30.9	22.0
Educational background	Primary school/lower	68.9	23.5	7.6
	Middle/High school	23.8	42.9	33.3
	University degree/above	6.2	27.9	65.9
Occupation	Blue collar	49.0	33.3	17.7
	White collar	15.5	35.7	48.8
	Student	6.4	26.9	66.7
Place of residence	Town	20.9	31.4	47.7
	Village	71.4	25.0	3.6
	Small town/Village	38.6	35.6	25.7
Total		**32.0**	**35.1**	**32.9**

Appendix 2. Language-competence in Laz (in terms of Gender and Age)

		Total	Black Sea / Marmara		Gender		Age		
			Black Sea	Marmara	Female	Male	<25 age	26-45 age	>46 age
Comprehension	None	2.2	.8	4.2	1.7	2.7	6.9	2.4	0.0
	Little	8.0	3.9	13.6	9.6	6.3	17.6	7.2	4.0
	Intermediate	21.6	23.2	19.4	24.0	19.0	33.3	26.4	13.5
	Good	23.6	28.2	17.3	19.7	27.6	20.6	28.0	22.4
	Very good	44.7	44.0	45.5	45.0	44.3	21.6	36.0	60.1
Speaking	None	5.6	1.2	11.5	6.1	5.0	12.7	5.6	2.2
	Little	13.8	11.6	16.8	17.0	10.4	33.3	13.6	4.9
	Intermediate	24.9	22.8	27.7	26.6	23.1	31.4	29.6	19.3
	Good	24.0	29.7	16.2	19.2	29.0	13.7	29.6	25.6
	Very good	31.8	34.7	27.7	31.0	32.6	8.8	21.6	48.0

Appendix 3. Language-competence in Laz
(in terms of Education, Occupation and Place of residence)

		Education			Occupation			Place of residence		
		Primary school	Middle–high school	University	Blue-collar	White-collar	student	city	village	city-village
Comprehension	None	.8	2.6	3.1	0.0	2.3	9.0	4.1	0.0	.5
	Little	.8	6.3	17.8	3.7	10.1	17.9	11.4	0.0	5.4
	Intermediate	10.6	22.8	31.0	16.5	24.8	32.1	24.5	3.6	20.8
	Good	23.5	28.0	17.1	26.3	21.7	17.9	15.9	25.0	31.7
	Very good	64.4	40.2	31.0	53.5	41.1	23.1	44.1	71.4	41.6
Speaking	None	.8	5.8	10.1	2.5	6.2	14.1	9.1	0.0	2.5
	Little	.8	10.6	31.8	3.7	20.9	33.3	18.2	3.6	10.4
	Intermediate	15.2	28.6	29.5	21.4	28.7	29.5	25.9	0.0	27.2
	Good	24.2	28.6	17.1	28.4	21.7	14.1	19.5	25.0	28.7
	Very good	59.1	26.5	11.6	44.0	22.5	9.0	27.3	71.4	31.2

Appendix 4. Which language is used with whom (Gender and Age)

		Total	Region / Marmara		Gender		Age		
			Black Sea	Marmara	Female	Male	<25	26-45	>45
Mother	Turk.	35.1	28.6	44.1	42.3	27.7	69.6	35.2	19.1
	Laz-Tr	23.9	19.7	29.8	21.1	26.8	23.5	29.6	20.9
	Laz	40.9	51.7	26.1	36.6	45.5	6.9	35.2	60.0
Father	Turk.	38.8	28.8	52.7	45.5	32.0	75.5	37.4	22.5
	Laz-Tr	21.4	19.5	24.2	17.0	26.0	17.6	30.1	18.3
	Laz	39.7	51.8	23.1	37.5	42.0	6.9	32.5	59.2
Siblings	Turk.	47.2	35.9	62.6	50.2	44.0	86.1	51.6	26.8
	Laz-Tr	20.1	18.8	21.9	18.1	22.2	11.9	21.3	23.2
	Laz	32.7	45.3	15.5	31.7	33.8	2.0	27.0	50.0
Spouse	Turk.	49.9	36.4	70.5	49.5	50.3	90.9	58.1	35.8
	Laz-Tr	17.3	17.3	17.3	14.8	19.9	9.1	16.3	19.8
	Laz	32.9	**46.3**	**12.2**	35.7	29.8	0.0	25.6	44.3
Children	Turk.	**59.4**	44.7	81.3	61.5	57.1	90.4	62.8	50.7
	Laz-Tr	**19.3**	23.6	12.9	15.1	23.8	5.8	23.1	21.2
	Laz	21.3	**31.7**	**5.8**	23.5	19.0	3.8	14.1	28.1
Grandmother	Turk.	30.4	21.4	43.6	36.3	24.4	62.0	25.7	16.7
	Laz-Tr	18.0	18.5	17.2	16.2	19.8	19.0	26.6	12.5
	Laz	51.6	60.1	39.3	47.5	55.8	19.0	47.7	70.8
Grandfather	Turk.	29.5	19.8	44.0	34.8	24.2	59.4	25.2	17.1
	Laz-Tr	18.4	20.3	15.7	17.7	19.2	21.9	26.2	12.4
	Laz	52.0	59.9	40.3	47.5	56.6	18.8	48.6	70.5
Laz friends	Turk.	36.9	27.3	50.6	42.7	31.0	70.0	36.3	21.4
	Laz-Tr	23.7	22.7	25.3	18.8	28.7	23.0	28.2	21.4
	Laz	39.4	50.0	24.2	38.5	40.3	7.0	35.5	57.1
Laz acquaintance	Turk.	35.9	27.1	48.4	40.2	31.5	70.0	33.3	21.7
	Laz-Tr	26.5	25.9	27.5	23.2	30.0	24.0	33.3	24.0
	Laz	37.5	47.1	24.2	36.6	38.5	6.0	33.3	54.4

Laz neighbours	Turk.	36.8	27.3	50.0	41.0	32.4	71.0	35.0	22.0
	Laz-Tr	25.3	25.0	25.8	22.5	28.2	24.0	30.8	22.9
	Laz	37.9	47.7	24.2	36.5	39.4	5.0	34.2	55.0
Laz relatives	Turk.	34.9	26.3	46.7	39.1	30.4	69.4	32.2	20.9
	Laz-Tr	26.7	26.3	27.2	23.6	29.9	24.5	32.2	24.5
	Laz	38.5	47.5	26.1	37.3	39.7	6.1	35.5	54.5

Appendix 5. Which language is used with whom?
(Education, Occupation, Place of residence)

		Education			Occupation			Place of residence		
		Primary	Middle-high school	University	Blue-collar	White-collar	student	city	village	City-village
Mother	Turkish	12.1	32.8	62.7	17.7	46	71.8	44.5	10.7	28.4
	Laz-Tr	11.4	33.3	23	25.5	23	20.5	27.5	7.1	22.4
	Laz	76.5	33.9	14.3	56.8	31	7.7	28	82.1	49.3
Father	Turkish	12.9	38.8	66.7	20.7	50.8	75.6	53	7.1	28
	Laz-Tr	10.6	28.7	22	22	23.4	16.7	21.4	14.3	22.5
	Laz	76.5	32.4	11.4	57.3	25.8	7.7	25.6	78.6	49.5
Siblings	Turkish	14.4	52.4	73.8	28	59.5	85.9	60.2	14.3	37.7
	Laz-Tr	15.2	24.9	18.3	22.2	21.4	11.5	21.3	17.9	19.1
	Laz	70.5	22.7	7.9	49.8	19	2.6	18.5	67.9	43.2
Spouses	Turkish	17.2	58.3	84.9	32.9	68.4	92.9	65.4	7.7	41.2
	Laz-Tr	17.2	21.6	10.5	17.4	21.4	7.1	17.3	15.4	17.6
	Laz	65.6	20.1	4.7	49.8	10.2	0	17.3	76.9	41.2
Children	Turkish	34.8	69.8	82.9	47.7	73	92.5	74.4	3.8	53.4
	Laz-Tr	23.5	18.7	13.2	21.1	22.5	2.5	16.9	34.6	19.3
	Laz	41.7	11.5	3.9	31.2	4.5	5	8.8	61.5	27.3
Grandmother	Turkish	9.2	30.2	53.1	15.6	36.3	62.3	41.7	3.7	23
	Laz-Tr	9.2	21.3	22.1	15.6	22.1	18.2	18.7	11.1	18.2
	Laz	81.5	48.5	24.8	68.7	41.6	19.5	39.6	85.2	58.8
Grandfather	Turkish	8.3	29.8	52.8	15.2	36	60.8	39.7	3.6	23.4
	Laz-Tr	8.3	22.6	23.1	15.6	22.5	20.3	19	14.3	18.5
	Laz	83.3	47.6	24.1	69.2	41.4	18.9	41.3	82.1	58.2
Laz friends	Turkish	8.7	37	65.3	19.6	47.2	73.7	46.9	3.6	31.2
	Laz-Tr	13.5	32.1	21.8	22.1	30.1	18.4	28	14.3	20.6
	Laz	77.8	31	12.9	58.3	22.8	7.9	25.1	82.1	48.2
Laz acquaintances	Turkish	7.8	38.6	61.3	19.7	45.5	71.4	45.7	3.6	30.2
	Laz-Tr	17.8	33.7	25	24.7	33.9	20.8	30	17.9	24.1
	Laz	74.4	27.7	13.7	55.6	20.7	7.8	24.3	78.6	45.7
Laz neighbours	Turkish	8.3	38.9	64.5	20.5	46.7	71.4	46.6	3.6	31.2
	Laz-Tr	17.4	32.4	23.1	23.8	30.3	22.1	30.3	14.3	21.8
	Laz	74.2	28.6	12.4	55.6	23	6.5	23.1	82.1	47
Laz relatives	Turkish	8.4	36.8	60.2	19.6	43.5	69.3	44.1	3.6	29.5
	Laz-Tr	17.6	33.5	26	23.8	34.7	22.7	31.3	14.3	23.5
	Laz	74	29.7	13.8	56.7	21.8	8	24.6	82.1	47

Appendix 6. Use of Laz and Turkish in other social domains (%)

		Total	Black Sea/Marmara		Gender		Age		
			Black Sea	Marmara	Female	Male	<25	26-45	>46
Home	Turkish	48.2	39.0	60.7	51.1	45.2	69.6	44.8	40.4
	Laz-Tr	26.9	23.2	31.9	24.5	29.4	23.5	33.6	24.7
	Laz	24.9	37.8	7.3	24.5	25.3	6.9	21.6	35.0
Neighbourhood	Turkish	52.2	34.0	77.0	57.2	47.1	77.5	53.6	39.9
	Laz-Tr	19.3	22.4	15.2	15.3	23.5	18.6	20.0	19.3
	Laz	28.4	43.6	7.9	27.5	29.4	3.9	26.4	40.8
Shopping Bazaar	Turkish	60.9	46.7	80.1	65.5	56.1	89.2	63.2	46.6
	Laz-Tr	22.7	26.6	17.3	18.3	27.1	6.9	24.8	28.7
	Laz	16.4	26.6	2.6	16.2	16.7	3.9	12.0	24.7
Weddings	Turkish	49.6	42.1	59.7	53.3	45.7	78.4	49.6	36.3
	Laz-Tr	31.1	30.1	32.5	28.4	33.9	12.7	36.0	36.8
	Laz	19.3	27.8	7.9	18.3	20.4	8.8	14.4	26.9
Funerals	Turkish	48.7	42.5	57.1	53.3	43.9	79.4	46.4	35.9
	Laz-Tr	31.6	31.7	31.4	27.5	35.7	12.7	36.8	37.2
	Laz	19.8	25.9	11.5	19.2	20.4	7.8	16.8	26.9
School	Turkish	87.8	85.3	91.1	89.1	86.4	93.1	88.8	84.8
	Laz-Tr	7.8	9.3	5.8	6.1	9.5	5.9	7.2	9.0
	Laz	4.4	5.4	3.1	4.8	4.1	1.0	4.0	6.3
Workplace	Turkish	86.4	83.4	90.6	87.8	85.1	93.1	89.6	81.6
	Laz-Tr	9.1	10.4	7.3	7.4	10.9	5.9	8.0	11.2
	Laz	4.4	6.2	2.1	4.8	4.1	1.0	2.4	7.2
Local public places (e.g. hospital, municipality)	Turkish	90.7	88.0	94.2	92.1	89.1	94.1	90.4	89.2
	Laz-Tr	6.9	8.5	4.7	5.7	8.1	4.9	8.0	7.2
	Laz	2.4	3.5	1.0	2.2	2.7	1.0	1.6	3.6
Official places	Turkish	92.7	91.1	94.8	93.4	91.9	96.1	91.2	91.9
	Laz-Tr	5.8	6.9	4.2	5.2	6.3	2.9	8.0	5.8
	Laz	1.6	1.9	1.0	1.3	1.8	1.0	.8	2.2

Appendix 7. Family language spoken during childhood

		Language of communication between the parents			Language addressed to the participants until primary school years		
		Laz	Laz-Turkish	Turkish	Laz	Laz-Turkish	Turkish
Regions	Black Sea	52.9	34.7	12.4	41.7	40.5	17.8
	Marmara	37.2	41.9	20.9	23.6	40.8	35.6
Age	<25	15.7	50.0	34.3	2.9	51.0	46.1
	26-45	40.8	45.6	13.6	23.2	48.8	28.0
	>46	63.2	27.8	9.0	54.3	31.4	14.3
Education	Primary school	79.5	14.4	6.1	73.5	16.7	9.8
	Middle-High school	37.0	47.6	15.3	24.3	54.5	21.2
	University/above	25.6	47.3	27.1	7.8	45.0	47.3
Occupation	Blue-collar	61.3	29.6	9.1	52.3	34.2	13.6
	White-collar	38.0	46.5	15.5	17.8	49.6	32.6
	Student	12.8	48.7	38.5	3.8	46.2	50.0
Place of residence	City	36.8	40.9	22.3	23.6	39.5	36.8
	Village	78.6	17.9	3.6	75.0	25.0	0.0
	City/Village	52.0	37.1	10.9	39.6	44.1	16.3
Total		**46.2**	**37.8**	**16.0**	**34.0**	**40.7**	**25.3**

Appendix 8. Children's knowledge of Laz in terms of socio-demographic variables

		Do/Does your child/ren know Laz?		
		No	Some	Advanced
Regions	Black Sea	13.0	52.7	34.3
	Marmara	50.0	43.9	6.1
Age	<25	100.0	0.0	0.0
	26-45	43.1	47.7	9.2
	> 46	22.7	50.0	27.3
Education	Primary school	10.3	46.8	42.9
	Middle-High School	29.1	60.9	10.0
	University-above	72.3	27.7	0.0
Occupation	Blue-collar	20.6	50.7	28.7
	White-collar	48.6	44.6	6.8
	Student	0.0	0.0	0.0
Place of residence	City/small town	40.3	46.3	13.4
	Village	8.3	25.0	66.7
	Small town-Village	18.4	56.8	24.8
Total		**27.9**	**49.1**	**23.0**

Appendix 9. The use of Laz with children (%)

How often do you address your children in Laz?

		Never	Rarely	Sometimes	Always
Regions	Black Sea	11.2	21.3	42.6	24.9
	Marmara	38.6	31.6	22.8	7.0
Age	<25	50.0	0.0	50.0	0.0
	26-45	23.1	29.2	41.5	6.2
	> 46	21.8	24.5	32.4	21.3
Education	Primary school	6.3	21.4	40.5	31.7
	Middle-High school	28.2	29.1	34.5	8.2
	University-above	51.1	27.7	19.1	2.1
Occupation	Blue-collar	19.6	22.5	36.8	21.1
	White-collar	29.7	33.8	28.4	8.1
	Student	0.0	0.0	0.0	0.0
Place of residence	Small town	31.3	29.9	28.4	10.4
	Village	4.2	4.2	37.5	54.2
	Small town-Village	16.0	24.8	40.8	18.4
Total		**22.3**	**25.4**	**34.6**	**17.7**

Chapter 2

On the Significance of Laz for Theoretical Research in Linguistics

Ömer Demirok
Boğaziçi University, Turkey

Balkız Öztürk
Boğaziçi University, Turkey

Abstract

This chapter discusses the potential of the Laz language for theoretical research in linguistics. Theoretical linguistics is empirically-driven and aims to understand the workings of grammars as mental systems by thoroughly investigating linguistic data that come from natural languages across the world. While all languages are important for theoretical research, Laz does genuinely stand out in terms of its potential to contribute to various theoretical debates in linguistics. It does so with its often typologically rare linguistic features, and the sheer number of notions it grammaticalizes. Devoting a section to each, this chapter highlights three of these domains in which Laz has the potential to contribute to theoretical research: the case and agreement system, the verb classification system, and the verbal spatial-marking system. Each section briefly describes the system from a theory-neutral point of view and elaborates on the potential of the empirical facts for specific theoretical questions.

Keywords: *Case, ergativity, spatial marking, thematic suffixes, theoretical linguistics, morphosyntax*

***

1. Introduction

Theoretical linguistics aims to understand the workings of grammar as mental systems by thoroughly investigating the vast space of linguistic data from natural languages across the world. While there is no doubt that all languages are equally crucial for theoretical research, some of them stand out in their potential to advance our understanding of certain research areas. This is because linguistic variation is a fact, and different languages naturally stand out in other respects. That said, in terms of its potential to contribute to various theoretical debates in linguistics, Laz does genuinely stand out. It does so with its often typologically rare linguistic features and the sheer number of notions it grammaticalizes. These include, among others, a typologically rare case-system, a rich verbal agreement-system, a largely semantic verb classification-system, a rich and intricate valency-marking system, a large set of markers that encode spatial information related to events, and a sentence-embedding system that challenges the typical assumptions about the way grammars establish co-variance between forms. Devoting a section to each, this chapter highlights three of these domains in which Laz has the potential to contribute to theoretical research: the case- and agreement-system, the verb-classification system, and the verbal spatial-marking system. Each section briefly describes the system from a theory-neutral point of view and elaborates on the potential of the empirical facts for specific theoretical questions.

2. Case and Agreement in Laz

This section has two parts. In the first part, we discuss the case-system of Laz,[1] focusing on the question of what the correct characterization of the ergative case should be. In the second part, we discuss the complex agreement-system of Laz, focusing on the question of how agreement realization-patterns in Laz can inform theoretical research about the syntactic hierarchy of non-subject NPs and the interaction between case and agreement-calculus in grammar.

2.1. Does Laz challenge the idea that ergative is uniform?

In varieties of Laz that have preserved overt case-marking (e.g., Pazar Laz), the morphological case-differentiation of Noun Phrases (NPs) presents a typologically rare system, attested in only a handful of languages. In this

---

[1] All Laz data that appear in this chapter come from the Atina/Pazar dialect of Laz. We gratefully acknowledge the help of our primary native speaker consultant Ismail Avcı Bucaklişi.

section, building on the important insights in earlier works on South Caucasian case (Harris, 1985; Hewitt, 1987; Holisky, 1991, Boeder, 2005), we discuss the case system of Pazar/Atina dialect of Laz, which is a system where case, at least on the surface, does not seem to be a morphological manifestation of a relation *between* NPs. Instead, it appears that the case in Laz is the morphological manifestation of the semantic relation an NP bears to the event of which it is a participant (Dixon, 1994; Woolford, 2006). This kind of case-system is called split-S or active-ergative in that the sole NP of an intransitive verb is differentially marked, depending on the role the NP has in the event. Compare the subject cases in (1b) and (1c). If the sole NP is an initiator/controller of the event, we see the ergative (ERG) case marking $-k$ on the NP. Otherwise, we see its absence, labelled nominative (NOM). For example, from this perspective, the fact that the subject *bere* 'child' in (1b) and the object *urdzenepe* 'grapes' in (1a) are both NOM (i.e., unmarked) is not surprising, for both are NPs that *undergo* an event that befalls them and over which they have no control. Similarly, the fact that the subject *bere* 'child' in (1c) and (1a) are both ERG, is again not surprising, for both are NPs that initiate/control the event.

(1) Laz
a. Bere-k   urdzen-epe   çinax-u
   child-erg   GRAPE-PL.NOM   CRUSH-PAST.3SG
   'The child crushed the grapes.'
b. Bere   col-u
   child.NOM   fall-PAST.3SG
   'The child fell.'
c. Bere-k   i-gzal-u
   child-ERG   PRV-walk-PAST.3SG
   'The child walked.'

The active-ergative case-system contrasts with accusative and (purely-) ergative case systems. As shown in (2) and (3), accusative and ergative case-systems differ from the active-ergative case-system in Laz in treating subjects of intransitives invariably.[2] Notably, unlike active-ergative systems, accusative and ergative systems are cross-linguistically widely attested.

---

[2] Departing from the common practice that refers to the unmarked case in ergative systems as absolutive, we label the unmarked case nominative (NOM) regardless of the case alignment.

(2) Turkish: accusative case-system

a. Çocuk   üzüm-ler-i   ye-di.
   child.NOM grape-PL-ACC   eat-PAST.3SG
   'The child ate the grapes.'
b. Çocuk   düş-tü.
   child.NOM fall-PAST.3SG
   'The child fell.'
c. Çocuk   yürü-dü.
   child.NOM walk-PAST.3SG
   'The child walked.'

⇒ only the object NP of a transitive predicate bears a different case, i.e., ACC.

(3) Shipibo: ergative case-system (examples [1]-[5] in Baker and Bobaljik 2017)

a. Maria-**nin**   ra   ochiti   noko-ke
   Maria.ERG   PRT   dog.NOM   find-PRF
   'Maria found the dog.'
b. Maria   ra   mawa-ke
   Maria.NOM   PRT   die-PRF
   'Maria died.'
c.. Rosa   ra   bewa-ke.
   Rosa.NOM   PRT   sing-PRF
   'Rosa sang.'

⇒ only the subject NP of a transitive predicate bears a different case, i.e., ERG.

Recently, the typological rarity of the active-ergative case-system that we see in Laz has become even more interesting, as it defies an otherwise successful theory, known as Dependent Case Theory (DCT hereafter) (Marantz, 1991; Baker & Vinokurova, 2010; Baker & Bobaljik, 2017, among others). DCT sees case, in particular the ERG case, as a relation between NPs. More concretely, in this kind of theory, ERG must be a dependent case that we should only see when there is another NP in the same domain with it. The DCT-perspective on ERG is widely and independently supported across languages where ERG is reserved for the subject NP in transitives and is never observed on the NP in intransitives, as Baker and Bobaljik (2017) extensively argue. That is, if Laz were, in fact, like in (3), it would directly support the DCT-view on ERG. However, Laz is different. In Laz, we do see ERG on subjects of transitives and subjects of some intransitives, as was illustrated in (1). It appears that case-marking is not about transitivity in Laz but derives from the semantic relation NPs bear to the event (Woolford, 2015). Hence, at least on the surface, Laz is a prime example of a linguistic system that profoundly challenges a uniform DCT-perspective on ERG.

Perhaps ironically, Laz *also* presents empirical evidence for the obvious way to explain an active-ergative case-system (as in Laz) within the scope of the idea that ERG is uniformly a dependent case. Under DCT, for ERG to be conditioned on an NP, there has to be another element that enters the so-called 'case-calculus,' the algorithm which determines the morphological case-values on NPs. The problematic example for DCT is (1c) (and, of course, its analogues within Laz and other languages with active-ergative systems). That is, the problem is systematic and arises in a class of intransitive verbs called unergatives, which (1c) exemplifies. Unergatives are traditionally intransitive verbs; therefore, the fact that their subject bears ERG poses a challenge to this uniformly dependent-case view on ERG. Unergatives simply lack another NP, which could explain the appearance of ERG under DCT. However, unergatives have a unique linguistic feature in Laz. As shown in (1c), the verb has a valency prefix *i-*. This prefix *i-*, elsewhere in the language, has a variety of synchronic functions such as reflexivization and argument-suppression, which can be unified under the label '*a placeholder for a regular NP.*'

Interestingly, *i-* is lexically required in a subset of unergatives in Laz, as shown by the impossibility of omitting it in (4). The reconciliation should now be straightforward. If *i-* is genuinely a placeholder for an NP, then perhaps it enters the case-calculus just like a regular NP, which would explain how we get to see ERG in (4) despite the apparent absence of another NP in the clause. This is the DCT-account Baker and Bobalijk (2017) and Nash (2017) sketch for active-ergative systems like Laz, highlighting the NP-placeholder status of *i-*.

(4)
a. Bere-k   i-gzal-u
    child-ERG   PRV-walk-PAST.3SG
    'The child walked.'
b. *Bere-k   gzal-u
    child-ERG   walk-PAST.3SG
    Intended: 'The child walked.'

The question, then, is: does Laz refute a uniform dependent-case view on ERG because we can see ERG only on NPs with a specific semantic role (i.e., initiator, controller of the event)? Or, does Laz support the idea that ERG is uniformly a dependent case because unergatives may be concealed transitives with a placeholder for an object NP that enters the case-calculus?

One good thing about theoretical research is that it urges us to formulate further questions which do not necessarily come up while writing a descriptive grammar of the language. DCT is a theory, and it makes testable predictions. In particular, it allows us to test independently whether an element enters the 'case-calculus' or not. One such domain is case-competition between objects. For example, in causative constructions, the causee may marked by the dative (DAT) in Laz, which can be analyzed as a dependent case because it is licensed only if there is another object NP. To illustrate, we see DAT on *Gubaz* in (5b) because the NP *dişk'a* 'wood' is in the same domain with it. This is a well-known pattern that was analyzed from a dependent case theoretic perspective in Baker and Vinokurova (2010), which deals with DAT marking on causees in Sakha. Their proposal is directly applicable to Laz, as well.

(5)
a. Gubazi-k   dişk'a   çit-u
   Gubaz-ERG   wood.NOM chop-PAST.3SG
   'Gubaz chopped wood.'
b. Xordza-k   Gubazi-s   dişk'a   o-çit-ap-u
   woman-ERG Gubaz-DAT wood.NOM CAUS-chop-CAUS-PAST.3SG
   'The woman made Gubaz chop wood.'

Then, the question is: what happens when we causativize unergatives? If they are like transitives and instead of an object NP, they have an NP placeholder that enters the case-calculus, we should get to see DAT on the causee when we causativize an unergative predicate. We test this on an especially problematic case where there is not even an overt prefix *i-* that can condition the ERG case on the subject in (6). As we have shown above, some unergatives appear to have the supposed NP placeholder *i-* overtly. This is an example that crucially lacks it.

(6)

Dida-k   barbal-am-s
old.woman-ERG   talk.alot-IMPF-PRES.3SG
'The old woman is rambling/talking a lot.'

But we do have evidence that the verb in (6) might be underlyingly transitive. As shown in (7) below, despite the absence of *i-*, DAT (as opposed to ERG or NOM) appears on the causee NP when (6) is causativized. That is, the unergative verb behaves as if it is transitive.

(7)

K'oçi-k   dida-s   var   o-barbal-ap-u
man-ERG   old.woman-DAT   NEG   caus-talk.alot-CAUS-PST.3SG
'The man did not let the old woman ramble/talk a lot.'

How is this possible? One possibility is a null version of the prefix *i-*, which would be an assumption hard to justify independently. There is another alternative, which also has some theoretical backdrop. Unergatives may often have an internal structure as in (8), where the verbal root (e.g., 'barbal' in (6)) is underlyingly a noun (phrase) and gains a verbal meaning by combining with a light verb like v_{do}.³ This sort of structure was hypothesized to be the underlying structure of unergatives in a seminal work by Hale and Keyser (2002) and was argued for Laz in Öztürk and Erguvanlı Taylan (2017).

(8)

Figure 2.1 - Underlying structure of unergative verbs derived from nouns

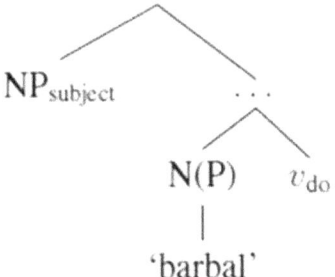

To summarize, from the perspective of DCT, it is not surprising after all that we see an ERG subject in (6). Whatever conditions ERG in (6) also conditions DAT in (7). If (8) is the structure of the event in (6), then *barbal*, by virtue of being an NP underlyingly, can participate in the case-calculus and condition ERG in (6) and DAT in (7).

Notably, there is further evidence for the transitivity of unergatives in Laz, the causative marker *-ap* itself. As was shown in (5b), *-ap* appears when a transitive predicate is causativized. We see that Laz has a different causativizer *-in* for

---

³ This is a cross-linguistically common pattern. For example, in Turkish *dırdır et-* 'to ramble', *et-* is a light verb meaning 'do' and *dırdır* is a noun.

transitivizing intransitivies. Hence, the fact that *-ap* is used in (7) is another support for the transitivity of unergatives. See the data in (9).

(9)
a. K'oğona ğur-u.
   mosquito.NOM die-PAST.3SG
   'The mosquito died.' intr

b. Bere-k k'oğona o-ğur-**in**-u.
   child-ERG mosquito.NOM CAUS-die-CAUS_{intr}-PAST.3SG
   'The child killed the mosquito.'

c. Dida-k bere-s k'oğona o-ğur-**in**-**ap**-u.
   old.woman-ERG child-DAT mosquito.NOM CAUS-die-CAUS_{intr}-CAUS_{trns}-PAST.3SG
   'The old woman made the child kill the mosquito.'

That said, an exhaustive testing of unergatives in Laz is needed to ensure that the pattern reported here is robust and replicable. We have been informed by our language consultant that (7) is preferred, but (10) is not out, either. We would, of course, expect (10) if unergative was an intransitive predicate. This optionality, then, predicts a correlation with the possibility of dropping ERG in (6). While we have anecdotal evidence of the omissibility of ERG on subjects of unergatives, understanding the extent to which this is possible in the grammar of Laz awaits further research.

(10)
K'oçi-k dida var o-barbal-in-am-s
man-ERG old.woman.NOM NEG CAUS-talk.alot-CAUS_{int}-IMPF-PRES.3SG
'The man does not let the old woman ramble/talk a lot.'

2.2 How does agreement realization inform us about syntactic prominence?

Laz has an intricate verbal agreement-system that encodes the person/number-information of the participants of an event. What is particularly noteworthy about the agreement-system of Laz is that not only the subject NP but also a non-subject NP occasion agreement on the verb. But the way agreement-information is realized on the verb is subject to a morphological hierarchy, as Demirok (2013) argues. To illustrate, we see the prefix *b-* cross-referencing a first-person singular subject in (11d) and the prefix *g-* cross-referencing a second person singular object in (11a). However, their simultaneous realization is not possible. As shown by the ungrammatical example in (11e). This means that, when both *b-* and *g-* are licensed to be on the verb individually, *g-* wins over *b-*. One way to state this is to say that *b-* is only insertable when the object-agreement is with a third person, which has no overt marking in the language, as shown in (11f). See also Tuite (1998), Hewitt (2004), Boeder (2005), Lacroix (2009, 2011), Kiria et al. (2015) among others for discussion of these facts or similar facts across South Caucasian.

(11)
a. Ma si g-dzir-i.
   I you 2OBJ-see-NON3SUBJ.PAST
   'I saw you.'
b. Si ma m-dzir-i.
   you I 1OBJ-see-NON3SUBJ.PAST
   'You saw me.'
c. Bere-k ma m-dzir-u.
   child-ERG I 1OBJ-see-3SUBJ.PAST
   'The child saw me.'
d. Ma bere b-dzir-i.
   I child.NOM 1SUBJ-see-NON3SUBJ.PAST
   'I saw the child.'
e. *Ma si g-b-dzir-i.
   I you 2OBJ-1SUBJ-see-NON3SUBJ.PAST
   Intended: 'I saw you.'
f. Gubazi-k bere dzir-u.
   Gubaz-ERG child.NOM see-3SUBJ.PAST
   'Gubaz saw the child.'

While agreement realization in Laz informs morphological theories (Blix, 2020), it also answers difficult syntactic questions. The basic idea in syntactic theories of agreement is that the NP which is more prominent in the syntactic hierarchy, will determine the agreement (Comrie, 1974; Keenan & Comrie, 1977). A well-known formalization of this basic idea in the generative tradition involves positing an agreement probe relatively high in the clausal structure that performs a search-operation downwards and agrees with the closest eligible NP in its search space (Chomsky, 2000; Baker, 2008; Preminger, 2014, among others). Given that subjects are universally more prominent (i.e., structurally higher) than objects as depicted in (12), this basic idea explains the universal preference to agree with subjects over objects in languages where there is agreement only with one NP. This is illustrated by the Turkish data in (13).

(12)

Probe » Subject NP » Object NP   [» = structurally higher]

(13)

Ben   sen-i   gör-dü-m   /   *gör-dü-n
I   you-ACC   see-PAST-1SG   /   see-PAST-2SG
'I saw you.'   Turkish

We find the same basic pattern regarding which NP determines the realization of the suffixal agreement in Laz. As shown in (14), the value of the suffixal agreement is determined by the subject NP, not the object NP.

(14)

a. Si   ma   m-dzir-i.
    you   I   1OBJ-see- NON3SUBJ.PAST
    'You saw me.'
b. Bere-k   ma   m-dzir-u.
    child-ERG   I   1OBJ-see-3SUBJ.PAST
    'The child saw me.'

However, Laz tells us much more than that. The possibility of non-subject NPs to agree in Laz allows us to ask many interesting questions whose answers are much less well-known. This is because simple syntactic tests that can determine the hierarchy between the subject NP and the object NP are not always informative when we use them to determine the hierarchy between non-subject NPs. Laz proves to be quite informative in this respect by showing us which non-subject NP determines agreement when two or more non-subject NPs are present, revealing the hierarchy between them. Suppose that in languages where agreement with two NPs is possible, there is a second lower Probe$_{OBJ}$ situated just below the subject NP, as shown in (15). If the basic idea that explains the universal preference to agree with subjects over objects (in languages where there is agreement only with one NP) is correct, then we expect that Probe$_{OBJ}$ will agree with Object NP1 rather than Object NP2, hence revealing the syntactic hierarchy between them.

(15)

Probe$_{SUBJ}$ » Subject NP » Probe$_{OBJ}$ » Object NP1 » Object NP2

Let us test this idea on Laz and determine the hierarchy between *causee* NPs and *beneficiary* NPs. Note that Laz allows agreement both with causee objects as shown in (16a) and with *beneficiary* objects as in (16b).

(16)

a. Arte-k   si   dişk'a   g-o-çit-ap-u.
    Arte-ERG you   wood.NOM   2OBJ-CAUS-chop-CAUS-PAST.3SG
    'Arte made you chop wood.'

b. Arte-k   ma   dişk'a   m-i-çit-u.
    Arte-ERG I   wood.NOM   1OBJ-APPL-chop-PAST.3SG
    'Arte chopped wood for me.'

Furthermore, it is possible to construct sentences where *causee* and *beneficiary* objects are both present. Such sentences allow us to test which of the two NPs is structurally higher. As shown by the data in (17), the agreement realization reveals that the *causee* object is higher than the *beneficiary* object (Demirok, 2013). We infer this hierarchy based on the finding that the causee object determines the prefixal agreement in the presence of an additional *beneficiary* object.[4]

(17)

a. Arte-k   ma   si   dişk'a   m-o-çit-ap-u.
    Arte-ERG I   you   wood.NOM   1OBJ-CAUS-chop-CAUS-PAST.3SG
    Available interpretation: 'Arte made **me** chop wood for you.'
    Unavailable interpretation: 'Arte made you chop wood for **me**.'

b. Arte-k   si   ma   dişk'a   g-o-çit-ap-u.
    Arte-ERG you   I   wood.NOM   2OBJ-CAUS-chop-CAUS-PAST.3SG
    Available interpretation: 'Arte made **you** chop wood for me.'
    Unavailable interpretation: 'Arte made me chop wood for **you**.'

---

[4] Notably, there are also pre-root vowels that appear on the verb when we introduce additional objects. We observe that their realization is also subject to the same syntactic hierarchy as that to which object-agreement realization is subject. While the pre-root vowel *i-* is required when a beneficiary object is introduced, the pre-root vowel *o-* is required when a beneficiary object is introduced. However, when both are present in the structure, it is the pre-root vowel *o-* that gets realized, suggesting that they are subject to the same hierarchy that we find in agreement realization. Same facts hold in case of full NPs instead of pronouns. See also Boeder (1969) and Öztürk and Pöchtrager (2011).

Hence, the possibility of both subjects and objects agreeing in Laz provides valuable data for theoretical research, informing it in ways many other languages could not. However, there are also challenges that it raises. For instance, some constructions in Laz exhibit non-canonical agreement realization, cross-referencing subjects as if they were objects. For example, in the perfect construction, the suffixal agreement, which in previous examples has cross-referenced the subject NP, shows default third person agreement, while the subject is cross-referenced as an object. This is illustrated in (18). It should be clear that this data challenges the hypothesized hierarchy of NPs and the two agreement probes in (15).

(18)

a. Ma si **m**-i-dzir-ap+un
I you 1OBJ-APPL-see-3SG.PERF
'I have seen you/I have the experience of seeing you.'

b. Si ma **g**-i-dzir-ap+un
You I 2OBJ-APPL-see-3SG.PERF
'You have seen me/You have the experience of seeing me.'

One possible way to accommodate the data in (18) is to assume that the subject NP in the perfect construction is an unusual kind of subject and it is syntactically lower than Probe$_{OBJ}$. This would allow Probe$_{OBJ}$ to find the subject of this construction and agree with it (before Probe$_{SUBJ}$ can). While this assumption would indeed require further justification, there are also data that suggest it is not the right path to take. There are other non-subject NPs, such as *affectee* NPs, which can appear to be higher than some subject NPs (in particular, nominative subjects) but cannot block agreement with the subject NP. These are illustrated in (19) below.

(19)

a. Ma bere m-i-ğur-**u**
I child.NOM 1.OBJ-APPL-die-3SUBJ.PAST
'The child died on me' (~the child died, which badly affected me.)

b. Ma si m-i-ğur-**i**
I you 1.OBJ-APPL-die-NON3SUBJ.PAST
'You died on me' (~you died, which badly affected me.)

These contradictory facts about the syntactic hierarchy of Probes and different kinds of NPs can be reconciled if agreement-calculus is assumed to be performed on the output of the case-calculus (Preminger, 2014). Relativizing agreement probes to different case-values allows us to have minimality-violating agreement-configurations. For example, if we stipulate that what we have labelled Probe$_{SUBJ}$ can see ergative and nominative NPs but not dative NPs, we can explain that the nominative subject can be agreed with by-passing the *affectee* NP (which would simply be invisible to it). Even though the dative case is not visible in the first- and second-person pronouns, it is visible on a third person NP, as shown in (20).

(20)

Gubazi-s   bere   u-ğur-**u**
Gubaz-DAT   child.NOM   3.OBJ.APPL-die-3SUBJ.PAST
'The child died on Gubaz' (~the child died, which badly affected Gubaz.)

To conclude, the agreement- and case-systems of Laz is highly informative for theoretical research. Studying the interaction of these two systems in Laz provides valuable insights into the mechanics of case and agreement-calculus in natural languages.

3. The Verbal Classification-system in Laz

Verbal roots in Laz belong in different inflection-classes, which is detectable in imperfective forms. Excluding derived transitives and derived intransitives, we have four distinct inflection-classes that can be inferred from the variation in the imperfective morpheme and, in one case, the pre-root vowel *o-*.[5] We assign them to three main classes, from CLASS.I to CLASS.III, based on the imperfective suffix the roots select, and we further split CLASS.II into two sub-classes based on the presence/absence of the pre-root vowel *o-*. While this is a purely morphological classification, it turns out to be *not* idiosyncratic (i.e., predictable to a great extent). The discussion that follows is based on Demirok and Öztürk (2021) and builds on some of the findings reported in Erguvanlı Taylan and Öztürk (2014) and Öztürk and Erguvanlı Taylan (2017).

---

[5] This pre-root vowel also appears in derived transitives (causative structures) in combination with a causative suffix. However, notably, there is no intransitive base for the set of roots that take *o-* but not a causative suffix. Hence, we take this class of roots to be underived.

(21)

a. K'oçi-k   lu   mezlap'-**um**-t'-u
   man-ERG   cabbage.NOM   mash-IMPF-AUX-3SUBJ.PAST
   'The man was mashing cabbage.'   CLASS.I

b. Bere-k   toyç'i   zd-**am**-t'-u
   child-ERG   rope.NOM   pull-IMPF-AUX-3SUBJ.PAST
   'The child was pulling the rope.'   CLASS.II-A

c. Aşela-k   kva   **o**-t'oç-**am**-t'-u
   Aşela-ERG   stone.NOM   CAUS-pull-IMPF-AUX-3SUBJ.PAST
   'Aşela was throwing stones/the stone.'   CLASS.II-B

d. Oşk'uri   kts-**ur**-t'-u
   apple.NOM   rot-IMPF-AUX-3SUBJ.PAST
   'The apple was rotting.'   CLASS.III

The roots in CLASS.III are systematically all intransitive verbs with nominative theme subjects, i.e., unaccusative verbs. While most roots in this class denote a change-of-state event, some stative verbs also belong here. The imperfective marker -*ur* that is used to define CLASS.III surfaces as -*un* when fused with third-person singular agreement and the present tense. Some examples of roots with change-of-state semantics are in (22a), while some examples of roots with stative semantics are in (22b).

(22)

a. mç'ox-un   'X is going sour.'
   burd-un   'X is solidifying.'
   t'rox-un   'X is breaking.'
   nçx-un   'X is getting warmer.'
   ç'urt'-un   'X is wrinkling.'
   nç'-un   'X is drying.'

b. dg-un   'X is standing.'
   sk'ud-un   'X is living.'
   nuxond-un   'X is enduring.'

The other two major classes all systematically require ergative subjects. The roots in CLASS.I are characterized by their selection of the suffix -*um* in the imperfective, while the roots in CLASS.II are characterized by their selection of the suffix -*am* in the imperfective.

What distinguishes the roots in CLASS.I is a typologically unusual feature. Although there are some exceptions to this generalization, as shown in (23b), a large body of roots in CLASS.I have a theme that undergoes a physical change in form during the event, as the set of examples in (23a) illustrates.

(23)
a. xorx-um-s   'X is pruning Y.'
    lağun-um-s   'X is chewing Y.'
    goç'-um-s   'X is roasting Y.'
    xut'or-um-s   'X is trimming Y.'
    t'ax-um-s   'X is breaking Y.'
    şol-um-s   'X is kneading Y.'
    xon-um-s   'X is ploughing Y.'
    cib-um-s   'X is cooking, boiling Y.'
    britz-um-s   'X is wearing Y away/out.'
    berg-um-s   'X is hoeing Y.'
    ğerğ-um-s   'X is nibbling Y.'
b. tor-um-s   'X is carrying Y.'
    [expected in CLASS.II-A as *tor-am-s]
    tsad-um-s   'X is taking care of Y.'
    [expected in CLASS.II-A as *tsad-am-s]
    gor-um-s   'X is looking for Y.'
    [expected in CLASS.II-A as *gor-am-s]

Underived roots in CLASS.II are characterized by their selection of the suffix -*am* in the imperfective. What morphologically divides this class into two subclasses is the pre-root vowel o-, absent in CLASS.II-A roots and present in CLASS.II-B roots.

CLASS.II-A roots include agentive dynamic events, which may be transitives or unergatives. Crucially, transitive CLASS.II-A roots differ from transitive CLASS.I roots in that they do not have themes that undergo a physical change in form. Some unergative roots in this class are in (24a), some transitive roots in this class are in (24b), and a form expected to be in CLASS.I due to its semantics is in (24c).

(24)
a. barbal-am-s   'X is nagging.'
    farfal-am-s   'X is glowing.'
    p'et'el-am-s   'X is roasting Y.'
    dits-am-s   'X is laughing.'
    k'i-am-s   'X is screaming.'
    şaşal-am-s   'X is burbling.'
    ts'umin-am-s   'X is barking.'
    dardal-am-s   'X is shaking.'
b. ts'-am-s   'X is extracting/removing Y.'
    ç-am-s   'X is feeding Y.'
    ç'-am-s   'X is sewing Y.'
    do-rg-am-s   'X is planting Y.'
    mo-ğ-am-s   'X is bringing Y.'
    zd-am-s   'X is pulling Y.'
    go-nts'-am-s   'X is opening Y.'
c. z-am-s   'X is mashing Y.'   [expected in CLASS.I as *z-um-s]

Roots in CLASS.II-B are transitive and differ from the CLASS.II-A and CLASS.I transitive roots. They are characterized by denoting two-phase events where the initiation of the event is followed by a process outside the agent's control. For example, a throwing event has an initiation component which is the initial displacement of an object by an agent and has a process-component on which the agent has no control. This is, for example, quite different from a carrying event where the initiation and process-components are co-temporal in that the agent controls the trajectory of displacement throughout the event. Events like throwing have been referred to as transitive achievements in the literature. While the core examples that fit the description of transitive achievements are in (25a), there are also some exceptions, as shown in (25b). Finally, a small number of underived transitive roots denote scalar change-of-state events in this class but do not have themes that undergo any physical change in form (unlike roots in CLASS.I). These are illustrated in (25c).

(25)
a. o-t'oç-am-s   'X is throwing Y.'
    o-tzir-am-s   'X is showing Y.'
    o-pin-am-s   'X is laying Y.'
    o-gz-am-s   'X is igniting Y.'

	o-rgin-am-s	'X is rolling Y.'
	o-kt-am-s	'X is spinning Y.'
	o-k'apin-am-s	'X is dropping Y.'
	o-ncğon-am-s	'X is sending Y.'
	d[o]-o-b-am-s	'X is pouring/spilling Y.'
	c[e]-o-ninkt-am-s	'X is toppling Y.'
	ey[o]-o-mpun-am-s	'X is letting Y overflow.'
b.	o-xosar-am-s	'X is stalking Y.'
	[expected in CLASS.II-A as *xosar-am-s]	
	o-val-am-s	'X is shaking Y.'
	[expected in CLASS.II-A as *val-am-s]	
c.	o-nçxun-am-s	'X is heating Y.'
	o-nç'un-am-s	'X is drying Y.'
	o-sar-am-s	'X is paling/yellowing Y.'

Overall, the verbal classification-system in Laz, despite exceptions, seems quite robustly non-idiosyncratic. More importantly, the classification is demonstrably sensitive to notions such as whether the theme undergoes a physical change in form and whether the initiation and process sub-events of an event are co-temporal. These observations are still largely unnoticed in theoretical research and have much potential to inspire inquiry into the grammatical relevance of these notions.

Moreover, in the verbal classification-system of Laz, we also find overt morphological evidence of argument/event-structure, which is quite central to theoretical research and has fundamentally reshaped our understanding of how verbal meaning is constructed in grammar (Perlmutter, 1978; Rothstein, 2004; Borer, 2005; Ramchand, 2008; Travis 2010; Beavers & Koontz-Garboden, 2020, among others). For example, in Laz, the split between unergatives and unaccusatives is encoded in case-marking and inflection-classes of verbal roots. Notably, diagnosing these categories typically requires involved tests in many other languages, while Laz simply shows it morphologically and in more than one place. Needless to say, such robust confirmation of the existence of hypothesized categories in language has much value in theoretical research.

4. Spatial Prefixes in Laz

Another both typologically and theoretically significant property which Laz exhibits is the highly elaborate system of spatial relations encoded via 27 spatial prefixes in the verbal complex (Holisky, 1991; Kutscher 2003, 2011; Boeder,

2005; Öztürk & Pöchtrager, 2011; Eren, 2016; Öztürk & Eren, 2021), as exemplified in (26):

(26)

Bere   k'ut'i-şe   {ama-/gama-/ce-/e-/go-/mo-}-ul-un.
child.NOM   box-ALL   SM-go-PRES.IMPF.3SG
'The child is going in/out/down/up/around/towards the box.'

Spatial prefixes in Laz encode information regarding: i) whether the event proceeds vertically or horizontally as in (27), ii) whether the event is directed towards or away from the speaker (deixis), i.e., the thither-hither orientation as in (28), and iii) the relative orientation of a specific object or entity that is involved in the event as in (29) (cf. Eren, 2016):

(27)

Bere   ey-ul-un / gol-ul-un.
child.NOM   SM-go-PRES.IMPF.3SG
'The child is going up (vertically) / forward (horizontally)'

(28)

Amedi   m(o)-ul-un / me-l-un.
Ahmet.NOM   SM-go-PRES.IMPF.3SG
'Ahmet is coming/ going.'
Lit: 'Ahmed is going towards or away from the speaker.'

(29)

Katu   masa-s   {k'ots'o-/ ela- / mok'o-}ren.
cat.NOM   masa-NOM   SM-is
'The cat is in front of/ next to/ behind the table.'

In this section, we will discuss the implications of such a spatial system with respect to two theoretical debates in the literature: i) the internal composition of adpositions (Svenonius, 2006; 2007) and ii) the path-based typology for motion-verbs (Talmy, 2000a,b).

4.1. The internal composition of adpositions

Focusing on the cross-linguistic expression of spatial relations, Svenonius (2007) argues for a functional category called P, which encompasses both adpositions and particles. Given the syntactic, semantic and phonological similarities between adpositions and other adposition-like elements, such as particles and affixes, Dikken (1995), Asbury *et al.* (2007) and Gehrke (2008) also group all these categories under one single category, namely P.

Relying on the general assumption in the literature that PPs are internally complex (Riemsdjik, 1990; Koopman, 2000; Gerhke, 2008, among others), Svenonius (2006) splits the functional category P and argues for a fine-graded layered structure for P, as given in (30):

(30)

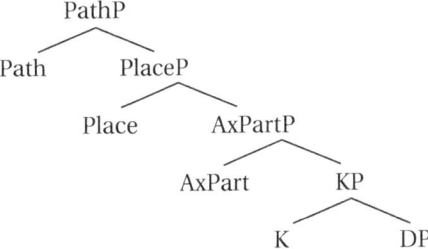

PPs are assumed to involve at least two hierarchically ordered projections, namely PathP and PlaceP associated with directional and locative meanings. In addition, Svenonius (2006) argues for the introduction of a projection called Axial Part Phrase (AxPartP), introduced under the PlaceP as seen in (30). AxPart refers to a set of spatial or locative nouns, such as *front, back, top, bottom, sides*, which exhibit both N-like and P-like properties, referring to a space defined regarding an object. As seen in (30), these projections are introduced above KP (case phrase), embedding a DP.

As extensively discussed in Eren (2016) and Öztürk and Eren (2021), the complex spatial prefix system of Laz provides support for the split P approach by Svenonius (2006). Table 1 illustrates the full list of these morphemes with rough English translations:[6]

---

[6] Table 2.1 is a modified version of the table given in Kutscher (2011).

Table 2.1 - Spatial Prefixes in PL

Directional Domain	Deictic Domain
Horizontal Domain	Deictic
ama-: 'into, inwards.' *gama-:* 'out of, outwards.' *gola-:* 'horizontally forward.' *meşk'a-:* 'into, through a narrow, cramped space.' *moşk'a-:* 'out of a narrow, cramped space.'	*me-:* 'thither, targeting a vertical surface.' *mo-:* 'hither'
Vertical Domain	Deictic +Directional
e-: 'up, upwards.' *ce-:* 'down onto, downwards.' *do-:* 'down onto the ground.' *dolo-:* 'into, down through.' *cela-:* 'diagonally down.' *ela-:* 'diagonally up.' *eşk'a-:* 'up (through), amidst.' *eyo-:* 'onto a higher surface.' *goyo-:* 'onto a lower surface.'	*mola-:* 'hither along, into a closed space.' *meyo-:* 'across thither, on top of' *moyo-:* 'across hither.'
Projective	
ets'o-: 'under, below.' *kots'o-:* 'in(to) front of, bottom.' *ç'eşk'a-:* 'middle/centre' *mok'o-:* 'behind, back.' *ek'o-:* 'behind, back + upwards.' *k'oşk'a-:* 'in between, amidst.' *ç'ek'o-:* 'at the tip of the backside of.'	
Circum	
go-: 'around'	

The spatial prefixes of Laz are divided into two basic groups based on their morphological complexity: i) Simplex Forms, and ii) Complex Forms (cf. Öztürk & Pöchtrager, 2011). The simplex prefixes are monomorphemic, whereas the complex prefixes are derived by combining the simplex form with another affix. Based on a detailed study of around 500 spatial prefix-verb combinations available in Laz dictionaries and data-elicitation sessions with informants, Eren (2016) concludes that the affixes which follow the simplex forms in complex prefixes denote information related to the different sides of the Ground-referent, hence the axial parts, as illustrated in the figure below.

Figure 2.2 - The AxPart affixes of PL

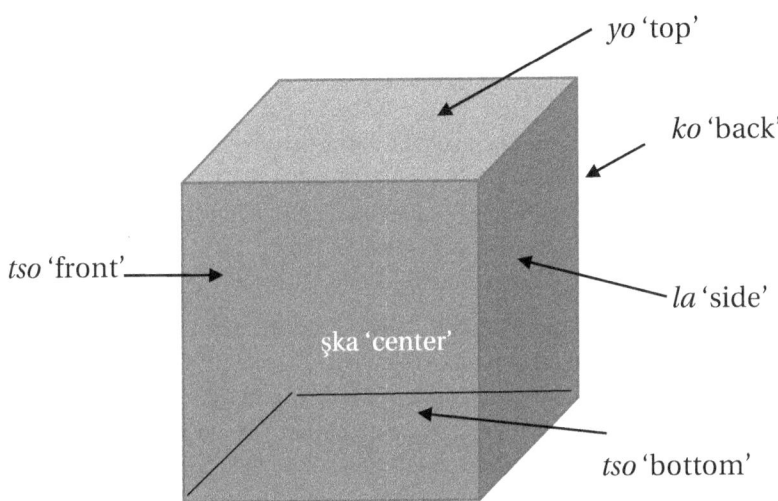

Table 2.2 shows how the complex prefixes are derived with the simplex ones:

Table 2.2 - The Simplex and Complex Prefixes of PL

Simplex Forms	AxPart Prefixes				
	Back/behind	Side/near	Centre/middle	Front/bottom /under	Top
	-k'o/-xo	-la	-şk'a	-ts'o	-yo
ce- 'down'	c'ek'o	Cela	c'eşk'a	----	----
e- 'up'	ek'o	Ela	eşk'a	ets'o	Eyo
go 'around'	----	Gola	k'oşk'a	k'ots'o	Goyo
me 'thither'	----	Mela	meşk'a	----	Meyo
mo 'hither'	mok'o	Mola	moşk'a	----	Moyo

Eren (2016) shows that while the first morpheme of the spatial prefixes in the complex form spells out the PathP and PlaceP, the second morpheme is for AxPartP. Thus, Laz supports the representation in (30).

Interestingly, however, the projections embedded under AxPartP in (30), namely, KP and DP are lexicalized independent of the spatial prefixes. As shown in (31), the DP *oxori* 'house' bears the allative case marker, which heads the KP. The spatial prefix encodes how the movement is configured concerning 'house':

(31)

Ali [ₖₚ oxori-şe] am(a)-ul-un.
Ali.NOM house-ALL into-go-PRES.IMPF.3SG
'Ali is going into (entering) the house.'

This indicates that different layers of the structure in (30) are lexicalized on two different lexical items. While PathP, PlaceP and AxPartP, the projections which constitute the spatial prefixes, are realized on the verbal complex, KP is lexicalized separately on DP. This might come as a challenge for the representation in (30), where AxPartP strictly selects and embeds KP.

Even though spatial prefixes and the KP are lexicalized on different lexical items, namely the DP and the verbal complex, there is still a selectional relation between them, which supports the representation in (30). Eren (2016) groups spatial prefixes into two, as dynamic and non-dynamic based on their compatibility with simple stative predicates (cf. Folli & Ramchand, 2005; Son, 2009; Svenonius 2010; Acedo Matellán, 2016, among others). If a prefix is not compatible with a stative predicate like *be* or *remain*, that prefix is taken to be inherently dynamic. The modification of stative predicates with a specific class of prefixes leads to ungrammaticality due to the semantic mismatch between the meaning of the prefix and that of the verb. The relevant prefixes are *ama-, gama-, meşk'a, moşk'a-, meyo-, moyo-, e-, me-, mo-, ela-, cela-, gola-*, which are exemplified in (32). These examples show us that these prefixes always require dynamic eventualities because of their semantics, as illustrated in (33). That is why Eren (2016) calls them dynamic prefixes:

(32)

a. Xordza mektebi-s *{ama-/gama-/meşk'a-/moşk'a-}{ren/squd-u}.
   woman.nom school-loc SP-is/ remain.PAST.3SG
   Intended meaning: 'The woman is/remained in(side)/out(side) the school.'
b. K'oç'i xinci-s *{meyo-/moyo-}-ren.
   man.NOM bridge-LOC SP-is
   Intended meaning: 'The man is over the bridge.'
c. Ali-k k'va e-t'oç-u. *K'va e-ren.
   Ali-erg stone.NOM SM-throw-PAST.3SG stone.NOM SM-is
   Intented meaning: Ali threw the stone up. The stone is up (in the air).'
d. Xordza *{me-/mo-}-ren.
   woman.NOM SM-is
   Intended meaning: 'The woman is (in an area) close to/away from me.'

e. Topi   *{ela-/cela-/gola-}-ren.
    ball.NOM   SM-is
    Intended Meaning: 'The ball is on an inclined or horizontal surface.'

(33)

Hasan   marketi-şe/*-s   am(a)-ul-un.
Hasan.NOM   market-ALL/-LOC   into-go-PRES.IMPF.3SG
'Hasan is going into (entering) the market.'

The spatial prefixes *eyo-/goyo-, c'eşk'a-, ela-, kots'o-, mola-, ko'şk'a-/e'şk'a-, mok'o-/eşk'o-, ets'o-, c'ek'o- an go-/gola-*, on the other hand, are non-dynamic prefixes. The common property of these prefixes is that they can be used with stative verbs, unlike the dynamic prefixes. Example (34) shows their compatibility with stative verbs:

(34)

K'avonozi   oxori-s/*şe   mok'o-{ren/squdu}.
bottle.NOM   house-LOC/-ALL   SM-is/remain.PAST.3SG
'The bottle is/remained behind the house.'

Looking at the examples in (33) and (34), we see that even though KP is realized separately on DP, it is still selected by the spatial prefixes. This is evidenced by the different case requirements of dynamic and non-dynamic spatial prefixes. As first noticed by Eren (2016), while dynamic prefixes require the use of the allative case-marker on the DP as in (33), but not that of the locative case, the DP is obligatorily marked with the Locative case with non-dynamic prefixes, but crucially never with an allative case as in (34). This indicates that the KP layer on top of the DP is closely related to the layers constituting the spatial prefix on the verbal complex.

Thus, while Laz supports the architecture in (30), it also presents an interesting challenge as different layers of the split P are realized on different lexical items, exhibiting a task-sharing between the DP and the verbal complex. The exact morphosyntactic derivation of this task sharing and its implications, especially for the syntactic approaches to morphology such as Nanosyntax or Distributed Morphology, require further research.

4.2 Spatial prefixes and the path-based typology of motion-verbs

Talmy (2000a, 2000b) proposes a typology of languages regarding how they express Motion Event. He argues that Motion has four basic components:

Figure, Ground, Path and Motion. The motion component, as the core unit, is expressed in the verb root. Figure is a moving or conceptually movable entity. On the other hand, Ground is a reference entity with respect to which the Figure moves to or is located. The path describes the relation between the Figure and the Ground and refers to the site occupied by or the path followed by the Figure concerning the Ground.

Under Talmy's path-based typology, languages fall into two different classes depending basically on which lexical component regularly expresses Path. If Path is encoded in the verb root in a given language along with Motion, as in Semitic and Romance languages, it is argued to belong to the verb-framed type. If Path is manifested through satellites as in Germanic and Slavic, then it is classified as a satellite-framed language. Talmy introduces the term 'satellite' to refer to the grammatical category of "any constituent other than a noun phrase or a prepositional phrase complement that is in sister relation to the verb root" (Talmy, 2000a, 101-102).

Elaborating on Talmy's typology, Acedo Matellán (2016) divides satellite-framed languages into two, as weak and strong, and argues for a three-way variation as: (i) verb-framed languages where Path is introduced in the verb root as in Romance, (ii) strong satellite-framed languages where Path is introduced as an independent DP/PP as in English or German and (iii) weak satellite-framed languages where Path is affixal and forms a single word with the verb as in Latin. Acedo Matellán (2016) presents several diagnostics to differentiate between satellite-framed and verb-framed languages, discussed below.

With respect to Talmy's path-based typology, focusing on the Ardeshen dialect of Laz, Kutscher (2011) argues that Laz should be classified as a satellite-framed language along with Germanic and Slavic, as the spatial prefixes express the path information separately and thus qualify as satellites. The fact that the spatial prefixes in Laz express information related to Path and are dependent on the verb root suggests that they qualify as satellites.

When a closer look is taken at their co-occurrence patterns with different types of motion verbs, it is seen that spatial prefixes in Laz behave quite differently from the satellites found in languages like English. In the literature, motion-verbs are classified into two separate groups, namely Manner of Motion Verbs (MVs) and Directed Motion Verbs (DMVs) (cf. Levin, 1993). While MVs conflate the Manner component of the motion event, the DMVs involve conflating the direction of motion, namely the Path component. These two classes exhibit different patterns cross-linguistically, as they have different syntactic and aspectual properties (Levin, 1993). MVs typically constitute activity-denoting unergatives, whereas DMVs denoting achievements exhibit an unaccusative pattern.

In well-studied satellite-framed languages like English, satellites are compatible with both MVs and DMVs as shown in (35):

(35)

a. John ran up.   MV
b. John went in. DMV

Eren (2016) and Öztürk and Eren (2021) show that this is not the case in Laz as spatial prefixes in Laz exhibit strict selectivity concerning the kind of motion-verbs with which they can co-occur. Spatial prefixes are only compatible with DMVs in Laz, which already encode Path-information in their lexical specification, but they are not felicitous with MVs which lack such information. The relevant co-occurrence restrictions are presented in examples (36) and (37). We see that while DMVs in (36) are compatible with dynamic spatial prefixes, such prefixes are strictly ungrammatical with MVs as shown in (37):

(36)

Bere   oxori-şe   am-ul-un.   DMV
child.NOM house-ALL   into-go-PRES.IMPF.3SG
'The child is going into (entering) the house.'

(37)

a. Bere-k   oxori-şe   *(am)-i-gzal-s.   MV
   child-ERG   house-ALL   into-PRV-walk-PRES.3SG
   Intended: 'The child is walking into the house.'
b. Çxomi-k   mosa-şe   *(am)-i-nçir-s.
   fish-ERG   net-ALL   into-PRV-swim-PRES.3SG
   Intended: 'The fish is swimming into the net.'

As shown above and discussed in Eren (2016) in detail, the dynamic prefixes of Laz are only compatible with DMVs but not with MVs. Crucially, note the alternation in the introduction of the Ground-referent in both types of verbs. While DMVs with dynamic prefixes take an allative case-marked Ground-entity, MVs require the Ground to be introduced through postpositional phrases, such as *şa(ni)* or *tere*, which mean 'towards' or 'in the direction of'.

Given the selective behaviour of spatial prefixes, which is not observed in well-known satellite-framed languages, Öztürk and Eren (2021) refute the account of Laz as a satellite-framed language by Kutscher (2011) and argue that Laz is a weak verb-framed language where Path is affixal and forms a single word with the verb. In addition to splitting the satellite-framed languages as strong satellite-framed languages and weak satellite-framed languages as proposed by Acedo Matellán (2016), they also suggest that verb-framed languages should also be classified into two, as strong and weak verb-framed languages. Hence, under this proposal, Laz typologically constitutes the fourth type and nicely complements the typology by Acedo Matellán (2016). Under the model by Acedo Matellán it is possible to hypothesize the existence of such a language. Still, there was no such language known in the literature to fulfil this missing fourth pattern. Thus, once again, Laz, as a typologically rare language, contributes significantly to the cross-linguistic understanding of the motion verbs, opening new venues for its theoretical research.

Note that the work by Öztürk and Eren (2021) only focuses on the interaction of spatial prefixes with motion-verbs in Laz, leaving the interaction of these markers with other verb-types to future studies, which we believe again has a significant potential for the theoretical research on topics, such as the internal composition of different verb-classes and their interaction with adpositional categories from the viewpoint of aspect and case.

5. Concluding Remarks

Theoretical research in linguistics has been informed by Laz and will continue to be so in different ways. More concretely, Laz provides a testing-ground for theoretical proposals, as we have seen in the discussion of the ergative case. Laz can also corroborate theoretical proposals by bringing in robust empirical evidence, as we have seen in the discussion of the syntactic hierarchy of non-subject NPs. Finally, Laz has a great potential to open up new debates with its typologically rare and understudied features, as we have seen in the discussion of its verb-classification and spatial marking systems. Hence, as an endangered language, Laz *is* valuable to theoretical research in many ways, giving us yet another purely scientific motivation for acting against language endangerment.

References

Acedo Matellán, V. (2016). *The morphosyntax of transitions: A case study in Latin and other languages.* Oxford: Oxford University Press.

Asbury, A., Gehrke, B. & Hegedus, V. (2007). One size fits all: Prefixes, particles, adpositions and cases as members of the category P. In Cem Keskin (ed.), *UiL OTS Yearbook*, 1-17. Utrecht: UiL OTS.

Baker, M. (2008). *The Syntax of Agreement and Concord*. Cambridge University Press.

Baker, M. & Bobaljik, J. D. (2017). On inherent and dependent theories of ergative case. In J. Coon and D. Massam (eds.) *Handbook of Ergativity*. Oxford: Oxford University Press.

Baker, M. & Vinokurova, N. (2010). Two modalities of case assignment: case in Sakha. *Natural Language & Linguistic Theory, 28*, 593-642.

Beavers, J. & Koontz-Garboden, A. (2020). *The roots of verbal meaning*. Oxford University Press.

Blix, H. (2021). Spans in South Caucasian agreement: Revisiting the pieces of inflection. *Natural Language & Linguistic Theory, 39*, 1-55.

Boeder, W. (1969). Über die Versionen des georgischen Verbs. *Folia Linguistica, 2*, 82-252.

Boeder, W. (2005). The South Caucasian Languages. *Lingua, 115*, 5–89.

Borer, H. (2005). *Structuring Sense*. Oxford.

Chomsky, N. (2000). Minimalist Inquiries: The Framework. In Roger Martin, David Michaels, Juan Uriagereka and Samuel Jay Keyser (Eds.), *Step by Step. Essays on Minimalist Syntax in Honor of Howard Lasnik*, 89-155. Cambridge, MA: MIT Press.

Comrie, B. (1974). Causatives and Universal Grammar. *Transactions of the Philological Society 73*(1), 1-31.

Demirok, Ö. (2013). *AGREE as a unidirectional operation: Evidence from Laz*. İstanbul: Boğaziçi University MA thesis.

Demirok, Ö. & Öztürk, B. (2021). Classifying lexically transitive verbs in Laz. Talk presented at the Workshop: Lexical Restrictions on Grammatical Relations at the University of Amsterdam, March 29-30, 2021.

Den Dikken, M. (1995). *Particles. On the syntax of verb-particle, triadic, and causative constructions*. New York and Oxford: Oxford University Press.

Dixon, R. M. W. (1994). *Ergativity*. Cambridge: Cambridge University Press.

Eren, Ö. (2016). *Spatial prefixes of Pazar Laz: A nano-syntactic approach*. İstanbul: Boğaziçi University MA thesis.

Erguvanlı Taylan, E. & Öztürk, B. (2014). Transitivity in Pazar Laz. *Acta Linguistica Hungarica, 61*, 271-296.

Folli, R. & Ramchand, G. (2005). Prepositions and results in Italian and English: An analysis from event decomposition. In Henk J. Verkuyl, Henriette De Swart & Angeliek van Hout (eds.), *Perspectives on aspect*, 81-105. Dordrecht: Kluwer Academic Publishers.

Gehrke, B. (2008). *Ps in motion: On the semantics and syntax of P elements and motion events*. Utrecht: LOT.

Hale, K. & Keyser, S. (2002). *Prolegomenon to a Theory of Argument Structure*. MIT Press.

Harris, A. (1985). Diachronic Syntax: The Kartvelian Case. (Syntax and Semantics. Vol. 18). Orlando: Academic Press, Inc.

Hewitt, G. (1987). Georgian: Ergative or Active? *Lingua, 71*, 319-340.

Hewitt, G. (2004). *Introduction to the Study of the Languages of the Caucasus.* München: Lincom Europa.

Holisky, D. A. (1991). Laz. In Alice. C. Harris (ed.), *The Indigenous languages of the Caucasus: The Kartvelian languages (Vol.1, 396-472).* Delmar, NY: Caravan Books.

Keenan, E. L. & Comrie, B. (1977). Noun phrase accessibility and universal grammar. *Linguistic Inquiry 8*(1). 63-99.

Kiria, Č., Ezugbaia, L., Memišiši, O., & Merab, Č. (2015). *Lazur-megruli gramat'ik'a. I. Morpologia [A Laz-Megrelian Grammar. I. Morphology].* Tbilisi: Meridiani.

Koopman, H. (2000). *The syntax of specifiers and heads.* London: Routledge.

Kutscher, S. (2003). Raumkonzeptionen im lasischen Verb: Das System der deiktischen und topologischen Präverbien. In Winfried Boeder, (ed.). *Kaukasische Sprachprobleme. Caucasica Oldenburgensia (223–245)*, 1. Bibliotheks- und Informationsystem der Universität Oldenburg.

Kutscher, S. (2011). On the expression of spatial relations in Ardesen-Laz. *Linguistic Discovery, 9*, 49-77.

Lacroix, R. (2009). *Description du dialecte laze d'Arhavi (caucasique du sud, Turquie). Grammaire et textes.* (PhD Dissertation, Sciences du langage, Lyon 2). Retrieved from: https://www.theses.fr/2009LYO20091

Lacroix, R. (2011). Ditransitive Constructions in Laz. *Linguistic Discovery 9*(2), 78–103.

Levin, B. (1993). *English verb classes and alternations: A preliminary investigation.* University of Chicago Press.

Marantz, A. (1991). Case and Licensing. *Proceedings of ESCOL91*, 234-253.

Nash, L. (2017). The Structural Source of Split Ergativity and Ergative Case in Georgian. In Jessica Coon, Diane Massam, and Lisa Demena Travis (eds.), *The Oxford Handbook of Ergativity.* Oxford University Press.

Öztürk, B. & Erguvanlı Taylan, E. (2017). Omnipresent little vP in Pazar Laz. In Roberta D'Alessandro, Irene Franco & Ángel Gallego (eds.), *The Verbal Domain*, 207-231. Oxford: Oxford University Press.

Öztürk, B. & Eren, Ö. (2021). Pazar Laz as a weak verb-framed language. *Linguistic Variation.* John Benjamins.

Öztürk, B. & Pöchtrager, M. A. (eds.). (2011). *Pazar Laz.* Münich: LINCOM: Languages of the World Materials.

Perlmutter, D. M. (1978). Impersonal passives and the unaccusative hypothesis. *BLS, 4,*157-89.

Preminger, O. (2014). *Agreement and its Failures.* MIT Press.

Ramchand, G. (2008). *Verb meaning and the lexicon: A first phase syntax.* Cambridge University Press.

Van Riemsdijk, H. (1990). Functional prepositions. In Harm Pinkster and Inge Genée (eds.), *Unity in diversity*, 229-241. Dordrecht: Foris.Rothstein, S. (2014). *Structuring Events: A Study in the Semantics of Lexical Aspect*. Blackwell.

Son, M. (2009). Linguistic variation and lexical parameter: The case of directed motion. *University of Pennsylvania Working Papers in Linguistics, 15*(1). 213-222.

Svenonius, P. (2006). The emergence of axial parts. *Nordlyd, 33*, 49-77.

Svenonius, P. (2007). Adpositions, particles and the arguments they introduce. In Eric Reuland, Tanmoy Bhattacharya and Giorgos Spathas (eds.), *Argument Structure*, 63-103. John Benjamins.

Svenonius, P. (2010). Spatial P in English. In Guglielmo Cinque & Luigi Rizzi (eds.), *Mapping Spatial PPs: The Cartography of Syntactic Structures* 6. Oxford.

Talmy, L. (2000a). *Toward a cognitive semantics: Concept structuring systems*, vol. 1, Cambridge: MIT Press.

Talmy, L. (2000b). *Toward a cognitive semantics: Typology and process in concept structuring*, vol. 2, Cambridge: MIT Press.

Travis, L. (2010). *Inner Aspect: The Articulation of VP*. Dordrecht: Springer.

Tuite, K. (1998). *Kartvelian morphosyntax: Number agreement and morphosyntactic orientation in the South Caucasian languages*. München: Lincom Europa.

Woolford, E. (2006). Lexical Case and Inherent Case and Argument Structure. *Linguistic Inquiry*, 37, 111-130.

Woolford, E. (2015). Ergativity and Transitivity. *Linguistic Inquiry*, 46, 489-531.

Appendix-1 ABBREVIATIONS	
AUX	auxiliary verb
APPL	applicative
ALL	allative
PRV	pre-root-vowel
VAL	valency marker
SP	spatial prefix
TS	thematic suffix
PERF	perfect
CAUS	causative
CAUSint	intransitive causitivizer
CAUStrns	transitive causitivizer
PL	plural marker
ERG	ergative
NOM	nominative
DAT	dative
1OBJ	first person object agreement
3SG	third person singular
SUBJ	subject agreement
PRES	present tense
NEG	negation

Chapter 3

A Spotlight on the 'Lazian' Lexis: Evidence from a 19th-Century Lexicographic Resource

Zaal Kikvidze
Tbilisi State University, Georgia

Levan Pachulia
Sokhumi State University, Georgia

Abstract

The chapter is a discussion of the Laz lexical data from 'Original Vocabularies of Five West Caucasian Languages' compiled by Demetrius Rudolph Peacock, a British diplomat residing in Batumi in the late 19th century, and published in the *Journal of the Royal Asiatic Society of Great Britain and Ireland* (1887). The lexicographic collection has the following organisation: Georgian, Megrelian (i.e., Mingrelian), Laz (i.e., Lazian), Svan (i.e., Swanetian), and Abkhaz translations accompany English headwords. The collection consists of 224 entries, including individual words (i.e., various parts of speech and lexico-semantic groups, word-forms, and sentences). The British diplomat and lexicographer compiled his resource based on word of mouth. Therefore, notwithstanding some apparent shortcomings, it can in no way be doomed to rejection since most of the Laz items are rendered rather adequately in terms of both transliteration and translation. Therefore, Demetrius Rudolph Peacock's 'Original Vocabularies of Five West Caucasian Languages' is a valuable source for the history of documentation of the Laz language.

Keywords: *Laz; D. R. Peacock; vocabulary; lexicographical resource*

* * *

1. Introduction

The history of linguistics knows a number of cases when rather valuable linguistic sources were disregarded, neglected, and stayed unnoticed. Scholars of larger languages with long-standing written traditions might have fallen prey to such behaviour when confronted by abounding numbers of relevant resources to be gleaned. However, this is hardly imaginable and forgivable when it is about an endangered and ever-shrinking language like Laz. The present chapter deals with a resource that was hardly unnoticed by many. Still, some disregarded, neglected, and even rejected this resource. The œuvre in question is a lexicographic collection including specimina from five languages and compiled by the British diplomat Demetrius Rudolph Peacock (1887). The collection presents 224 English headwords translated into Georgian, Megrelian, Laz, Svan, and Abkhaz. In the present chapter, we, of course, spotlight the Laz data, specifically lexis.

To consider the collection in question within the appropriate historical context, initially, we provide a historical overview of available linguistic resources on Laz before D. R. Peacock. Then, we discuss his life and work, with particular reference to the 'Lazian' lexis, specifically where Laz lexical items appear and how they are rendered. As in any other instance, alongside a handful of specific inadequacies, we identify and assess correct and adequate representations of the Laz lexical items in it.

Finally, we shall discuss reflections on D. R. Peacock's œuvre in subsequent publications on Laz to show whether and how his contribution was noticed, acknowledged, and appreciated.

2. A Historical Overview of Linguistic Resources on Laz before D. R. Peacock

It may come as a paradox that while the Laz people were recognised and repeatedly mentioned by numerous authors since antiquity, hardly any Laz linguistic material appeared until later centuries (i.e., at least, they have not come down to our days). One may argue that, as an unwritten language, it has been passed on only orally from generation to generation, this potentially being a principal cause for its unrepresented nature. However, if we consider the level to which other unwritten languages are represented, the argument above will not seem strong enough. For instance, Megrelian is rather well represented in Evliya Çelebi's *Seyahâtnâme*.

Whatever explanations may be offered, so far, no student of the history of linguistic studies of Laz has even mentioned any period prior to the 17th c. as a starting point. There is a poem in Evliya Çelebi's aforementioned book, regarded by some as a source for the oldest cohesive Laz material dating back to the 17th c. (Jikia, 1954). However, various scholars are not unanimous about its linguistic identity. 'The poem, contained on page 253a of the second volume of Evliya's book, occurs again in a nearly identical shape in vol. 8 (336b), where it forms part of the specimen of the Trabzon Greek dialect, and there are only Greek elements to be detected in it' (Gippert, 1992, p. 10). Due to the contradictions and uncertainty (see also Bleichsteiner, 1934; Dankoff, 1991), we must disregard the aforementioned work. Instead, we focus on the collection by the prominent Spanish philologist Lorenzo Hervás y Panduro (1735-1809). His multilingual lexicographic resource (Hervás & Panduro, 1787) is acknowledged as the earliest surviving record of Laz. However, most later students of the Laz language did not seem familiar with the specimina in question. The reason for neglect might have been an abuse of glossonyms by Hervás, as Aleksiva (2018, p. 74) logically assumed. The lexicographer identifies Laz linguistic data as *Lingua Lesga* ('Lezgian language'). Scholars were misled by the glossonym, having disregarded both the linguistic data cited and the subsequent clarifications provided by Hervás (1787, p. 65): 'Lingua Lasga, detta ancora Laza, e Lassa.' Notably, he provides data from two dialect-varieties of Laz: "*Kiemer, e Goine*" and "*Hope, o Crainza*" (ibid.).

More than 35 years later, Julius Heinrich von Klaproth published his linguistic compendium *Asia Polyglotta* in which he provided Laz translations of 67 German words (1823, pp. 122-124). The specimina are presented as data from three dialects: 'den von *Kiemer* oder *Gonia*' (Ki.), 'den von *Hope* oder *Krainza*' (H.), and 'den von *Trebisonde*' (Tr.) (op. cit., p. 111).

The next landmark is by Georg Rosen, who in 1843 presented his review of the Laz language to the German Academy of Sciences. This review appeared in a book-format, containing quite a comprehensive glossary of Laz nouns and adjectives (two columns per page) (Rosen, 1844, pp. 29-37) a year later. However, its representativeness is limited in dialectal diversity as the data come from a single dialect-variety (Atina (Pazar)). Chronologically, following G. Rosen's and preceding D. R. Peacock's collections, two, probably not very resourceful and still hardly explored, works including some Laz lexical specimina appeared. One of these works was written by a botanist (Koch, 1846) and the other by a linguist (Tsagareli, 1872).

These are the sources produced prior to D. R. Peacock's collection. Concerning the scarcity of the cited ones, it is more than evident that Laz is the most under-resourced and even under-studied language among the Kartvelian languages. Therefore, it is vital to scrutinise data from various sources, particularly those based on word of mouth, as with Peacock's collection.

3. Demetrius Rudolph Peacock and the 'Lazian' Lexis

3.1. Life and Work of D. R. Peacock

The lexicographic collection in question was published in the *Journal of the Royal Asiatic Society of Great Britain and Ireland*, Volume 19, Number 1. In this issue, there are two pages where the article's author is identified: p. III (i.e., table of contents) and p. 145 (i.e., the initial page of the article). Both pages communicate precisely the same information: 'Compiled on the spot by Mr. Peacock, Vice-Consul of Batúm, Trans-Caucasia, South Russia' (Peacock, 1887, pp. III, 145). Hence, the author is referred to only by his last name and position held; his other names do not appear. Of course, his full name can easily be found in various other sources: Demetrius Rudolph Peacock. On 26 September 1842, he was born to Charles Peacock and Concordia Peacock (née Schlegel). His birthplace is the village of Shakhmanovka, the governorate [gubernija] of Tambov, Russia. We came across the story of how the Peacocks got to Russia in the memories of Evgenia Peacock, our author's granddaughter (Horsbrugh-Porter, 1993, p. 105):

> Charles Peacock was the son of a Lancashire farmer, and his main interest was farming. When he married, he was looking for a job and happened to see an advertisement saying that someone in the Tambov province of Russia was looking for an estate manager. So Charles Peacock and his young wife went to Russia. They got on very well with the owner of the estate, who became a great friend. I cannot remember his surname, but his Christian name was Dimitri, and my grandfather was called after him, Dimitri Rudolph.

This is why his first name sometimes also appears as either Dimitri or Dmitry. Young Peacock was sent to school in England, and, after coming back to Russia, he entered Moscow University, where he studied law. As for his activities in Georgia, initially, he worked as a contractor in the construction of the Tbilisi-Poti railway. Later, he was employed at consular residences of the U.S.A. and Italy in Georgia. Afterwards, in 1881, D. R. Peacock started to work as a vice-consul at British Consular Service. In 1890, he was promoted to the post of Consul to reside in Batumi.

His years in Batumi seem to have been remarkable concerning his professional and personal relationships. Here is what Oliver Wardrop (1888, pp. 1-2) wrote about their encounter in Batumi:

I took an early opportunity of presenting myself at the British Vice-Consulate, a small, two-storey cottage, the lower half of which is of brick, the upper of corrugated iron sheets. Mr. Demetrius R. Peacock, the only representative of British interests in the Caucasus, is a man whose services deserve fuller recognition. It would be hard to find a post where more diplomatic tact is required, yet he contrives to make himself respected and admired by all the many races with which he is in daily contact. Mr. Peacock was born in Russia in that empire, but he is nevertheless a thorough Englishman. In Tiflis I heard a good story about him. On one occasion the French Consul-General jokingly said to him, 'Why, Peacock, you are no Englishman, you were born in Russia.' To which our representative replied, 'Our Saviour was born in a stable, but for all that he did not turn out a horse.'

As for his linguistic background and activities, we can once again refer to his granddaughter's narrative (Horsbrugh-Porter, 1993, p. 105):

He was supposed to know fifteen languages, which is probably an exaggeration. But he certainly knew several European languages and later, when he was working at the British consulate in Batum, he studied several Caucasian languages. He was friendly with the mountaineers of the Caucasus, and published original vocabularies of Georgian, Mingrelian, Lazian, Svanetian and Apkhazian.

In addition to 'Vocabularies' and diplomatic reports, it seems that there was another œuvre belonging to his pen, about which William R. Morfill (1895, p. 138) writes: 'According to the "Levantine Herald", as quoted by the "Athenaeum", he wrote a book on the Caucasus which was not approved by the foreign office, but his widow promised to publish it. It has not yet appeared.' Unfortunately, we failed to find any trace either of the aforementioned book or its manuscript.[1]

In 1891, he was appointed a consul-general and moved to Odessa; he 'had been in residence a few weeks when he died, as is reported, of Caucasian fever, the marshes which surround Batumi rendering that town very unhealthy. His

---

[1] There is a noteworthy record in a paper by W. Rickmer Rickmers, a German traveller and geographer: "When friends told me about his [Peacock's] trip to Karchkhal, I wrote to his widow, a daughter of Bakunin. She replied that her late husband had climbed the mountain but his diaries had been destroyed by fire" (Rickmers 1934, p. 475). Hence, that may have been the reason why the book was not published.

death occurred on 23 May 1892, at Odessa, and he was buried in the British cemetery there' (Morfill, 1895, 138).

3.2. D. R. Peacock's 'Original Vocabularies of Five West Caucasian Languages'

The publication 'Original Vocabularies of Five West Caucasian Languages' consists of three parts. The initial one is a note by Dr R. N. Cust (Peacock, 1887, p. 145):

> When I visited Trans-Caucasia in 1882 for the purpose of collecting information regarding the languages of the Caucasus, the result of which I published in Vol. XVII. of the Journal, I became aware of the scantiness of the Vocabularies, and I mentioned this to Mr. Peacock, the Vice-Consul of H.B.M. at Batúm, who had resided some time at Poti, and had made excursions into the regions not often traversed. He was good enough to undertake the duty of collecting Vocabularies, and I forwarded to him a copy of Standard Form of Words and Sentences prepared by the Bengal Asiatic Society. After some delay, owing to the heavy press of his official duties, and a visit to England, when I had a pleasure of seeing him, and again encouraging him on the subject, he has forwarded to me the subjoined Vocabularies, which are highly important.

Judging from the complete title, informing us that the vocabularies were compiled 'at the request of, and communicated by Dr R. N. Cust,' and the note, he was the one who both initiated the work and submitted it to the *Journal*. Hence, it is thanks to him that the reader has an opportunity to familiarise himself with the aforementioned *Instructions of Compiling Vocabularies and Sentences*, which is the second part of the publication (Peacock, 1887, 145).

> The enclosed List of English Words and Sentences has been prepared by the Bengal Asiatic Society to enable persons to compile exhaustive specimens of Languages spoken in any Region. Each sheet contains Five Languages, and those Languages should be selected for each sheet which are cognate to each other. When the whole is completed and printed, it becomes the basis for a further advance as regards those Languages of which we have no Grammars or Vocabularies. Care should be taken that all loan words from English, Arabic, Portuguese, etc., are excluded. Only *pure* words of each language should be entered. One system of transliteration should be adopted: the best is that of Lepsius; but at any rate one system should be adopted for Languages entered

A Spotlight on the 'Lazian' Lexis

upon the same sheet, and when Lepsius' system is not adopted, explanatory notes should be added, giving the exact value of each symbol, letter, or diacritical mark employed.

Hence, D. R. Peacock did not compile the word-list for his collection. Following the Leibnizian sampling preferences, he received a standard form and did his best to find their equivalents in the five languages.[2]

The third core part of the publication is the lexicographic resource. There are 224 entries, including 99 words on various parts of speech and lexico-semantic groups, 103 word-forms, and 22 sentences. The table is organised in the following way: the leftmost column is a list of English headwords being accompanied with translations into Georgian, Megrelian (i.e., Mingrelian), Laz (i.e., Lazian"),[3] Svan (i.e., Swanetian), and Abkhaz.

3.3. Laz Lexical Items in *D. R. Peacock's Collection*

The Laz sample in Peacock's collection is deficient; a handful of word-forms and sentences do not appear in the 'Lazian' column.

Fortunately, this is not the case with individual words presented as lemmas. Laz translations accompany all the 99 English words pertaining to various parts of speech and lexico-semantic groups. Hence, Table 3.1 is the representation of the English word-list and the Laz equivalents of the respective head-words:

Table 3.1 - English head-words and their "Lazian" translations

English	Laz
One	**Ar**
Two	**Jūr**
Three	**Sum**
Four	**Otkhu**
Five	**Khut**
Six	**Ashi**
Seven	**Shkit**
Eight	**Orvo**

---

[2] The word-list was published in the Society's journal and consisted of exactly the same items as D. R. Peacock's "Vocabularies" (Campbell, 1866).

[3] The glossonym (language-name) 'Lazian' seems to have been commonly used to refer to the language in either original or translated writings by Anglophone authors in the 19th century; see, for instance, 'Lazian' (Smith 1833, p. 325) or 'Lasian' (Wagner 1856, p. 262).

Nine	Tchkholo
Ten	Vit
Twenty	Etchi
Fifty	Jurnetchi da vit
Hundred	Oshi
I	Ma
Of me	Tchkimda
Mine	Tchkimiran
We	Tchku
Of us	Tchkunda
Our	Tchkuniran
Thou	Si
Of thee	Skandan
Thine	Skani
You	Tkwa
Of you	Tkwanden
Your	Skani
He	Kiamushiren
Of him	Hetepeshia
His	Hemushian
They	Hemtepe
Of them	Hemteps
Their	Hemtepeshia
Hand	Khe
Foot	Kutchkhe
Nose	Tchkhindi
Eye	Toli
Mouth	Nuku
Tooth	Kibiri
Ear	Udji
Hair	Toma
Head	Ti
Tongue	Nena
Belly	Kolba
Back	Shka
Iron	Demiri
Gold	Altuni
Silver	Ghemiish
Father	Baba
Mother	Nana
Brother	Djuma

A Spotlight on the 'Lazian' Lexis

Sister	Da
Man	Kotche
Woman	Okhordja
Wife	Tchili
Child	Berre
Son	Bidji
Daughter	Bozo
Slave	Rële
Cultivator	Makhatchkali
Shepherd	Tchkeshi
God	Tanghrï
Devil	Sheitan
Sun	Mjora
Moon	Tuta
Star	Muritskhi
Fire	Datchkhuri
Water	Tskhari
House	Okhori
Horse	Tskheni
Cow	Pudji
Dog	Djoghori
Cat	Rato
Cock	Mamuli-
Duck	Ordeghi
Ass	Guruni
Camel	Deve
Bird	Kintchi
Go	Tkzale
Eat	Tchkhomi
Sit	Dokhedi
Come	Mokhti
Beat	Getchi
Stand	Missadovi
Die	Doghuri
Give	Komomtchi
Run	Okhudkwatsini
Up	Jin
Near	Kholos
Down	Tude
Far	Mendra
Before	Tsokhle

Behind	**Okatchkhele**
Who	**Mik**
What	**Munoren**
Why	**Mushene**
And	**Do**
But	**Mara**
If	**Si**
Yes	**Ko**
No	**Var**
Alas	**Eivakh**
A father	**Baba**
Of a father	**Babashi**
To a father	**Babassi**
From a father	**Babashi**
Two fathers	**Jur baba**
Fathers	**Babape**
Of fathers	**Babapeshe**
To fathers	**Babapes**
From fathers	**Babapeshe**
A daughter	**Tsiraskwa**
Of a daughter	**Bososhe** (also **Bozo**)
To a daughter	**Bozos**
From a daughter	**Bozoshe**
Two daughters	**Jur bozo**
Daughters	**Bozope**
Of daughters	**Bozopeshe**
To daughters	**Bozopes**
From daughters	**Bozopeshe**
A good man	**Kai kotchi**
Of a good man	**Kai kotchishe**
To a good man	**Kai kotchish**
From a good man	**Kai kotchishe**
Two good men	**Jur kai kotchi**
Good men	**Kai kotchepe**
Of good men	**Kai kotchpeshe**
To good men	**Kai kotchepes**
From good men	**Kai kotchepeshe**
A good woman	**Kai okhordja**
A bad boy	**Altchaghe berre**
Good women	**Kai ohkordjalepe**
A bad girl	**Altchaghe bozo**

A Spotlight on the 'Lazian' Lexis

Good	**Kai**
Better	**Utchghishi**
Best	**Iris utchghin**
High	**Maghali**
Higher	Demushen maghali
Highest	**Tëli maghali**
A horse	Tskheni
A mare	Zura
Horses	Tskhenepe
Mares	**Zurape**
A bull	**Khodji**
A cow	**Pudji**
Bulls	Khodjepe
Cows	**Pudjepe**
A dog	Djoghori
A bitch	
Dogs	Djoghorepe
Bitches	
A he-goat	Botchi
A female	
Goats	Botchepe
A male deer	**Mskweri**
A female deer	Zura mskweri
Deer	Mskweri
I am	Ma bore
Thou art	Si ore
He is	He yaren
We are	**Tchku boret**
You are	Tkwa ret
They are	**Hentepe renan**
I was	Ma borti
Thou wast	**Sin orti**
He was	He yatu
We were	**Tchku bortit**
You were	Tkwa tit
They were	**Hemtepe tes**
Be	Boret
To be	
Being	
Having been	Borti
I may be	Ma mkhvenen borti

I shall be	Ma bortare
I should be	Ma bortare
Beat	Ghetchi
To beat	Ghetchi
Beating	
Having beaten	
I beat	Ma ghebtchare
Thou beatest	Sin ghetchi
He beats	Hemuk ghetchas
We beat	Tchku ghebtchat
You beat	Tkwan ghetchit
They beat	Hemtepe ghetchaman
I am beating	
I was beating	
I had beaten	
I may beat	
I shall beat	
I should beat	
I am beaten	
I was beaten	
I shall be beaten	
I go	Ma bidare
Thou goest	Si idi
He goes	Heya idassen
I went	Man mendabti
Thou wentest	Si mendakhti
He went	Heya mendakhtas
Go	Igzale
Going	Magzale
Gone	Mendakhtu
What is your name?	Li mukdjokhons djokho
How old is this horse?	Mutchomperi badi tskheni?
How far is it from here to ---?	Hakolen nako mendrare ---?
How many sons are there in your father's house?	Baba skanish okhoris nako bereren?
I have walked a long way today	Andgha dido gza
The son of my uncle is married to his sister	Djumadi tchkimishi berre gamatkveriren hemush dasha
In the house is the saddle of a white horse	Okhirishi eyeri ktche tskhen isheren
Put the saddle upon his back	

A Spotlight on the 'Lazian' Lexis

I have beaten his son with many stripes	**Hemushe berres dido gebtchi**
He is grazing cattle on the top of the hill	**Hemuk pudjepe odjunams sirtis**
He is sitting on a horse under that tree	**Hemuk khatchkumsdjash tude**
His brother is taller than his sister	**Hemushi djuma damushishen maghar liren**
The price of that is two pounds and a half	**Hemush pakha djur da gverdi**
My father lives in that small house	**Baba tchkimi ham tchuta okhoris molakhen**
Take those pounds from him	**Roy tchopi ham funti**
Give this pound to him	**Rometchi hemus funti**
Beat him well and bind him with ropes	**Bigazeri getchi koreri tokita**
Draw water from the well	**Kuishe tskari esheghi**
Walk before me	**Tsokhle tchkimi igzale**
Whose boy comes behind you?	**Mush berre mulun skani okatch khele?**
From whom did you buy that?	**Mis yutchopi haya?**
From a shopkeeper of the village	**Këdish dukhandjis**

Although we are going to spotlight D. R. Peacock's "Lazian" lexis in the present chapter, we have sampled only those items occurring as lemmas, having discarded all the word-forms and sentences:

Table 3.2 - "Lazian" lexis in D. R. Peacock's collection

English	Laz
One	**Ar**
Two	**Jūr**
Three	**Sum**
Four	**Otkhu**
Five	**Khut**
Six	**Ashi**
Seven	**Shkit**
Eight	**Orvo**
Nine	**Tchkholo**
Ten	**Vit**
Twenty	**Etchi**

Fifty	**Jurnetchi da vit**
Hundred	**Oshi**
I	**Ma**
Mine	**Tchkimiran**
We	**Tchku**
Our	**Tchkuniran**
Thou	**Si**
Thine	**Skani**
You	**Tkwa**
Your	**Skani**
He	**Kiamushiren**
His	**Hemushian**
They	**Hemtepe**
Their	**Hemtepeshia**
Hand	**Khe**
Foot	**Kutchkhe**
Nose	**Tchkhindi**
Eye	**Toli**
Mouth	**Nuku**
Tooth	**Kibiri**
Ear	**Udji**
Hair	**Toma**
Head	**Ti**
Tongue	**Nena**
Belly	**Kolba**
Back	**Shka**
Iron	**Demiri**
Gold	**Altuni**
Silver	**Ghemiish**
Father	**Baba**
Mother	**Nana**
Brother	**Djuma**
Sister	**Da**
Man	**Kotche**
Woman	**Okhordja**
Wife	**Tchili**
Child	**Berre**
Son	**Bidji**
Daughter	**Bozo**
Slave	**Rële**
Cultivator	**Makhatchkali**

A Spotlight on the 'Lazian' Lexis

Shepherd	**Tchkeshi**
God	**Tanghrï**
Devil	**Sheitan**
Sun	**Mjora**
Moon	**Tuta**
Star	**Muritskhi**
Fire	**Datchkhuri**
Water	**Tskhari**
House	**Okhori**
Horse	**Tskheni**
Cow	**Pudji**
Dog	**Djoghori**
Cat	**Rato**
Cock	**Mamuli-**
Duck	**Ordeghi**
Ass	**Guruni**
Camel	**Deve**
Bird	**Kintchi**
Up	**Jin**
Near	**Kholos**
Down	**Tude**
Far	**Mendra**
Before	**Tsokhle**
Behind	**Okatchkhele**
Who	**Mik**
What	**Munoren**
Why	**Mushene**
And	**Do**
But	**Mara**
If	**Si**
Yes	**Ko**
No	**Var**
Alas	**Eivakh**
Good	**Kai**
High	**Maghali**

As Table 3.2 demonstrates, the overwhelming majority of the Laz lexical items are provided rather adequately. This is particularly true of their correspondence with respective English head-words. However, non-speakers of Laz would hardly identify the accurate pronunciations of a handful of words, predominantly because of transliteration-conventions. D. R. Peacock does not mark distinctions between aspirated and ejective (glottalised) stops and affricates. This feature is essential for the phonemic system of Laz; hence, it should be regarded as a significant shortcoming in his transliteration-conventions. In addition, one is unable to observe graphic distinctions not only between the aspirated (k) and glottalised (k') velar stops but also between the two and the uvular ejective (q'): all of them are rendered by the character k; likewise, both the voiced velar stop (g) and the voiced velar fricative (γ) are represented as either g or gh.

Table 3.3 - D. R. Peacock's transliteration conventions

I.P.A. symbols	D. R. Peacock's conventions	Illustrations
ɑ	a	Ar
b	b	Baba
g	g	Guruni
d	d	Datchkhuri
ɛ	e	Deve
v	v, w	Vit, Tkwa
z	z	Bozo
t	t	Toma
i	i	Tchili
k'	k	Kotche
l	l	Altuni
m	m	Mara
n	n	Nena
j	y	Yutchopi
ɔ	o	Orvo
p'	p	-
ʒ	j	Jin
r	r	Okhordja
s	s	Si
t'	t	-
u	u	Udji
p	p	Pudji
k	k	Ko
ɣ	gh	Maghali
q'	k	-
ʃ	sh	Shka
t ʃ	tch	Datchkhuri

t s	ts	**Ts**kheni
d z	ts	-
t s'	ts	**Ts**okhle
t ʃ	tch	**Tch**keshi
x	kh	**Kh**olos
d ʒ	dj	**Dj**uma
h	h	**H**aya
f	f	-

Aside from the shortcomings mentioned earlier in the transliteration system, one would in all likelihood notice two specific cases in the graphic representations of some Laz words. The first case is the labio-dental *v* and its de-dentalized allophone *w*, for instance, in *Vit* and *Tkwa*. In our opinion, this in no way should be considered a transliteration-error, but rather a reflection of variation. Another is associated with the following items: *Rële* and *Rato*. The occurrence of the *ë* (e-diaeresis) seems rather unexpected because such a sound occurs neither in Laz nor in Turkish. However, when we look at the respective English headword (*Slave*), it becomes clear that this is a Turkish loan in Laz *köle* 'a slave:' the *ë* is used to render the Turkish *ö*, and the *r* is just a typo (similarly, in *Rato* (*Katu*), and a handful of words in other languages in D. R. Peacock's specimina). These inadequacies are not so detrimental as to make the 'Lazian' words unidentifiable.

4. Reflections on D. R. Peacock's Œuvre

It would be inadequate to state that the work in question has been rather famous and oft-cited in the literature on respective Caucasian languages;[4] however, it has in no way been that neglected as it may seem initially.

As far as we are concerned, the earliest mention of D. R. Peacock's collection is found in Volume 1 of *The Exploration of the Caucasus* by his fellow countryman Douglas Freshfield (1896, p. 221), who cites it when examining Svan:

> The Suanetian language resembles Old Georgian. It has some affinity also with the dialects spoken by the more eastern highlanders, the Pshavs, Chevsurs, and the Tushians. The late Mr D. R. Peacock, H.B.M.'s

---

[4] For instance, in his rather representative book on the Caucasian languages, R. von Erckert (1895) does not even mention D. R. Peacock and his collection, probably because he was not aware of its existence.

Consul at Batum, prepared a limited vocabulary of the Georgian, Mingrelian, Laz, Suanetian, and Abkhasian dialects for the Royal Asiatic Society.

What comes next chronologically is immediately associated with Laz. This is a comprehensive study of the Laz language by Hrachia Adjarian (sometimes also spelt as Acharian) published in French in 1898. It should be noted that Adjarian (1898, p. 447) extensively applied Peacock's lexical data and commented as:

> When this study was in press, I learned about the existence of another work on the Laz language. It is a collection of a hundred words published in the *Asian Journal of London*, XIX (1887) by Mr. Peacock, consul of England in Batoum. These forms are almost always identical to those indicated here as Bt. I was able to include some of Mr. Peacock's forms in the *Dictionary*, indicating them as P. Others are found in the *Addenda* below.

Reviews written by Antoine Meillet (1899, p. 516) and Hugo Schuchardt (1902, 380) soon followed H. Adjarian's seminal publication. Both reviews recognised Peacock's collection as one of the sources for the study under review.

Another seminal and very remarkable work on Laz belongs to the pen of Nicolas Marr. In the review of literature on the Laz language, when talking about Peacock's collection, the author comments on it with utter criticism: "Peacock's work is too insignificant to be dealt with" (Marr, 1910, p. XXIV). However, he goes on to say that "[i]t still has one advantage: he was in Lazistan and heard the real Laz" (op. cit., p. XXIV); in a footnote, he adds the following: "In Arkabe, I met a Laz man who was involved in Peacock's activities; according to him, Peacock stayed there for three days" (op. cit., p. XXIV). This is all that Marr says about Peacock and his work. Yet, "[i]rrespective of this utterly negative assessment, Nicholas Marr communicates rather notable information about D. R. Peacock's fieldwork: he collected his resource based on word of mouth. Therefore, notwithstanding obvious shortcomings, it can in no way be doomed to total rejection" (Kikvidze & Pachulia, 2020, p. 194). Since the publication contains no narrative text by D. R. Peacock, there is no hint about his visit to Arkabe. One can only assume that he described his visit and fieldwork in Lazistan in his diary, later destroyed by fire.

In his review of N. Marr's book mentioned above, H. Adjarian (1911a, pp. 363, 366, 370)[5] lists Peacock among other predecessors (*devanciers*) of Marr.

There is a notable reflection on Peacock's Svan collection by Wardrop (1911), who was one of the first to comment on the work in question. Wardrop (1911, p. 589) states: "More than twenty years ago the late Mr. D. Peacock included Svanetian among the five languages of which he published vocabularies in the Journal of the Royal Asiatic Society, but the material was scanty, and a large number of errors are found in it."

Two other early authors, Kluge (1913, p. 265) and Kipshidze (1914, p. XXXI) only place Peacock's publication in their lists of references.

In addition to D. R. Peacock and his provision of vocabularies of five languages, various authors have dwelt upon individual collections in individual publications. For instance, Orlovskaya (1994; 2013) discussed the Georgian language data, Genebashvili (2000) analysed the Svan vocabulary, and Kikvidze and Pachulia (2018) provided a discussion of Peacock's resource as one of the earliest landmarks in the history of English-Megrelian lexicography.

Notably, whether owing to the under-resourcefulness of Laz or not, D. R. Peacock's work has rather frequently been cited in publications dealing with the Laz people and their language, both earlier (e.g., Minorsky, 1993, 22) or later, in the 1960s (e.g., Bryer, 1966, 184) and in this century (e.g., Lacroix, 2009, 6; Akkuş & Akkuş, 2020, 123).

5. Conclusion

It is more than evident that a student of Laz, an endangered and under-resourced language, could hardly afford to ignore and reject any lexicographic source containing its specimina. This is particularly applicable to Demetrius Rudolph Peacock's "Vocabularies of Five West Caucasian Languages," especially with its 'Lazian' segment. Starting from a general background, one should pay attention to the fact that the Bengal Asiatic Society furnished the word-list. Moreover, judging from its composition, the list follows the trend of word-collecting from various languages initiated by G. W. Leibniz (e.g., Pedersen, 1924; Gulya, 1974; Robins, 1990). Hence, Peacock's collection should be considered in the context of this well-known trend. Therefore, the resource in question is notable for the history of lexicography and linguistics.

---

[5] See also Adjarian 1911b (p. 415).

As for the 'Lazian' lexis contained in the collection, without forgetting a handful of apparent shortcomings, it should be unambiguously stated that most of them appear in their correct forms. This is not to say that correct forms simply outnumber incorrect ones, but that the overwhelming majority of the Laz words are rendered adequately. What can be assumed is that an inadequate translation is frequently an outcome of how a word is recorded. That is, the conventions of transliteration imposed on D. R. Peacock do not seem to be sufficient for the phonemic system of Laz, and its consonantism in particular. Among other shortcomings, the lack of distinctions between aspirated and ejective (i.e., glottalised) stops and affricates has been the most conspicuous. However, this drawback persists in later works (e.g., Adjarian, 1898).

D. R. Peacock's 'Lazian' collection has an evident and rather significant advantage: it is based on word of mouth. Moreover, chronologically it is the first-ever English-Laz glossary, and hence the earliest landmark in the history of English-Laz lexicography.

References

Adjarian, H. (1898). Étude sur la langue laze. *Mémoires de la Société Linguistique de Paris, X,* 165-448.

Adjarian, H. (1911ₐ). [rev.] I. Илья Чкония. *Грузинский глоссарий.* [Élie Tchkonia. *Glossaire Géorgien.*] II. Н. Марръ. *Грамматика ч'анскаго (лазского) языка.* [N. Marr. *Grammaire de la langue laze.*] – Saint-Pétersbourg, 1910. *Journal Asiatique, 17,* 361-371.

Adjarian, H. (1911ᵦ). [Rev.] Н. Марръ. – Грамматика чанскаго (лазского) языка, С. П. 1910. *Ararat, 5,* 414-420. [in Armenian]

Akkuş, M. & Akkuş, B. (2020). A multilingual 'contact' hub in which Altai faces Caucasia in the north eastern Turkey: Laz encounters Turkish in Artvin. *Artvin Araştırmaları, 2,* 117-132.

Aleksiva, İ. Ç. (2018). Lorenzo Hervás'ın 1787 tarihli çokdilli sözlüğündeki Lazca malzemeler (İnceleme - sözlükçe - tercüme). *Ogni Skani Nena, 8,* 74-99.

Bleichsteiner, R. (1934). Die kaukasischen Sprachproben in Evliya Çelebi's Seyahetname. *Caucasica, 11,* 84-126.

Bryer, A. (1966). Some notes on the Laz and Tzan (I). *Bedi Kartlisa, Revue de Kartvélologie, 21-22,* 174-195.

Campbell, J. (1866). Appendix A.–List of words and phrases to be noted and used as test words for the discovery of the radical affinities of languages, and for easy comparison. *Journal of the Asiatic Society of Bengal, 35/2*(1-3), 201-203.

Dankoff, R. (1991). *An Evliya Çelebi Glossary: Unusual, dialectal and foreign words in Seyahat-name.* Cambridge, MA: Department of Near Eastern Languages and Civilizations, Harvard University.

Freshfield, D. W. (1896). *The exploration of the Caucasus* (Vol. 1). London & New York: Edward Arnold.

Genebashvili, K. (2000). Original Vocabularies of Five West Caucasian Languages. *Issues of Linguistics, 1,* 120-124. [in Georgian]

Gippert, J. (1992). The Caucasian language material in Evliya Çelebi's travel book: A revision. In G. Hewitt (Ed.). *Caucasian perspectives,* (pp. 8-62). Unterschleissheim/München: Lincom Europa.

Gulya, J. (1974). Some eighteenth-century antecedents of nineteenth century linguistics: The discovery of Finno-Ugrian. In D. Hymes (Ed.). *Studies in the history of linguistics: Traditions and paradigms,* (pp. 258-276). Bloomington: Indiana University Press.

Hervás y Panduro, L. (1787). *Vocabolario poligloto con prolegomeni sopra più di cl. Lingue: dove sono delle scoperte nuove, ed utili all'antica storia dell'uman genere, ed alla cognizione del meccanismo delle parole.* Cesena: G. Biasini.

Jikia, S. (1954). Evliya Çelebi about the Laz and Laz language. *Ibero-Caucasian Linguistics, 6,* 243-256.

Klaproth, J. (1823). *Asia polyglotta.* Paris: J. M. Eberhart.

Kikvidze, Z. & Pachulia, L. (2018). An early landmark in the history of English-Megrelian lexicography: D. R. Peacock's contribution. *8th International Research Conference on Education, Language and Literature. Proceedings Book,* 490-496. Tbilisi: IBSU.

Kikvidze, Z. & Pachulia, L. (2020). Laz lexical data from D. R. Peacock's Collection: Representations, reflections, translation. *General and Specialist Translation / Interpretation: Theory, Methods, Practice: International Conference Papers, 189-196. Kyiv: Agrar Media Group.*

Kipshidze, I. (1914). *A grammar of the Mingrelian (Iverian) language with a reader and vocabulary.* Saint Petersburg: Imperial Academy of Sciences. [in Russian]

Kluge, Th. (1913). Materialen zu einer Lazischen Grammatik nach Aufnahmen des Dialektes Trapezunt. *Nachrichten der Königlichen Gesellschaft der Wissenschaften zu Göttingen. Philologisch-historische Klasse,* 264-324. Göttingen: Commissionverglag der Dietrich'schen Verlagsbuchhandlung.

Koch, K. (1846). *Wanderungen im Oriente, während der Jahre 1843 und 1844: Reise im pontischen Gebirge und Türkischen Armenien.* Weimar: Druck und Verlag des Landes-Industrie-Comptoirs.

Lacroix, R. (2009). *Description du dialecte Laze d'Arhavi (Caucasique du sud, Turquie): Grammaire et texte.* [Unpublished doctoral dissertation, Université Lumière de Lyon 2].

Marr, N. (1910). *A grammar of the Chan (Laz) language with a reader and vocabulary.* Saint Petersburg: Imperial Academy of Sciences. [in Russian]

Meillet, A. (1899). [rev.] L'*Étude sur la langue laze. Revue Critique d'histoire et Littérature, 47,* 516.

Minorsky, V. (1993). Laz. In M. Th. Houtsma, A. J. Wensinck, E. Lévi-Provençal, H. A. R. Gibb, W. Heffening (Eds.). *Brill's first encyclopedia of Islam, 1913-1936,* (Vol. 5), (pp. 20-22). Leiden: E. J. Brill.

Morfill, W. R. (1895). Peacock, Dmitri Rudolph. In S. Lee (Ed.). *Dictionary of national biography*, (Vol. XLIV), (pp. 137-138). London: Smith, Elder & Co.

Orlovskaya, N. (1994). Some notes about the Georgian language in 19th century England. *Mnatobi, 1*(2), 174-176. [in Georgian]

Orlovskaya, N. (2013). *Essays on literary relations*. Tbilisi: Russian Club. [in Russian]

Peacock, D. R. (1887). Original vocabularies of five West Caucasian Languages (Georgian, Mingrelian, Lazian, Swanetian, and Abkhazian). *Journal of the Royal Asiatic Society of Great Britain and Ireland, (19)*1, 145-156.

Pedersen, H. (1924). *Sprogvidenskaben i det nittende aarhundrede, metoder og resultater.* København: Gyldendalske Boghandel.

Rickmers, W. R. (1934). Lazistan and Ajaristan. *The Geographical Journal, 84*(6), 465-478.

Robins, R. H. (1990). Leibniz and Wilhelm von Humboldt and the history of comparative linguistics. In T. De Mauro & L. Formigari (Eds.). *Leibniz, Humboldt and the origins of comparativism* (pp. 85-102). Amsterdam & Philadelphia: John Benjamins.

Rosen, G. (1844). *Über die sprache der Lazen.* Lemgo: Meyersche Hofbuchhandlung.

Schuchardt, H. (1902). [Rez. von:] MH Adjarian, Étude sur la langue laze. *Wiener Zeitschrift für die Kunde des Morgenlandes, 16*: 379-404.

Smith, E. (1833). *Researches of the Rev. E. Smith and Rev. H.G.O. Dwight in Armenia including a journey through Asia Minor, and into Georgia and Persia, with a visit to the Nestorian and Chaldean Christians of Oormiah and Salmas.* Boston: Crocker and Brewster.

Tsagareli, A. (1872). *A comparative review of the morphology of the Iberian group of the Caucasian languages.* Saint-Petersburg. [in Russian]

Wagner, M. (1856). *Travels in Persia, Georgia and Koordistan: with sketches of the Cossacks and the Caucasus.* London: Hurst and Blackett.

Wardrop, O. (1888). *The Kingdom of Georgia. Notes of travel in a land of women, wine, and song.* London: Sampson Low, Maarston, Searle, and Rivington.

Wardrop, O. (1911). English-Svanetian vocabulary. *Journal of the Royal Asiatic Society of Great Britain and Ireland, 16*, 589-634.

Chapter 4

Linguistic Variation and Complexity in Laz

Ömer Eren
University of Chicago

Abstract

This study investigates the synchronic and dialectal variation in Laz in relation to the notion of language-complexity. Firstly, focusing on the differences between different generations of Laz speakers in terms of forming reflexive constructions, I reveal that Laz is evolving into a more analytic structure with less linguistic complexity. The decrease in the number of available patterns for reflexivization constitutes an instance of pattern-regulation (Dahl, 2004; 2009), leading to a decrease in system-complexity because only one pattern, rather than two, suffices to express reflexivity. Secondly, the examination and comparison of two particular dialects of Laz, namely Ardeshen and Pazar Laz (AL and PL henceforth), in terms of their morpho-syntactic properties indicate that the loss of inflectional morphology in AL does not necessarily correlate with less overall complexity. Instead, I argue that the lesser (overt) morphological complexity is counterbalanced by the greater syntactic complexity (McWhorter, 2001) and hidden complexity (Bisang, 2014).

Keywords: *South Caucasian, endangerment, variation, linguistic complexity, simplification*

* * *

1. Introduction

Laz is an endangered and understudied language spoken mainly in Northeastern Turkey. It belongs to the South Caucasian language family (see Hewitt 2004 for a thorough introduction to Caucasian languages in general and Holisky 1991 and Boeder 2005 for more details on South Caucasian languages) together with Georgian, Svan and Mingrelian, which is the closest sister language of Laz (see Kiria, Ezugbaia, Memišiši & Čuxua 2015 for a recent grammar of Laz and Mingrelian). All these languages are mainly spoken in

Georgia with the exception of Laz, which is the only member of the language family that is spoken predominantly outside of Georgia (Hewitt, 2004, 19).[1] Almost all speakers of Laz are bilingual as they also speak the socio-economically more prestigious language, namely Turkish. Haznedar et al. (2018) note that there is a direct correlation between the age of speakers and their use of Laz or Turkish. That is, as the age of the speakers increases, their tendency and frequency to speak Laz also increases. The study by Haznedar et al. (2018) additionally statistically indicates the endangerment of Laz as it is not transmitted to, and spoken by, younger generations: Of the 107 younger generation speakers, who participated in their study, 28% do not know Laz at all, 49% have only passive knowledge, and only 23% know Laz well. In other words, younger generation speakers of Laz (age 26 or younger) are more proficient and prefer speaking Turkish rather than Laz. As far as the domains in which Laz is used are concerned, Laz is primarily confined to the private sphere, especially in rural areas, being mainly used in familial interactions in home-settings, while Turkish prevails in the public sphere and urban settings (Kutscher, 2008). Thus, that the Laz population have gradually been switching to a socio-economically more advantageous vernacular manifestly indicates that the Laz population is undergoing a language-shift.

Through adopting an ecological approach (Mufwene, 2001), this study aims to investigate the current situation of Laz as an endangered language and the synchronic variation it exhibits. Along with the changes that generated the relevant linguistic differences, Laz exhibits extensive dialectal variation to the extent that there are clear differences in terms of case-alignment. While AL has lost its morphological case-system and patterns with Nominative-Accusative languages like Turkish, all other varieties have overt morphological case-markers, exhibiting an Ergative-Absolutive system (Öztürk, 2008). In relation to the notion of linguistic complexity, this study focuses on this particular dialectal morpho-syntactic and intergenerational variation in Laz, which is the result of an ongoing language-change.

This study is organized as follows: in Part 2, adopting an ecological approach to language-endangerment and loss (Mufwene, 2001; 2017), I show the significance of contact-ecology in giving rise to the current status of Laz as an endangered language. I specifically focus on the changes in the socio-

---

[1] Note that there are Laz speakers in Georgia, albeit low in number, and also in other parts of Turkey, i.e., the Marmara Region. Since I did not have access to these speakers along with those who reside in Georgia, the varieties of Laz spoken in these areas are not included in the present study.

economic and population structure (Mufwene, 1996; 2001) before and after the foundation of the Turkish Republic and then discuss the implications of the relevant facts for the linguistic complexity of Laz. In Part 3, I briefly explain the methodology employed for data-collection in the present study. In Part 4, I turn to an ongoing change observed in Laz and show that affixation as a strategy to form reflexive constructions is falling out of use and is being gradually replaced by pronoun-strategy for two reasons. First, younger generations either are not familiar with the former at all or have only passive knowledge of this strategy. Second, second-generation speakers tend to favour pronoun-strategy over affixation. I consider this to be an instance of linguistic simplification (McWhorter, 2001; Dahl 2004; 2009). Following that, Part 5 focuses on the dialectal variation in Laz and specifically examines the effects of the loss of the case-system in AL in relation to language-complexity. Lastly, Part 6 summarizes and concludes the discussion in this study.

2. The Endangerment of Laz: An Ecological Perspective

Laz is an understudied South Caucasian language spoken in Northeastern Turkey. It is classified as 'definitely endangered' by the UNESCO *Atlas of the World Languages in Danger*. All speakers of Laz are bilingual in that they also speak Turkish, which is the socio-economically prestigious language in the area. On the other hand, younger generations are mostly monolingual speakers of Turkish, or a small percentage of them have only passive knowledge of Laz (Haznedar et al., 2018). Kutscher (2008) notes that, while Laz is mainly confined to the private sphere, Turkish dominates the semi-public and the public sphere. Additionally, Laz is primarily spoken in rural areas, while Turkish has instead penetrated more and more domains of interaction in which Laz has been spoken, thus confining Laz to being spoken either by only the elderly in the rural areas or with the elderly in private home-settings.

Following this, it can be claimed that the Laz population is undergoing a language-shift (see Fishman, 1991; Pauwels, 1996; Mufwene, 2020a). More specifically, they have adopted and gradually switched to a new vernacular that is politically and economically more prestigious than their heritage-language. The abandonment of Laz for Turkish has come about due to the gradual contraction of the former's domain of uses, ultimately restricting Laz to home-settings and familial interactions. This is in line with Fishman's domain-analysis (1966.); language-shift gradually proceeds from domain to domain, comprised of three essential components. In the case of Laz, the 'role relation between participants' mainly corresponds to 'grandparent-(grand)child', 'place of interaction' to home/villages, and 'topic of interaction' to familial and culture-specific issues. As far as the first component is concerned, we see that 'parents' are missing between the two generations in the sense that younger generations mainly do not interact or refrain from interacting with their parents in Laz. As for the second component, Laz seems to be less preferred in interactions in urban settings. In the last component, too, we see a similar kind of contraction in the domains in which Laz is used. This situation is also in line with Mufwene (2020a), who defines language-shift as 'the outcome of fewer and fewer opportunities or motivations that particular speakers have to practise their heritage vernacular.'

In the remainder of this section, I will focus on the changes in the ecology of Laz before and after the foundation of the Turkish Republic to account for the endangerment of Laz under the ecological approach (Mufwene, 2001). For this purpose, I first present the socio-historical facts, which show the changes in the ecology of Laz. In light of this discussion, I then show how these changes have eventually given rise to the endangerment of Laz. In this regard, I focus on two main ecological factors: i) population-structure and ii) socio-economic structure. Lastly, I turn to the effects of ecological changes on linguistic complexity.

2.1. Socio-historical Background

Turkey comprises a wide range of ethnic groups. Thus, there are a number of diverse minority languages spoken within its borders along with the national language of the country, namely Turkish. These languages, including Armenian, Pontic Greek, Hemshin, Kurdish, Pomak and Laz, have shared the same (or a similar) geographical area since at least Ottoman times.

Lasting more than 600 years, the Ottoman Empire (OE hereafter) took Anatolia as its centre and extended its influence into south-eastern Europe as well as the Middle East. As a result, there was a wide array of diverse ethnic minorities living under the rule of the OE. Compared to its counterparts, namely other imperial powers, the OE stood out for its tolerance and protection of the minority groups (Ceylan, 2002). The administration of the OE was decentralized in that the empire was divided into regions governed by local governors called *pashas*. As for the status of the minorities, the OE adopted a system called *millet* (cf. Arabic *nation*) that ruled religiously and ethnically different communities. Every *millet* in the OE had its own ruler selected by the communities themselves and approved by the Sultan. These rulers, who used to act as mediators between the Ottoman government and their fellow co-religionists, were held responsible for their communities' legal, financial, and administrative activities. As long as these minority groups fulfilled their duties, such as paying their taxes and abiding by the regulations of the Ottoman government, they were free to speak and even receive education in their ethnic languages and also to keep their ethnic identity and traditions alive (Özfidan et al., 2018). Additionally, these groups did not need to interact with the Ottoman government, whose official language was Turkish (or, more precisely, Ottoman Turkish), thanks to their intermediary leaders (Ceylan, 2002).

Another noteworthy fact regarding the minorities in the OE is that, although these groups co-existed with other ethnic groups, they used to live in separate quarters within cities and in different villages. Furthermore, it is often the case that different ethnicities were competent and ethnically associated with different occupations (Hidayat, 2014). For example, Armenians were (predominantly) competent craftsmen, and Greeks were fishermen.

After the collapse of the 600-year-old OE at the end of World War I, the Republic of Turkey was founded in 1923. The newly founded republic adopted *westernization* as a policy and tried to incorporate this policy in all domains of life by launching reforms that followed the following principles: nationalism, secularism and modernism (Akyol, 2006). For this purpose, and importantly for our purposes, although the Turkish Republic inherited a multilingual and pluricultural structure from the OE, it constructed its nationalistic policy on a monolithic ethnicity and on a single language: Turkishness and the Turkish language. For instance, the Act of Unification of Education approved one year after the foundation of the republic combined all educational institutions under a single institution (viz., the Ministry of Education) and forbade the formal teaching of any language other than Turkish. (Özfidan et al., 2018)

As for its economic policies, the Republic adopted a liberal approach and started industrialization to establish a financial structure that is nationally self-sufficient. For this purpose, a series of new factories were founded to mass-produce various goods, including textile, sugar, and cement, in the early years of the republic (Habib, 1951; Asiliskender, 2009; Güler, 2011). These developments were accompanied and supplemented by some infrastructure improvements like the construction of modern roads that connected the internal parts of the country. All these developments also contributed to the formation of cities and fostered the urbanization-process that the country underwent after the foundation of the republic (Keles, 1980).

2.2. Ecological causes of the endangerment of Laz

In this section, adopting an ecological approach to language-endangerment and loss (Mufwene, 2001), I argue that the language-shift that Laz has gradually faced over the last century results from the changes in its ecology after the foundation of the Turkish Republic. In other words, I demonstrate the significant role that certain non-linguistic factors interacting with one another play in determining the current status of Laz as an endangered language.

2.2.1. Population-structure

Population-structure, originally a term used in population-genetics, is invoked by Mufwene (1996, 2001) as an important ecological factor that explains the differential outcomes of contact-situations between languages in the context of different styles of colonization-situations (e.g., whether we observe the emergence of certain creoles or language-shift and why). The term is mainly used to address the nature of socialization-patterns among members of a population (i.e., whether different members of a community can freely interact with one another or not, and if they can, to what extent and what the dynamics of this social interaction are). More clearly, the idea is that the contact-outcomes are likely to be different for populations with a (racial or residential) segregated structure than those that are integrated.

The geographical area populated by Laz people (i.e., Northeastern Turkey) is highly mountainous, hence steep and uneven. The region has lots of water-sources, which led to a more scattered type of settlement. It is also often the case that there is a 1 km difference between the two houses in a (so-called) village. Also, these natural conditions made it difficult for Laz people to go to town-centres to trade with others (Taşkın, 2011). These factors have made it difficult for the members of the Laz community to interact not only among themselves but also with the members of other communities, which suggests a more segregated type of population-structure due to natural conditions.

The situation described above, however, seems to be more valid for Ottoman times because there have been significant changes in it since the foundation of the Turkish Republic. As of the early days of the republic, the country has undergone a process of industrialization. As part of this process, the Turkish government decided to make investments for establishing tea-factories in North-eastern Turkey, where the climate and geography were most suitable for tea-cultivation and production.

The introduction of the tea-industry has been a catalyst in that it has led to significant changes in the life of Laz people socially, economically and culturally. For example, these changes made Laz people more dependent on, and subsidiary to, the state, enhancing the official interaction between the Laz and the government, whose official language is Turkish. Likewise, the Laz people engaged in close and intense contact with the rest of the population around the same area through these changes, which is particularly significant for this study (Taşkın, 2011).

The latter came as a result of the fact that state-investments were supplemented by specific significant infrastructure-improvements like the building of modern roads both along the Black Sea coast and also in the internal parts of North-eastern Turkey, replacing the pathways that were not wide enough for vehicles needed for tea-production. The construction of these roads, combined with the availability of motorized vehicles, made it easier for people to move about and go to the city or town-centres more often than before. As a result, Laz people came into contact with the members of other populations, which created a more integrated population-structure.

Urbanization is another significant effect of the introduction of the tea industry in the lives of Laz people. Turkey's industrialisation process went hand-in-hand with urbanization (viz., the establishment of cities, which were also the main centres of modern life and economic opportunities as opposed to the rural areas). During this period, a flow of migration from rural areas to city-centres prevailed across the entire country. Taşkın (2011) and Bucaklishi (2002) note that tea-farming did not prevent Laz people from migrating to the city-centres for several reasons. Firstly, the tea-industry has lost its valuable income-generating status due to the liberal economic policies that reduced the effect of the state on tea-production, especially from the 1980s onwards. This situation has resulted in a significant decrease firstly in the unit-price of tea. The prices decreased from $0.62 in 1978 to $0.34 in two years (Bucaklishi, 2002, p. 60), thus decreasing the tea-producing Laz people's income. Secondly, the patrimonial inheritance-customs combined with the increase in the population-growth thanks to the improvements in the health-conditions caused the fragmentation of the agricultural lands into tiny parcels, making it difficult for people to sustain their lives only on tea-agriculture. Also, tea-agriculture only lasts for five months of the year and is mostly conducted by women, making it necessary for especially men to look for other and better job-opportunities. All these factors contributed to the massive migration from the rural areas to developing city-centres. Bucaklishi (2002, p. 3) notes that North-eastern Turkey is the region that has been influenced by this process the most since it exhibited the highest rate of migration compared to other parts of the country.

The underlying reasons for migration were mainly economic, which also affected the population-structure. Migrating to urban centres has significantly increased the interaction of Laz people with other ethnic groups and languages, leading incrementally to an ever more integrated population-structure. Citing Demirtaş et al. (1996, p. 40), who suggest that the modern cities that are designed for nation-states are like a melting-pot where all differences disappear, Taşkın (2011, p. 39) argues that urban life assumes a kind of fusion, leading to the abandonment of cultural traits and linguistic features associated with certain ethnicities.

At this point, the significance of population-structure becomes even more evident because urbanization *per se* does not necessarily entail a language-shift. More precisely, whether there is residential segregation or not bears a great deal of significance because, in the presence of residential segregation, the amount of interaction across different ethnic groups could be rather limited, yielding a segregated population-structure in an urban setting. Mufwene (Mufwene, 2020b) invokes residential segregation as one of the most ecological factors in explaining the maintenance of the African-American ethnolects as opposed to the loss (or shift) of the continental European languages in the New World (Mufwene, 2020b, p. 13). To the best of my knowledge, as far as Laz is concerned in this respect, it is not easy to talk about segregated residential neighbourhoods in urban areas in Turkey[2]. In that respect, Laz seems to pattern more with the continental European languages in the present-day USA, most of which have been replaced with the socio-economically more prestigious language, English, mainly due to the integrated population-structure.

The development of the tea-industry and its effects on the population-structure of the Laz community is quite similar to the development of the textile-industry in 18th-century Ireland. Mufwene (2020b) notes that the majority of the Irish population was rural before the 18th century, with the English colonists' presence being restricted to the urban centres. However, the introduction of the textile-industry as part of the Industrial Revolution led to a significant change in this situation in that it brought the Irish in closer and more intense contact with the Anglophone manufacturers and employees. Furthermore, as we also observe in the case of Laz, the industrialization-process also resulted in the migration of the Irish population to the urban centres that were gradually becoming more and more industrial, and hence also more promising in terms of holding better and well-paid jobs. Mufwene (2020b) argues that these demographic changes and urbanization gave rise to a more integrated population-structure as opposed to the pre-18th-century era. Consequently, Irish people started to communicate more and more in English.

---

[2] The absence of (official) demographic information on this issue makes it hard to make any robust claim on this issue.

This situation, combined with the fact that the socio-economic structure only functioned in English, resulted in the loss of Irish, whose existence remained restricted to the substrate influence it left on English.

2.2.2. Integration into Socio-economic Ecology

In this section, I focus on the significance of the integration of Laz people into the socio-economic structure of the newly founded Republic, which has one national language (viz., Turkish), for the current status of Laz. Following Mufwene (2001, 2020a, 2020b), I argue that the language-shift that Laz has faced can be explained to a great extent as an adaptive response of the Laz speakers to the changing socio-economic structure (i.e., in the hope of a better socio-economic future for themselves as well as their children).

Bucaklishi (2002) notes that Laz people were engaged in occupations like fishing and cattle-breeding, mainly because the geography where they lived was mountainous, and hence not suitable for agriculture of many products other than especially maize, collards and beans. Moreover, the highly steep nature of the environment, combined with the absence of roads other than small pathways, prevented Laz people from economic interaction and trade with other communities. As a result of this economic and social isolation, Laz people pursued a self-sufficient way of life during Ottoman times and most probably even before that. In this respect, the lifestyle of the Laz people seems to be reminiscent of the Pomak people, who also led a more isolated lifestyle on the Rhodope Mountains, as reported by Adamou (2010), rather than the Romani, who were primarily engaged in trade, and hence interacted more with outsiders.

However, the introduction of the tea-industry has significantly changed this situation in that the Laz people ended up being more dependent on the state for their economic life. Taşkın (2011, p. 13) argues that the establishment of tea-factories eliminated the aforementioned hitherto-closed economy, rendering the Laz community's economic position less autonomous and more subsidiary to the state. Moreover, tea-farming and industry turned out not to be sufficient to meet the demands of the growing Laz population, especially after the 1980s. Consequently, Laz people (along with other residents of North-eastern Turkey) started to migrate to big urban areas where there were better job-opportunities. Given also that tea-agriculture is carried out only for a limited period of the year and primarily by women, the migrations mostly affected the male population, who needed to be engaged in other occupations in the cities and to stay there for most of the year (Bucaklishi, 2002; Taşkın 2011).

What is more crucial for our purposes is that the socio-economic structure was only allowed to function in Turkish (i.e., the national language). As noted in Part 1.1, other ethnic languages were forbidden in public and official settings in the early days of the Turkish Republic. This regulation necessitated that Laz people learn Turkish to function in the socio-economic structure as opposed to the case during the OE.

Taşkın (2011) also notes that most Laz people, especially women, also showed a great interest in migrating to the urban areas where a more modern style of life prevailed compared to the rural areas. On the other hand, this also required a full integration into the city-life and the socio-economic atmosphere, making Turkish even more critical for social and economic reasons. As a result, Turkish became more advantageous than Laz in that it was understood to be a key to a better social and economic life, while Laz was only spatially associated with, or useful in, the heritage-villages, especially to communicate with the elderly.[3]

The shift and loss of Laz can be interpreted as simply a strategy that Laz speakers employ to adapt to the changing socio-economic structure (Mufwene, 2001). In other words, it seems that the Laz speakers simply avoid(ed) using their heritage-language in the presence of an economically and socially more advantageous alternative, namely Turkish. The necessity of integration into the new socio-economic world-order and its effects on language-endangerment and loss are also evidenced by the cases of Irish, continental Europeans in the New World along with the Native Americans where we also see the role of economic and political marginalization of these languages by the dominant or politically more powerful ones in giving rise to their endangerment and loss (Mufwene, 2001).

2.3. Effects of ecological factors on linguistic complexity

Linguistic complexity is neither easily defined nor easily measured. The main reason for this is that complexity has been invoked in reference to such various factors as computational complexity, structural complexity, or system-complexity. Computational complexity is defined as the amount of time and effort required to process certain utterances, while structural complexity is the variety and elaborateness involved in arranging different units and components linearly and hierarchically (see Sinnemaki, 2011 for an overview

---

[3] There is also another side of this issue, namely, the perception of Laz as being detrimental to Turkish that prevails among the Laz people.

of different modes of complexity). The third factor, system-complexity, is defined as the length of the description of a given language (Dahl, 2009). Depending on the type of complexity to be measured, different metrics have been proposed in the literature (see Kortmann & Szmrecsanyi, 2012 for an overview).

The existence of a wide range of metrics mainly follows from the modular structure of linguistic systems. That is, metrics are usually intended to assess complexity in a certain module. The overall complexity of a given language (or global linguistic complexity in Miestemo's 2008 terms), in turn, is dependent on the relevant complexity in each of its modules. In that regard, assessing overall complexity is an enormous and ambitious task, even 'a hopeless endeavour'. However, measuring the complexity of a specific domain (e.g., morphology or syntax) within local linguistic complexity (Miestemo, 2008) is relatively more doable (Kortmann & Szmrecsanyi, 2012).

What complicates the picture is that different modules are dependent on one another and interact with each other in complicated ways. Mufwene et al. (2017) highlight the significance of this interaction in contributing to the subject-matter of the complexity of a given language. They also criticize certain interpretations of complexity that solely rely on counting the number of the parts and components in a language (cf. McWhorter, 2001).

The relation of the complexity with the sociolinguistic factors and context where speakers of a language are embedded is also significant. In other words, the question is how complexity is affected by external factors of language like population-size, high- and low-contact speech-communities. Details aside, there seems to be a consensus in the literature that small and isolated communities tend to preserve internal language-complexity, whereas high-contact leads to simplification (see Baechler & Seiler, 2016 for an overview). The main factor giving rise to this situation is argued to be the role played by L2 learners. Trudgill (2011), for instance, argues that the simplification induced by contact comes as a result of the high number of L2 learners in high-contact situations. Adult L2 learners are assumed to be 'imperfect language learners' and hence fail to notice and/or preserve structurally complex constructions. In contrast, children, who are the masters of language-acquisition, do not have any problems with structurally complex grammatical structures.

Leaving aside the question of what exactly gives rise to a decrease in complexity in high-contact situations, focusing on how this claim might inform us about the complexity of Laz is also necessary. The changes in the ecology of Laz after the fall of the OE leads to a prediction that one expects to find a trend towards more simplification in Laz in present-day Turkey, unlike in the OE. Laz communities mainly remained in geographical, social and economic isolation during Ottoman times, when they were low-contact communities. However, the industrialization- and urbanization-process after the foundation of the Turkish Republic ended this isolation and brought Laz communities in close contact and interaction with mainly Turkish speakers. Therefore, the previously low-contact community gradually became a high-contact one, which might have led to a decrease in the structural complexity.

Before discussing one potential example for this in Part 2, a word of caution is in order. The term 'complexity' here is intended in its theoretical sense. That is, certain constructions are more complex than others with respect to certain theoretical assumptions. Therefore, a decrease in complexity does/cannot render a language less sophisticated or less worthy/easier to be learned, as claimed for creoles, which are also argued to exhibit a low rate of complexity (McWhorter, 2001).

3. Methodology

Data reported in the present study (unless cited otherwise) were collected on an online-basis from 8 anonymous Laz speakers[4] as a result of the worldwide pandemic COVID-19. The language-consultants were firstly contacted via the group on social media (Facebook, Şurimşine Lazuri), and data were collected by using the chat-function and online-video and/or audio-conversations. The judgments of the language-consultants were cross-checked after data-collection, which resulted in the generalizations about Laz reported in the remainder of the present study.

3.1. Intergenerational variation in Laz

In this section, I focus on the reflexive constructions in Laz, which can either be formed via reflexive pronouns or verbal affixes. The main focus is on my observation that verbal prefixes are not actively used by younger generations, who appear to have passive knowledge of them and understand them but do not actively use them. Instead, they prefer to use reflexive pronouns.

There are two main strategies in Laz to form reflexive constructions. One can either use a reflexive pronoun, as shown in example (1a) or a verbal reflexive marker, namely {-i}, as shown in example (1b). The affixation strategy is falling out of use because either younger generations are not familiar with it or are

---

[4] I would like to express my deepest gratitude to all my language consultants, without whom the present study would not have come into existence.

familiar with it but do not actively use it. Instead, they prefer the reflexive-pronoun strategy.

(1)

a. *Reflexive Pronoun Strategy*
Ali-k   yali-s   ti-muşi   dzir-u.
Ali-erg mirror-loc himself   see-pst.3sg
'Ali saw himself in the mirror.' (PL)

b. *Verbal reflexive Marker Strategy*
Ali-k   yali-s   i-dzir-u.
Ali-erg mirror-loc refl-see-pst.3sg
'Ali saw himself in the mirror.' (PL)

Adapting the notion of 'gene-pool' in biology, Mufwene (2001) argues that the feature pool involves 'all the parts and components of a language, from which idiolects and languages select materials for their systems.' The idea is that different features frequently stand in a competitive relationship, and one of them is selected over the others, being the winner of the competition. Analyzing Laz facts under the ecological approach, we can say that both of the two possible strategies are morpho-syntactic variants in the feature pool of Laz; the competition is resolved in favour of the reflexive-pronoun strategy.

Table 4.1 - Reflexivization in Laz

Feature Pool	
Verbal prefix	Competition
Reflexive pronoun	Winner: Reflexive pronoun strategy

Making a similar observation regarding the use of verbal prefixes such as the ones that are used to form locational constructions, Kutscher (2008) argues that using verbal affixes to form certain constructions is a distinguishing typological property of South Caucasian languages in comparison to, for instance, Turkish, which does not have any such markers but uses free forms for the same functions. Based on this idea, Kutscher (2008) also argues that younger speakers of Laz do not fully command the morpho-syntactic constructions and forms typical of South Caucasian languages.

In the case of Laz reflexivization, we see another example of competing typologies within the same language. More specifically, the decay of the verbal reflexive by affixation constitutes an instance of typological realignment, which is a shift from one typological type to another (Mufwene et al., 2017), at least for those verbs that have traditionally preferred affixation. Furthermore, the relevant realignment seems to be taking place under the influence of Turkish (cf. Kutscher, 2008), where the dominant reflexivization-strategy is to use a reflexive pronoun. Note that, while the reflexive-pronoun strategy can replace the verbal suffixation-strategy in Turkish as shown in (2), the opposite is not licensed as in (3).

(2)

a. Ali   yıka-n-dı.
   Ali   wash-refl-pst.3sg
   'Ali showered.'

b. ?Ali   kendi-ni   yıka-dı.
   Ali   self-acc   wash-pst.3sg
   'Ali showered.'

(3)

a. *Ali   yak-ın-dı.
   Ali   burn-refl-pst.3sg
   'Int: Ali burnt himself.'

b. Ali   kendi-ni   yak-tı.
   Ali   self-acc   burn-pst.3sg
   'Ali burnt himself.'

Therefore, the preference for using a free form (i.e., a pronoun) over a bound form for reflexivization in Laz seems plausible given that younger generations of Laz are more fluent in Turkish, where the primary strategy is to use a free form. What we see here is Laz realigning typologically with Turkish on this particular parameter.

A similar kind of change seen in the case of Laz has indeed been attested in many languages, especially in the heritage-languages spoken by younger generations. Heritage-speakers cross-linguistically have been noted to favour analytical constructions over synthetic ones because the former consists of a more direct mapping between form and meaning (Boumans, 2006; Brehmer & Czachór, 2012; Polinsky, 2018). This becomes significant in the case of Laz because the so-called reflexive verbal marker is indeed syncretic in that it also occurs in constructions that lack an overt external argument as well as in unergatives. These facts are illustrated in (4a) and (4b) (Öztürk & Taylan, 2017, examples (23) and (37) respectively).

(4)

a. Cami   i-t'ax-e-n.
   glass.nom   val-break-TS-pres.3ps
   'The glass is broken/breaks/breakable.'

b. Ali-k   i-çaliş-am-s.
   Ali-erg   val-work-TS-pres.3ps
   'Ali is working.'

In Eren (2021), I argue that the so-called reflexive marker[5] is indeed an expletive; it is simply a syntactic argument with no referential meaning. Thus, it leads to an asymmetry between syntax and semantics (i.e., a direct violation of one-to-one correspondence between meaning and form).

Details aside, what is more crucial for our purposes here is the effect of the decay of the reflexivization function of this marker, which is present in the baseline varieties of Laz (i.e., older generations) and absent in the heritage-varieties, on the linguistic complexity of these relevant varieties. As noted in Part 1.3, there are different interpretations of complexity, which are accompanied by different metrics. However, the kind of change observed in the case of Laz reflexivization would be treated as a case of simplification in many accounts of complexity as it involves a shift towards more analyticity via the loss of an inflectional marker. One of such accounts that relies on the quantity of inflectional markers is McWhorter's (2001), which has then been referred to as bit-complexity (DeGraff, 2009). Likewise, in this case, we see a decrease in the number of available patterns in Laz. Therefore, it constitutes an instance of pattern-regulation (Dahl, 2004; 2009), leading to a decrease in system-complexity because only one pattern, rather than two, suffices to express reflexivity.

A word of caution for this argument is in order for two reasons. Firstly, any claims on the complexity of Laz, and endangered languages in general, needs to be approached with scepticism given the fact that endangered languages are usually under-described. This being the case, we are unfortunately in no position at this point to know i) what kind of a division of labour there exists between the pronoun- and affixation-strategy in Laz before and after this ongoing change has taken place, and ii) the exact rate and profile of speakers who have abandoned the affixal strategy. It is very likely that such a change is correlated with the proficiency of speakers in that it is only or more likely to be attested in low-proficiency speakers, where heritage-speakers would fall into (Haznedar et al., 2018). Secondly and relatedly, the argument proposed here relies not only on the judgments of a relatively small group of speakers but also on a data collection process that was mediated through social media, which comes with its own costs and limitations because when recruitment is done via social media, it becomes hard to keep certain sociolinguistic variables under control for the identification of correlations between certain sociolinguistic

---

[5] Lacroix (2009) refers to this marker as middle voice marker due to its syncretic nature. See Boeder (1969) and Nash (2021) *inter alia* for a discussion of version vowels in Georgian.

and grammatical variables. This is mainly concerned with the fact that not all the participants who took part in this study currently reside in the same geographical area, despite being born and raised in the same area at one point where they were first exposed to Laz. The differences in the residential neighborhood are likely to lead to differing language contact experiences, which then result in differences in linguistic practices and proficiency. All these factors make it difficult to firmly assert that the grammar of Laz is becoming less complex due to language contact. Nevertheless, such a change is still attested in at least some speakers. Given that similar changes are cross-linguistically observed in heritage-speakers, the relevant argument stands as a reasonable hypothesis to be verified with further in-depth research.

4. Dialectal variation in Laz: AL vs PL

In this section, I take a closer look at Laz and focus on AL in more detail. The crucial fact is that while PL still retains its case-morphology, AL has lost it. The examples in (5) show that while PL, along with other dialects of Laz like Arhavi (5c), still marks its core-arguments with overt case-markers (5a), core-arguments are not case-marked in AL (5b) (Öztürk, 2008). Tables 4.2 and 4.3 show that AL stands as an outlier in the South Caucasian language family because all members of the family still mark core arguments with overt case morphology despite the existence of certain exceptions based on agentivity, verb classes and/or screeves in certain dialects (See Tuite 1998 for a thorough examination of case and agreement systems of South Caucasian languages. Also see Hewitt 1987 for Georgian exhibiting an Ergative alignment rather than the 'active-inactive' system proposed in Harris 1985). As far as Laz is concerned, Tuite 1998 (p. 209), for instance, notes that subjects of certain verbs can optionally remain unmarked rather than being marked with ergative case. Yet, this particular pattern is only concerned with and restricted to a limited set of verbs and ergative case in this particular Laz variety. What we see in AL is, on the other hand, the complete loss/absence of all core-case morphology, which makes it stand out in the entire South Caucasian language family.

(5)

a. PL
Ali-**k** Amedi-**s** a mutxa utzu.
Ali-erg Ahmet-dat one thing told
'Ali told Ahmet something.'

b. AL
Ali Amedi mutxa duʒu.
Ali Ahmet thing told
'Ali told Ahmet something.'

(5c)

Mtuti-k arkadaši-muši-s uži el-u-d-u.
bear-ERG friend-POSS3SG-DAT ear PV-II3.VAL u-put-AOR.I3SG
'The bear applied his ear to his friend.' (LaCroix 2011, 87 cited from Dumézil, 1972)

Table 4.2 [6] - Distribution of case-markers based on semantic roles in Laz
(Öztürk 2008, p. 4)

	PL	AL
Agents/Causers	Ergative	Nominative
Theme	Nominative	Nominative
Experiencers/Benefactives	Dative	Nominative

Table 4.3 - Partial paradigm of Comparative Case Forms
(Common Kartvelian kac 'man') (Harris, 1985, p. 388)

	Standard Georgian[7]	Standard Laz[8]	AL
Nominative	kac-i	koçi[9]	koçi
Narrative/Ergative	kac-ma	koçi-k	koçi
Dative	kac-s	koçi-s	koçi

What we see here is another instance of typological realignment. More specifically, unlike PL, the case-system of AL has changed from an ergative-absolutive system to nominative-accusative system without case-markers while retaining the agreement-marker for the indirect object on the verb. This appears to be due to contact with Turkish, which exhibits the latter system.

---

[6] An anonymous reviewer has pointed out that AL features a bare stem rather than nominative case. Nothing hinges on this distinction for the purposes of the analysis proposed in the present study. Therefore, here I simply adopt and cite the case system proposed in Öztürk (2008) and focus only on the fact that different core arguments are not case-marked overtly and differently in AL.

[7] The Georgian data here are represented in Latin script as cited in the original source.

[8] A reviewer has pointed out that the use of this term is confusing given the absence of a standard variety of Laz. I believe the term in the original source is meant to refer to all varieties of Laz other than AL, which stands as an outlier due to having lost its morphological case system.

[9] Note that Harris (1985) argues that the epenthetic vowel 'i', which comes at the end of words ending with a consonant, used to be the nominative case marker in Old Laz (p. 73).

Interestingly, despite the loss of case-morphology, the verbal complex in the two varieties has remained similar, with all inflectional markers in the verbal domain kept intact. Therefore, the loss of inflectional morphology in AL seems to be only restricted to the nominal domain.

In this section, I discuss this morpho-syntactic discrepancy concerning the notion of language-complexity, following Hawkins (2005) and Steels & Beuls (2017). For this purpose, I first identify the morpho-syntactic differences between AL and PL that have come about due to the loss of the case-system in AL.

4.1. Morpho-syntactic variation

The first piece of evidence for the fact that the syntax of AL is more configurational comes from the data in (6), where scrambling of main constituents in a ditransitive clause is not possible in AL as opposed to PL, where we can switch the position of the subject and indirect object. This is also consistent with a nominative-accusative system without case-marking. Additionally, the data in (7) show us that while AL exhibits superiority-effects, PL does not. While the position of the wh-question words relative to one another is fixed in AL (viz., *mi* 'who' has to precede *mu* 'what'), the constraint does not apply in PL.

(6)

a. {Fatma Ayşe /*Ayşe Fatma}   bere   ko-me-ç-u.   (AL)
　 Fatma   Ayşe   child Aff-PV-give-pst.3sg
　 'Fatma gave the child to Ayşe.'

b. {Fatma-k Ayşe-s /Ayşe-s Fatma-k} bere ko-me-ç-u. (PL)
　 Fatma-erg Ayşe-dat   child Aff-PV-give-pst.3sg
　 'Fatma gave the child to Ayşe.'

(7)

a. *Mu mi   şkom-u?   (AL)   b. Muya mi-k   şkom-u?   (PL)
　 what who eat-pst.3sg   what who-erg eat-pst.3sg
　 Intended: 'Who ate what?'   'Who ate what?'

The same kind of syntactic rigidity that we observe in the sentential domain also holds in the nominal domain. (8a) shows that possessors cannot be extracted in AL, whereas extracting possessors in PL is totally fine, as seen in the example (8b).

(8)

a. *Mişi si baba gaziri? (AL)   b. Mişi si baba dziri? (PL)
   whose you father saw   whose you father saw
   'Intended: Whose father did you see?' 'Whose father did you see?'

Likewise, the DP internal constituents in AL also exhibit superiority-effects in that quantifiers cannot precede possessors in AL (9a), whereas there is more flexibility in this respect in PL, as shown in (9b).

(9)

a. {şkimi alai / *alai şk imi} kalemepe (AL)
   my every / every my pencils
   'every pencil of mine'
b. {şk imi iri / iri şk imi} kalemepe (PL)
   my every / every my pencils
   'every pencil of mine'

All these facts show us that the loss of the case-system has given rise to a more configurational syntax in AL as opposed to PL. In the remainder of the present study, I relate all these facts with the notion of language-complexity.

4.2. Pragmatic effects of morpho-syntactic variation

This section aims to show the significance of pragmatic inferences in resolving ambiguities, which adds to the overall complexity of languages. By contrasting AL with PL, it is shown that the loss of the case-morphology has increased the number of ambiguous constructions in AL. As a result, this particular variety has become more context-dependent and costly to process (i.e., requires more cognitive efforts to make sense out of sentences), hence more complex.

In the literature (see Thomason, 2008 and the references therein for an overview), it was argued that the loss of inflectional morphology leads to an overall simplification in the language. For instance, McWhorter (2001) argues that a greater number of inflectional morphemes is correlated with greater complexity based on a quantity-based approach to complexity. This argument was then shown to be problematic (DeGraff, 2001; 2009), and instead, it was argued that there is an inverse correlation between the amount of inflectional morphology and complexity of a language (Hawkins, 2005).

The examination of AL facts contributes to this discussion and lends further support to the latter claim. As shown in Part 3.1, the loss of the case-morphology in AL has given rise to a greater number of syntactic rules regulating the position of constituents. Thus, under McWhorter's quantity-based metric and understanding of quantity-based complexity, referred to as 'bit complexity' by DeGraff (2001, 2009), AL exhibits more syntactic complexity than PL.

What complicates the picture more comes from the data in (10a), where world-knowledge overrides the syntactic ordering rules (i.e., the subject can optionally follow the object because a non-human argument, namely the bee, is the subject of the clause, and this is recoverable from world-knowledge). Note that both orderings are acceptable in PL due to the presence of case markers (10b).

(10)

a. {Bʼtuci Ali / Ali bʼtuci} nomsku. (AL)
   bee Ali stung
   'Ali was stung by bee (lit: A bee stung Ali)'

b. {Bʼtuci-k Ali-s / Ali-s bʼtuci-k} nomtsxu. (PL)
   bee-erg Ali-dat stung
   'Ali was stung by bee (lit: A bee stung Ali)'

Moreover, agreement can also impact on the flexibility of the order of constituents in AL. Example (11a) shows that, when the subject and object bear different person-values, the cross-referencing of these features on the verb allows flexibility in word order in AL. Note that such flexibility is already available in PL with all types of arguments, as one can see in (11b).

(11)

a. {Ma Ayşe / Ayşe ma} bere ko-me-p-ç-i. (AL)
   I Ayşe child Aff-PV-1sg.subj-give-pst.2sg
   'I gave the baby to Ayşe.'

b. {Ma Ayşe-s / Ayşe-s ma} bere ko-me-p-ç-i. (PL)
   I Ayşe-dat child Aff-PV-1sg.subj-give-pst.2sg
   'I gave the baby to Ayşe.'

These facts show us that the loss of case-morphology in AL has given rise to more complexity in its syntax. Thus, this is an instance of what is referred to as equilibrium (Mufwene et al., 2017) (i.e., less complexity in one module is balanced by greater complexity in another).

A significant fact at this point regards ambiguities, which shows us the significance of pragmatics in computing complexity. Note that both AL and PL allow argument-drop to the extent that it is recoverable from the context. This is illustrated in example (12), where dropping the indirect object is licensed in both varieties when this information is recoverable from the context.

Context: *Fatma is Ayşe's daughter. Ayşe takes care of her grandson when Fatma is at work. Every morning, Fatma takes her son to her mother's place.*

(12)

a. Fatma-k   (Ayşe-s)   bere   ko-me-ç-u.   (PL)
   Fatma-erg   (Ayşe-dat)   child   Aff-PV-give-pst.3sg
   'Fatma gave the child to Ayşe.'

b. Fatma   (Ayşe)   bere   ko-me-ç-u.   (AL)
   Fatma   (Ayşe)   child   Aff-PV-give-pst.3sg
   'Fatma gave the child to Ayşe.'

However, the two Laz varieties differ regarding the number of available interpretations associated with such constructions. In (13), a ditransitive verb requires both a theme-object and a locational complement, but one of these arguments is missing. Note that while the AL example in (13a) is ambiguous, it is not the case in PL, as you can see in (13b). This example clearly illustrates that the loss of case-morphology in AL gives rise to a greater number of possible interpretations that can only be resolved by reference to context. This renders AL a more context-dependent language, where pragmatic considerations play a more significant role in processing the meaning of sentences.

(13)

a. Ali telefoni keʒu-d-u. (AL)   b. Ali-k tilifoni-s   ketzo-d-u.   (PL)
   Ali phone   under-put-pst.3sg   Ali-erg phone-loc   under-put.pst.3sg
i. 'Ali put it under the phone'   'Ali put it under the phone.'
ii. Ali put the phone under
    something.

Moreover, this kind of ambiguity is not restricted only to argument-drop cases; it is more prevalent in AL. (14a) shows that *mektebi* 'school' could be interpreted either as a predicate or a locational complement of the copula. This is, however, not the case in PL, as seen in (14b), in which the presence of the locative marker eliminates a potential ambiguity as we see in the case of AL.

Given these, it becomes clear that pragmatic considerations and rules must be considered in any metric aiming to measure the complexity of a language.

(14)

a. Him   mektebi'n.   (AL)   b. Him   mektebi-s   on.   (PL)
   s/he/it   school-is   s/he/it   school-loc   is
   i. S/he/it is at the school. /   'S/he/it is at the school.'
   ii. It is a school.

In both cases in AL, there is a structure that has fewer overt markers. However, the relevant structures are compatible with more than one construction; hence they are open to more than one interpretation. The resolution of this kind of ambiguity relies on a complex background of potential inferences. Bisang (2014) proposes that such cases constitute an instance of hidden complexity as opposed to overt complexity; they contribute to the overall complexity of a language. In the case of AL, then, we see that the apparent overt simplicity is counterbalanced by hidden complexity (viz., less is said, but consequently, it takes longer to process the utterance, factoring the non-linguistic context, including knowledge of the world).

We can conclude that poorer inflectional morphology increases the complexity of languages, as suggested by Hawkins (2005). This shows that complexity cannot be reduced to how crowded a system's space is with morphemes and rules. Instead, complexity should have more to do with how different units, rules, and *all* the modules in a system involving pragmatics interact with one another. Additionally, the role of interpretative and computational efforts and mechanisms should also be considered in measuring complexity.

4.3. An interplay between different types of complexity

In this section, I turn to a specific interpretation of complexity in the literature, where complexity is understood as the interplay between different types of complexity. Building on Hawkin's analysis (2005), Steels and Beuls (2017) first identify different types of complexity and then argue that human languages ideally evolve in a way to minimize complexity at all of these levels, but often what happens is a complex interplay between them. Before seeing an example of such an interplay, let us take a quick look at the different types of complexity they propose.

The first kind of complexity is called inventory-complexity. It is about the number of units and rules in a language; that is, inventory-complexity is the same as McWhorter's understanding of complexity (2001). On the other hand, form-complexity is about the length of utterances, where the idea is that the longer an utterance (word or phrase) is, the more complex it is. Processing complexity is about the cognitive effort that is needed to interpret an utterance. Lastly, population-level complexity is mainly concerned with idiolectal variation and how this is resolved. Based on these assumptions, Steels and Beuls (2017) show that losing agreement-markers might reduce the inventory-complexity, but this results in an increase in processing-complexity.

Adopting the ecological approach, I argue that different word-orders are variants in the feature-pool of AL as in (15).

(15)

F1: S-IO-DO, **F2:** IO-DO-S, **F3:** S-DO-IO
F4: IO-S-DO, **F5:** DO-IO-S, **F6:** DO-S-IO
(where S=subject, IO=indirect object, DO=direct object)

We see when there is more than one possible word-order, as in (16), that inventory-complexity reduces processing-complexity, as also suggested by Steels and Beuls (2017), and the competition between different variants is not resolved because agreement-markers readily resolve a potential ambiguity.

(16)

| {Ma | Ayşe / | Ayşe | ma} | bere | ko-me-p-ç-i. | (AL) |
| I | Ayşe | | | child | Aff-PV-1sg.subj-give-pst.2sg | |

'I gave the baby to Ayşe.'

However, when there are no agreement-markers, as in (17), where all arguments are 3rd person, competition arises, and only one of the variants ends up being the winner. What we see here is that the reduction of inventory- and form-complexity increases processing-complexity.

(17)

| {Fatma | Ayşe / | *Ayşe | Fatma} | bere | ko-me-ç-u. | (AL) |
| Fatma | Ayşe | | | child | Aff-PV-give-pst.3sg | |

'Fatma gave the child to Ayşe.'

There is another way in which this kind of ambiguity and processing-complexity is resolved. This is shown in (19), where different personal pronouns, or more specifically suffixes, are used to resolve the ambiguity in (18).

(18)

a. Him   mektebi'n.   (AL)
   s/he/it school-is
   i. S/he/it is at the school.
   ii. It is a school.

b. Him   mektebi-s   on.   (PL)
   s/he/it school-loc is
   'S/he/it is at the school.'

(19)

a. Him   mektebi'n.
   3ps-animate school-is
   'S/he/it is at the school'

b. Him-**u**   mektebi'n.
   3ps-inanimate   school-is
   'It is a school.'

However, this is only at an idiolectal level because only one of my informants reported this sentence to me and added that this strategy exists only in their village, which indicates a lot more dialectal variation than has been assumed in the literature so far. This variation could generate complexity if anybody proceeds to model Laz in a computer to understand how norms arise because these different idiolects would interact with one another in specific and complicated ways (Steels & Beuls, 2017).

5. Conclusion

In this study, I have closely examined the endangerment of Laz under the ecological approach (Mufwene, 2001) and discussed the implications of the changes in its ecology for its linguistic complexity. Firstly, I have also shown that Laz is undergoing a change towards more analyticity and less linguistic complexity in terms of how reflexive constructions are formed. Given the under-described nature of the Laz language, it becomes hard to indicate the full scope of the aspects of Laz grammar that tend to become more analytical, as observed in the case of reflexive constructions. Yet, one possible candidate could be affixal constructions with no external argument (see (4a) above). Recall that these constructions are established with the same verbal prefix, namely {-i}, which is also used in reflexive constructions (see Eren 2021 for an analysis of this syncretism). More specifically, it is likely that the same speakers who prefer analytical reflexive constructions over affixal ones might produce active constructions with impersonal subject pronouns like *mitxa* 'somebody' or *null* third person pronoun, rather than dropping the subject of the clauses and marking the verb with the verbal affix to convey a passive or middle reading. I have left this issue to further studies.

Secondly, I have argued that the examination of AL with respect to the notion of complexity clearly shows that the loss of inflectional morphology does not necessarily correlate with less overall complexity because lesser (overt) morphological complexity is counterbalanced by i) greater syntactic complexity and ii) hidden complexity (Bisang, 2014).

References

Adamou, E. (2010). Bilingual speech and language ecology in Greek Thrace: Romani and Pomak in contact with Turkish. *Language in Society, 39*(2), 147-171. http://www.jstor.org/stable/40606075

Akyol, M. (2006). *Kürt sorununu yeniden düşünmek*. İstanbul: Doğan.

Asiliskender, B. (2009). Cumhuriyet sonrası kalkınma hareketi olarak sanayileşme ve mekansal değişim. *Türkiye Araştırmaları Literatür Dergisi*, (13), 153-170

Baechler, R. & Seiler G. (Eds). (2016). *Complexity, isolation, and variation*. De Gruyter, 139-157.

Bisang, W. (2014). Overt and hidden complexity–two types of complexity and their implications. *Poznan Studies in Contemporary Linguistics, 50*(2), 127-143.

Boeder, W. (1968). Über die Versionen des georgischen Verbs. *Folia Linguistica, 2*, 82–252.

Boeder, W. (2005). The South Caucasian Languages. *Lingua*, 115, 5–89.

Boumans, L. (2006). The attributive possessive in Morccan Arabic spoken by young bilinguals in the Netherlands and their peers in Morocco. *Bilingualism: Language and Cognition, 9*(3), 213-231.

Brehmer, B., & Czachór, A. (2012). Formation and distribution of the analytic future tense in Polish-German bilinguals. *Multilingual individuals and multilingual societies, 13*, 297-314.

Ceylan, E. (2002). The millet system in the Ottoman Empire. In J.M. Upton-Ward (Ed.), *New Millennium Perspectives in the Humanities* (pp. 245-266). Global Humanities Press.

Dahl, Ö. (2004). *The growth and maintenance of linguistic complexity* (Vol. 71). John Benjamins Publishing.

Dahl, Ö. (2009). Increases in complexity as a result of language contact. In K. Braunmüller & J. House (Eds), *Convergence and divergence in language contact situations 8* (pp. 41-52), John Benjamins Publishing.

DeGraff, M. (2001). On the origin of creoles: A Cartesian critique of neo-Darwinian linguistics, *Linguistic Typology*, (5), 213-310.

DeGraff, M. (2009). Language acquisition in creolization and, thus, language-change: Some Cartesian: Uniformitarian boundary conditions. *Language and Linguistics Compass, 3*(4), 888-971.

Demirtaş, S., Diken, B., & Gözüaydın, İ. (1996). Mekan ve Ötekiler, *Defter, 28*, İstanbul: Metis Yayıncılık.

Dumézil, G. (1972). Textes en laze d'Ardeşen. *Bedi Kartlisa, vol. XXIX-XXX*.

Eren, Ö. (2021). Fake arguments as apparent valency-changers: Evidence from Laz. *Proceedings of WCCFL 38*
Fishman, J. A. (1966). *Language loyalty in the United States*. Mouton
Fishman, J. A. (1991). *Reversing language shift*. Multilingual Matters.
Güler, H. (2011). Türkiye'nin erken dönem sanayileşme serüveni. *Hitit Üniversitesi Sosyal Bilimler Enstitüsü Dergisi*, 4(1), 63-87.
Haznedar, B. (2018). Türkiye'de Lazca'nın mevcut durumu (Report). Laz Enstitüsü. Retrieved from: http://www.lazenstitu.com/rapor.pdf.
Habib, H. (1951). Industrialization in Turkey. *Pakistan Horizon*, 4(1), 40-51.
Harris, A. C. (1985). *Diachronic syntax: the Kartvelian case*. (Syntax and Semantics. Vol. 18). Orlando, FL: Academic Press Inc.
Hawkins, J. A. (2005). *Efficiency and complexity in grammars*. Oxford University Press.
Hewitt, G. (1987). Georgian: Ergative or Active? *Lingua*, 71, 319-340.
Hewitt, G. (2004). *Introduction to the Study of the Languages of the Caucasus*. München: Lincom Europa.
Hidayat, S. (2014). Minority groups in Ottoman Turkey before 1856: different arrangements of the Jews and the Christians under Millet system. *Indonesian Journal of Islam and Muslim Societies*, 4(1), 25-30.
Holisky, D. A. (1991). Laz. In A. Harris (Ed.), *The Indigenous Languages of the Caucasus. Vol. 1. The Kartvelian Languages* (pp. 396-472). Delmar/New York: Caravan Books.
Keles, R. (1980). Urbanization and environment: Turkey. *Ekistics*, 47 (284), 349-352.
Kiria, Č., Ezugbaia, L., Memišiši, O., & Čuxua, M. (2015). *Lazur-megruli gramat'ik'a. I. Morpologia* [A Laz-Megrelian Grammar. I. Morphology]. Tbilisi: Meridiani.
Kortmann, B., & Szmrecsanyi, B. (Eds.). (2012). *Linguistic complexity: Second language acquisition, indigenization, contact* (Vol. 13). Walter de Gruyter.
Kutscher, S. (2008). The Language of the Laz in Turkey: Contact-induced change or gradual language loss? *Turkic Languages*, 12(1), 82-102.
Lacroix, R. (2009). Description du dialecte Laze d'Arhavi (Caucasique du sud, Turquie): Grammaire et texte. [Unpublished doctoral dissertation, Université Lumière de Lyon 2].
Lacroix, R. (2011). Ditransitive Constructions in Laz. *Linguistic Discovery*, 9 (2), 78-103.
McWhorter, J. (2001). The world's simplest grammars are creole grammars. *Linguistic Typology*, 5(2), 125-66.
Miestamo, M. (2008). Grammatical complexity in a cross-linguistic perspective. In M. Miestamo, K. Sinnemaki & F. Karlsson (Eds.), *Language complexity: Typology, contact, change* pp (23-41). John Benjamins Publishing.
Mufwene, S. S. (1996). The founder principle in creole genesis. *Diachronica*, 13(1), 83-134.
Mufwene, S. S. (2001). *The ecology of language evolution*. Cambridge University Press.

Mufwene, S. S. (2020a). Language shift. *The International Encyclopedia of Linguistic Anthropology.* https://doi.org/10.1002/9781118786093.iela0357

Mufwene, S. S. (2020b). Population structure and the emergence of world Englishes. In E. Schneider, D. Schreier, & M. Hundt (Eds.), *The Cambridge handbook of world Englishes*, (pp. 99-119). Cambridge University Press.

Mufwene, S. S., Coupé, C., & Pellegrino, F. (eds.). (2017). *Complexity in language: Developmental and evolutionary perspectives.* Cambridge University Press.

Nash, L. (2021). Nonunitary structure of unergative verbs in Georgian. *Natural Language & Linguistic Theory*, 1-67.

Özfidan, B., Burlbaw, L. M., & Aydın, H. (2018). The minority languages dilemmas in Turkey: A critical approach to an emerging literature. *Journal of Educational Issues*, 4(1), 1-19.

Öztürk, B. (2008). *The loss of case system in Ardesheni Laz and its morpho-syntactic consequences.* [Conference session: Morphological Variation and Change in the Languages of the Caucasus]. 13th International Morphology Meeting. *University of Vienna, Austria.*

Öztürk, B. & E. Taylan, E. (2017). Omnipresent little vP in Pazar Laz. In R. D'Alessandro, I. Franco & A. Gallego (Eds.), *The verbal domain* (pp. 207-232), Oxford: Oxford University Press.

Pauwels, A. (2016). *Language maintenance and shift.* Cambridge University Press.

Polinsky, M. (2018). *Heritage languages and their speakers* (Vol. 159). Cambridge University Press.

Steels, L., & Beuls, K. (2017). How to explain the origins of complexity in language: A case study for agreement systems. In Salikoko S. Mufwene, Christophe Coupé, and François Pellegrino (Eds.), *Complexity in language: Developmental and evolutionary perspectives,* (pp. 30-47). DOI: 10.1017/9781107294264

Taşkın, N. (2011). *Representing and performing Laz identity: This is not a rebel song.* [Unpublished master's thesis]. Boğaziçi University.

Thomason, S. (2008). *Does language contact simplify grammars.* Paper presented at Deutsche Gesellschaft für Sprachwissenschaft.

Trudgill, P. (2011). *Sociolinguistic typology: Social determinants of linguistic complexity.* Oxford University Press.

Tuite, K. (1998). *Kartvelian Morphosyntax. Number Agreement and Morphosyntactic Orientation in the South Caucasian Languages.* München: Lincom Europe.

Özfidan, B., Burlbaw, L. M., & Aydın, H. (2018). The Minority Languages Dilemmas in Turkey: A Critical Approach to an Emerging Literature. *Journal of Educational Issues*, 4(1), 1-19.

Chapter 5

Stories of Perseverance: Using the Lazuri Alboni for the Emergence of Literary Genres in a South Caucasian Endangered Language

Peri Yuksel
New Jersey City University, New Jersey, USA

Irfan Cağatay Aleksiva
Laz Cultural Association, Istanbul, Turkey

Abstract

The severely endangered South-west Caucasian language Lazuri (a.k.a. Laz) has survived various historical conflict-driven forces (e.g., Iberian, Persian, Russian, Ottoman) as an indigenous oral language in today's concentrated Laz settlements along the North-eastern Black Sea region in Turkey and adjacent parts of Georgia. With the emergence of mass-communication and innovative technologies of the 20th century, it is a question of time, dedication, and ingenuity as to how the Laz community will take advantage of innovative digital tools to document their lore and legends before it is destined to vanish. In the current chapter, the authors discuss controversies in the development of a romanized Lazuri alphabet (i.e., the Lazuri Alboni) and report a content-analysis of fifty-eight literary books published from 1997-2021 in Turkey. Results highlight the emergence of a Lazuri literature encompassing a broad range of written genres (e.g., poetry, fairy-tales, essays, short stories, autobiographies, wisdom-books, translations of classics) of a rich dialectical representation, language-fluency, and stylistic expression (i.e., traditional vs. modern). The presented emerging Lazuri literature contributes to the world's diverse intellectual knowledge and provides a window into a community's sense of cultural identity and consciousness.

Keywords: *Lazuri Alboni, Laz alphabet, Laz authors, Laz literature, endangered language literature*

* * *

1. Introduction

About 97% of the world's people speak 4% of the world's languages, underscoring complex power relationships and privileges (Turin, 2012). Less than 10% of today's human languages are genuinely safe to survive into the next century (Krauss, 1992). Many of these endangered languages are entirely oral with little or no written literature, and thus at high risk of vanishing without a trace because they are no longer taught by new generations of speakers (Moseley, 2012). Although language-extinction (or linguicide) has been a natural phenomenon throughout history, modern linguistic diversity is disappearing at an unprecedented rate, causing tremendous loss to the world's biodiversity and traditional ecological knowledge. Every fortnight, one elder of an endangered language dies and carries into the grave their ancient tongue, leaving no descendants (Davis, 2009). At a loss is the rich cultural heritage, an 'old-growth forest of the mind, a watershed of thought, and ecosystem of spiritual possibilities'– humanity's intellectual legacy since the dawn of consciousness (Davis, 2009, p. 3).

A myriad of reasons contributes to language-loss, such as macro sociopolitical events, like the rise of nationalism in Western Europe at the beginning of the industrial revolution (Grenoble & Whaley, 2006). The group that has military and political power establishes the *lingua franca* of rule and shows less support towards indigenous (or local) languages for language-maintenance and development, such as an alphabet. Once members of the subordinate population gain access to the language of prestige, power, and privilege, they are likely to give up or abandon their ancestral language in the process unless the indigenous or local language has a positive reputation to preserve their intellectual wealth (Bernard et al, 2008).

The current chapter overviews early and contemporary attempts to craft a written script for the UNESCO-rated endangered South-west Caucasian language, Lazuri (Ch'an), which is facing severe language-extinction within the next generation if nothing is done to resist its alarming decline (Kutscher, 2008; Yuksel & Brooks, 2017). It takes a whole village to keep alive the communal practices of local languages while also requiring transliteracy to compete with the digital age of mass-communication. Promoting an *endographia* or indigenous literacy is an important development for language-maintenance and is essential to the language-documentation process of endangered languages and their vitality (Fishman, 1991).

1.2. Current Chapter

The existence of a writing system is a vital tool for an endangered speech-community to engage in important activities for language-maintenance and revitalization. Such supportive activities may include dictionary-writing, curriculum-development for language-literacy, documentation of intimate knowledge of local lore, legends, and biotic communities to understand how to interact and survive within the immediate environment. Any change from an oral language to a written language affects the society, while the dominant language-group's attitudes towards multilingualism and multiliteracy are crucial for language-survival of indigenous languages (Grenoble & Whaley, 2006). The efforts to formally represent Lazuri in Turkey trace back to the Lazuri Alboni in roman characters by Lazoğlu and Feurstein (1984). Most recent efforts focus on spreading awareness of a distinct Laz ethnic identity and heritage by creating foreign language-learning courses for adults at the Boğaziçi University in Istanbul. Voluntarily-run after-school language-learning programmes in Laz regions of Rize and Artvin (Lazona) were established in 2013 to teach Lazuri to children in a formal setting. Unfortunately, these formal language-learning services stopped in 2018 due to low student-enrolment, lack of language-teaching resources, and unsupported national education-systems for training teachers and staff.

The current chapter catalogues Lazuri literary books published in Turkey to highlight a collective effort across borders. This collective effort aligns with the 8-stage Graded Intergenerational Disruption Scale (GIDS) proposed by Fishman (1991), where the endangered language is further developed to be effectively used in written form. The following sections will briefly introduce the context of Lazuri in Turkey, the orthography of Caucasian languages with a focus on the development of the Lazuri Alboni (i.e., alphabet)– an effortful and vigorous response spearheaded by Laz activists and community-speakers to transform a traditionally oral language into a written language to preserve the local intellectual wealth.

2. The Case of Lazuri

Indigenous to the Lesser Caucasus region of the north-eastern Black Sea part of Turkey is Lazuri (also known as Ch'an), lacking a written script. Despite its tumultuous past, Lazuri has remained resilient to historically-rooted ethnic conflicts among the Caucasian tribes and attacks by Iberian, Pontic, Persian,

Ottoman, and Russian powers (but also outside-powers, such as the British) throughout antiquity and medieval times (Braund, 2003). Natural barriers separated for centuries the Laz people living in the Caucasian Mountains from other speakers from mainland Turkey (Hann, 1997). With the emergence of modern infrastructure in the 1950s that revolutionized transportation and communication and facilitated migration from rural areas to urban settings, the inter-generational transmission of Lazuri experienced disruptions (Ascherson, 1996; Hann, 1997; Karpat & Karpat, 1976). To date, it is difficult to estimate the true number of native Lazuri speakers. The most recent and last official Turkish census of 1965 showed that 26,007 people spoke Lazuri as their mother-tongue at home (Devlet İstatistik Enstitüsü, 1968). Other sources state that ethnic Laz people are estimated to be about 45,000 to 500,000: Feurstein (1983) suggests that 250,000 ethnic Laz live in the European Union and Turkey, Andrews and Benninghaus (1989) estimate that 45,000 of Turkish ethnic minorities are Laz, and Holisky (1991) offers quotes the figure of 5,000 ethnic Laz living in the village of Sarpi (Georgia). Along the eastern Black Sea towns of Rize and Artvin, concentrated Lazuri-speaking communities can be found in Pazar (Atina), Ardeşen, Fındıklı (Viçe), Arhavi (Arkabi), Borçka (Çxala), and Hopa (Xopa) (e.g., Bellér-Hann,1995; Kutscher, 2008).

Currently, Turkey does not officially recognize Lazuri as an ethnic language. When ethnic minorities, such as the Laz, lack prestige and power, they are motivated to quickly assimilate to the majority culture. Moreover, families might stop transmitting their home-language without being aware of the impact of their language behaviours on children's linguistic, social, and psychological patterns (Fillmore, 1991). The lack of language-recognition, combined with compulsory primary education, and increased access to modern technology, such as Turkish TV, or economically-driven emigration are contributing to the rapid assimilation into the mainstream-culture, thus severely altering ancestral language-practices among the Laz community living in Turkey (Kutscher, 2008; Yuksel & Brooks, 2017). Although older adult speakers restrict the usage of Lazuri to private communication amongst family-members or friends, recent field-studies show that more than 90% of parents or grandparents have stopped teaching Lazuri to their children to prepare them for school and higher status livelihoods, seeing no value in the teaching of a local ethnic language (Yuksel, Lowry, & Brooks, 2020). Consequently, Lazuri is rated as definitively endangered and is predicted to become extinct within the next generation (Kutscher, 2008; Moseley, 2012).

Children become competent members of their community through language-socialization (Schieffelin & Ochs, 1996). Lazuri children today are growing up in the context of language-loss, influenced by communal language-practices and the perceived low status of the Lazuri language in mainstream Turkish society. Fishman (1991) stressed the importance of children's early learning environments and applied the family-context to endangered languages through a scale used to measure the vitality of a language. He proposed the 8-stage Graded Intergenerational Disruption Scale (GIDS hereafter) in which inter-generational transmission in the home-language is key. Stage 8 and Stage 1 of Fishman's GIDS represent the ends of the scale: endangered language near-total extinction versus dominant language least disrupted. Stage 8 is associated with language-loss and requires a collaboration of experts and community-members for language-revitalization. Stage 1 is associated with a language that is widely used in various institutional domains. While Stages 1 to 5 refer to languages used in more formal institutions, Stage 6 highlights language use in communities and families with young children and, where possible, the language in written and oral forms. According to the GIDS, Lazuri is situated in Stage 7, where the child-bearing generation knows the language well enough to use it with elders but is not transmitting it to the next generation (i.e., children). Fishman's scale may be used to focus attention on critically important behaviours that occur at Stage 6, such as encouraging caregivers to use the home-language when interacting with their children. Parent-child interactions in Laz are vital to preserve the language and move up the scale toward a literacy-education in Lazuri. The written word in the Laz language or any other endangered language is vital for language pedagogy. Even if the Laz language is used among elders and traditionally transmitted orally to the childbearing generation whereas literacy skills are not being valued or taught, teachers and aspiring Laz language learners, for instance, depend on a writing system to design lesson plans and to learn the various rules and forms of the language, including orthography. Thematic teaching of an endangered language with the help of a writing system may contribute to language maintenance. Therefore, the contribution of Laz authors is fundamental to the development of a Laz corpus for further socio-linguistic study and dissemination of unique and valuable information. Such a corpus will provide a rich resource for psycholinguists, anthropologists, musicologists, folklorists, ethnologists, and anyone interested in learning about cultural heritage and memory. Language pedagogy and education are fundamental in sustaining endangered languages against the pressure of mainstream languages (Benzinger et al., 2003).

2.1. To Write or Not to Write in Laz?

As will be further discussed below, developing an orthography for previously undocumented languages, such as Laz, is burdensome, and poses pros and cons to the language community (Hinton & Hale, 2001; Guérin, 2008). Once an endangered language is written down, the misconception might be that the language is safe now. This misconstruction may alter the language transmission process. Writing the vernacular might even divide the language community among the ones who are literate and can use technological means to spread their words in the written text with other ones who believe that the best literature in the Laz language is the spoken version, taking its traditional oral language transmission for granted. Laz speakers who do not acquire skills in writing their mother tongue may feel a loss of agency over their spoken words because once spoken words are written down, they become fixed in time in the way an oral language is not. Needless to say, on the other hand, handwritten language pedagogy may help to widen the usage of the language for informal (wedding vows, love poems, children's rimes, family recipes, etc.) and formal purposes (dictionary, grammar books, orthography rules, etc.). Efforts and painstaking activities in the creation of orthographic conventions or standardized scripts in Laz are crucial for language revitalization. Once a language shift is near its completion, language revitalization can be facilitated if the language community or its heritage speakers have access to a corpus of Laz work. We hope that the results of the current study will contribute to the building of such.

3. Languages and Orthography in the Caucasus

At the intersection of Asia and Europe, a *mountain of tongues* stretches from the Caspian Sea to the Black Sea, viz. the Caucasian Mountains, where about 8 million people form a mosaic of languages and ethnic identities. The term *mountain of tongues* was first used by the 10th-century Arab geographer and historian, Abu al-Hasan Ali ibn al-Hussain al-Mas'udi, to express the multilingual embodiment of human wealth distributed over 7,000 named mountains (Catford, 1977). Close to 50 languages belong to five distinct language-families: Indo-European, Turkic, North-east Caucasian, North-west Caucasian, and South Caucasian. Lazuri is among the 37 indigenous South-west Caucasian languages that are believed to have been spoken for more than 4000 years at the foothills and plateaus of the Caucasian Mountains at the north-eastern part of the Black Sea of Turkey and adjacent areas of Georgia. There are two geographically and typologically independent groups of Caucasian languages: North Caucasian and South Caucasian (Tuite, 2008).

The North Caucasian languages are further divided into three indigenous groups: North-west Caucasian (Abkhazo-Adyghean), North Central Caucasian (Nakh), and North-east Caucasian (Daghestanian). The South Caucasian languages form a separate major group, which are also known in western publications by their Georgian-derived name Kartvelian and comprise Lazuri, Megrelian, Svan, and Georgian, of which only the last is an official and vital language spoken by about 4 million speakers in Georgia. Among the South Caucasian language-family, Georgian has been the only language with an official script for more than fifteen centuries (Hewitt, 1990). Svan (*lušnu nin*; 30,000) is spoken in the north-west of Georgia and the Upper K'odor valley in Abkhazia, Megrelian (Mingrelian; *margaluri nina*; 300,000) speakers live in the lowlands of western Georgia and south-eastern Abkhazia, and speakers of Lazuri (Ch'an; *lazuri nena*; 22,000) are concentrated in north-eastern Turkey in the provinces of Rize and Artvin, and in one part of the village of Sarpi in Georgia with approximately 2,000 speakers. The Georgian language is also the only one with its own standardized writing system (with an extensively documented literature reaching back to the fifth century) that is conventionally believed to have been invented around 400 A.D. by Mesrop Mashtots, an Armenian monk who is also credited with developing the Armenian and Caucasian Albanian alphabets (Catford, 1977).

Lazuri, Megrelian and Svan speakers alike lack official scripts and are not recognized as distinct ethnic groups, their languages being thus mistakenly regarded as dialects of Georgian by many in Georgia. Megrelian and Svan speakers in Georgia use Georgian as their written language. However, in Abkhazia the occasional newspaper *Gal* often publishes material in Megrelian using a slightly adapted form of the Georgian script. Modern Georgian uses the Mkhedruli orthography, whereas Old Georgian mainly ecclesiastical works were written in two varieties of the Georgian script called Asomtavruli (which is rounded in appearance) and the angular Nuskhuri (Dobrushina, Daniel, & Koryakov, 2020). Lazuri is written in the roman alphabet, as will be further discussed below.

4. Brief History of Laz Language-studies

4.1. Early Lazological Work by International Linguists

The oldest written record of the Laz language is attributed to the philologist Lorenzo Hervás whose work was (1787) entitled *Lingua Lesga, Detta Ancora Laza e Lassa* [Lesga Language, also Called Lazca, and Lassa]. In this work, he briefly describes the Laz language and lists eight Laz words, using the Spanish orthography (p. 65-66). Later, Georg Rosen's book, *Über die Sprache der Lazen* [On the Language of the Laz], was published in 1844 and used Arabic letters for the Laz orthography with German translation. The work comprises a broader list of Laz words by lexical category (e.g., verb, particle, adjective, noun) and a more detailed grammar-guide than the compilation by Hervás. Commissioned by the Russian Imperial Academy, Klaproth (1827), Peacock (1887), and Erckert (1895) each published short grammatical notes along with a complementary list of Laz vocabulary. Notably, Adjarian's long article, *Étude Sur La Langue Laze* [Studies of the Laz Language] (1899), surveryed previous publications and presented a richer dictionary, including extended grammatical descriptions. In all these seminal works of language-documentation, Laz words were not written in a canonical alphabet; more so, Laz words were distorted and often written with almost unrecognizable spellings.

However, Nikolay Marr's *Грамматика чанского (лазского) языка с хрестоматиуelo и словарем* [Ch'an (Laz) Grammar with Reader and Dictionary] (1910) was the first publication of Lazology in Russian with about 2,500 Laz words, using modern scholarly standards. In Marr's work, Laz is written in Georgian script and includes sections on grammar, a dictionary, as well as texts and constitutes one of the primary sources used in Laz studies. Through his travels and lexicographical work in the Transcaucasian district of the Ottoman Empire (formerly known as 'Lazistan'), Marr rejected his previous hypothesis that Lazuri is a dialect of Georgian. Instead, he stated that Lazuri is a part of the Kartvelian language-family with a distinct grammar and morphology, closely related to Mingrelian. Most notably, the Laz linguist Iskender Chitasi developed in 1928 the first Laz alphabet in Latin letters. Chitasi is famously known for having published the first newspaper completely in Lazuri in 1929, called "Mç'ita Murutsxi" [Red Star] in Abkhazia (then part of the Georgian SSR). Unfortunately, Chitasi could not further develop his grassroot-activities because he was killed soon afterwards.[1]

The work by Nikolay Marr increased interest in Laz studies in the Russian Empire, with comparative linguistic work by Chikobava (1929 = Ch'anuri T'ekst'ebi. Nak'veti P'irveli. Xopuri K'ilok'avi [Ch'an (= Laz) Texts. First Part. Khopa Dialect], 1936; 1938), laying the groundwork for the fundamental

---

[1] The Azeri alphabet in Transcaucasia has been modified four times through conquests and language-reforms from Arabic to Latin (1928-1938), to Cyrillic (1993-1991), and again to Latin (1991- present), which means that three generations spoke the same language but may have not been able to read each other's writings (Slavs and Tatars, 2009).

arguments about the linguistic kinship of Lazuri and Migrelian. Chikobava published the Laz texts compiled by Georgian linguist Ioseb Qipshidze (1915) and trained students, including Sergi Jghent'i and Irine Asatiani. Marr's work also attracted the interest of the French linguist and mythologist Georges Dumézil, who in 1930/31 recorded Laz folktales and stories of a 20-year-old Laz, Niazi Ban, living in Constantinople, and published *Contes Lazes* [Laz Tales] in 1937. Dumézil's work was used in the compilation of the Arkabi dialect of Lazuri by a Mingrelian/Georgian linguist, Guram Kartozia (1967), who has done valuable work on Laz language-preservation. Guram Kartozia collected texts from Soviet Laz speakers (1972), and his work was also published in Turkey after the opening of the Turkish-Soviet border (1993). His precious work *Lazuri Ena Da Misi Adgili Kartvelur Enata Sist'emashi, Nek'eri* [Lazuri and Its Place in the System of the Kartvelian Languages] was published in Turkey in 2005.

4.2. Contemporary Lazuri Alphabet: Lazoğlu Alboni

The Lazuri Alboni was developed in the 1980s by a German scholar named Wolfgang Feurstein and co-authored with Fahri Kahraman during a time when Turkey's laws prohibited the usage of any non-Turkish languages throughout the 1990s tracing back to the radical language-reforms under Atatürk when Turkish was declared the official language of the new republic in 1932. To form a homogenous national identity with one common language, the Turkish citizens had to adapt to the "*umumi hayat*" (public life) and exclusively speak Turkish to avoid being excluded from public life (Çolak, 2004, p. 81). To protect Fahri's identity, the new writing system became known as the Lazoğlu Alboni, and with the help of the Laz-German activists, such as Selma Koçiva, Feurstein further developed the newly established Lazuri alphabet and gradually delivered little Lazuri textbooks through clandestine channels to primary schools in Laz regions (Lazoğlu & Feurstein, 1984). For secretly infiltrating the Lazuri Alboni into Turkey, Feurstein was framed by the security-police for "illegally entering a frontier district" and imprisoned (Ascherson, 2007, p. 203). When holding the Lazuri alphabet while visiting Feurstein in Schopfloch, Ascherson felt as if he was holding "something like a seed but also like a bomb" (2007, p. 204) and described the witnessing of an emerging alphabet as follows (2007, p. 204-205):

> With an alphabet, a people – even a tiny one – sets out upon a journey. Ahead lie printed novels and poems, newspapers and concert programmes, handwritten family letters and love letters, angry polemics and posters, the proceedings of assemblies, the script of

Shakespeare translations for a theatre and of soap-operas for television, the timetables of ferries, the announcements of births and deaths. Perhaps, one day, laws. But perhaps, too, leaflets with a last speech from the condemned cell. This is a long journey, and it may be a dangerous one.

Ascherson's moment of awe captured above is now manifested in the work of contemporary bilingual Laz authors around the world who are awakening to a newly found self-awareness and appreciation of their Laz identity (Ascherson, 1996): the possibility to explore ancestral wisdom and knowledge through self-authorship by telling stories and writing them down. The following section portrays the rich literary work of Lazuri authors who are using the roman alphabet to creatively express their ideas, memories, and imagination in Lazuri in order to document the existence of a Laz identity.

5. Method

5.1. Design and Literary Book-selection

The current study used the inquiry-tradition of content-analysis, which provides an objective, systematic, and quantitative method of making valid inferences with text (Berelson, 1952; Weber, 1990). To provide a snapshot of the emergence of Lazuri literacy in Turkey, representativeness is an important criterion to generate valid evaluations in content-analysis. Therefore, we have only included literary books that have been published in Turkey and written in Lazuri. To the best of our knowledge, fifty-eight literary books were published in Turkey between 1997 through 2021 and written by Laz authors (see Tables 5 through 9). The Lazuri literary books were published by fourteen different publishers, with *Lazika Yayin Kolektifi* being the largest publisher (41.1%) and *Lazi Kültür Yayinlari* being the second-largest publisher (20.7%). A total of fifty-six books were re-read by the second author and were included in the content-analysis since they were also in his possession. We created a database and categorized each eligible book by year of publication, publisher name, title, author characteristics (i.e., name, gender, age, place of living, geographical location of Laz affiliation), authors' language-use (i.e., alphabet type, type of Lazuri dialect, Lazuri language-proficiency), type of genre, and style of expression (i.e., traditional vs modern).

5.2. Criteria for Distinguishing Lazuri Dialects

Based on early linguistic fieldwork (Marr, 1910), it is accepted that Lazuri has at least three distinct dialectical variations spoken between Batumi (Georgia) and Pazar (Rize, Turkey), namely Xopa-Çxala, Arkabi-Viçe, and Atina-Ardeşen. Although there is generally no consensus among the linguistic community as to the differentiation of dialects from languages, for the purpose of the current work, we used the Laz author's biographical sketches as a criterion to categorize their geographical homeland-affiliation, known in Lazuri as follows: Atina (Pazar), Ardeşen, Viçe (Fındıklı), Arkabi (Arhavi), Çxala (Borçka), and Xopa (Hopa). We retrieved the author's biographical information either from the published books or from websites launching book-publications or containing interviews.

The excerpts below (1-4) are taken from an illustrated Lazuri children's book for pre-schoolers (Yuksel-Sokmen & Wei, 2014). They exemplify distinct morphological and lexical differences that are likely to be found in Lazuri dialects spoken in Fındıklı (see excerpts 1, 3) and their corresponding translation into the Ardeşen dialect (see excerpts 2, 4), with English translation in italics.

Table 5.1 - Different Laz Alphabets with Equivalent IPA

Alphabets				Transcriptions	
Chitaşi (1928)	Chitaşi (1930)	Feurstein (1984)	Georgian	Transcript	IPA
a	a	a	ა	a	[ɑ]
b	b	b	ბ	b	[b]
c	j	c	ჯ	ǯ	[dʒ]
ç	ç	ç	ჭ	č	[tʃʰ]
ɾ	çh	č̣	ჯ̣	č̣	[tʃʼ]
d	d	d	დ	d	[d]
e	e	e	ე	e	[ɛ]
f	f	f	ჶ	f	[f]
g	g	g	გ	g	[g]
ğ	ɑı	ğ	ღ	ɣ	[ɣ]
ħ	x	x	ხ	x	[x]
h	h	h	ჰ	h	[h]

i	i	i	ი	i	[i]
j	ẓ	j	ჟ	ž	[ʒ]
q	q	k	ჲ	k	[kʰ]
k	k	k̆	კ	ḳ	[k']
-	-	q	ყ	q̇	[q']
l	l	l	ლ	l	[l]
m	m	m	მ	m	[m]
n	n	n̠	ნ	n	[n]
o	o	o	ო	o	[ɔ]
ṗ	p	p	პ	p	[pʰ]
p	ph	p̆	ჭ	ṗ	[p']
r	r	r	რ	r	[r]
s	s	s	ს	s	[s]
ş	ş	ş	შ	š	[ʃ]
ṭ	t	t	ტ	t	[tʰ]
t	th	t̆	თ	ṭ	[t']
u	u	u	უ	u	[u]
v	v	v	ვ	v	[v]
y	y	y	ჺ	j	[j]
z	z	z	ზ	z	[x]
ӡ	ӡ	ž	ძ	ӡ	[dz]
ჭ	c	ӡ	ც	c	[tsʰ]
ჭ	ch	ӡ̌	წ	ç	[ts']

Excerpt 1 (Fındıklı dialect)

Mota pencereṣen ožkes, Nandidi do Nina çumers. Mundeṣ moxtanen? Aha, **muluṉan koẓiru**! Nandidi **komox̱tu** do "Ma dido **domač̱ǩin̲du**"-ya, "Çai **ožilus̲** kap̆ula **mažǩunu**. **Haži** dopxedat do ar **ǩai** çai opṣvat."-ya.
(Yuksel-Sokmen & Wei, p. 12)

Stories of Perseverance

IPA Transcript

Mota **pencereşen ot s' k'es**, Nandidi do Nina **çumers. Mundes** moxtanen?

Aha, **mulunan kod ziru**! Nandidi **komoxtu** do "Ma dido domat ʃ k'indu"-ya,

"Çai ot s' ilus k'aP'ula mat s' k'unu. Hat s' i dopxedat do ar k'ai çai opşvat."-ya.

Excerpt 2 (translation into the Ardeşen dialect)

Monta **pencereşa gamaʒes**, Nandidi do Nina **uondray. Munde** moxṯanen?

Aha, **muluran kaziru**! Nandidi **komoxt̯u** do "Ma dido **domančinu**"-ya,

"Çai oʒilute kap̌ula maʒunu. Huy dopxedat do ar vorsi çai opşvat."-ya.

(Yuksel-Sokmen & Wei, 2014, p. 13)

IPA Transcript

Monta **pencereşa gamat s' es**, Nandidi do Nina **uondray. Munde** moxt'anen?

Aha, **muluran kaziru**! Nandidi **komoxt'u** do "Ma dido **domant ʃ inu**"-ya.

"Çai ot s' ilute k'ap'ula mat s' unu. Huy dopxedat do ar vorsi çai opşvat."-ya.

(Yuksel-Sokmen & Wei, 2014, p. 13)

Mota looks into the window, waiting for Nandidi [grandma] and Nina. When will the come? Ha, they are coming, he saw them! Grandma came and says "I am very tired.

My back hurts from plucking tea leaves. Now, let's sit and drink some good tea."

Excerpt 3 (Fındıklı dialect)

Pap̌ulik Motas "**Handğa** Mota **çkimik** çai **dovu**! Hayde Mota **çkimi**, otxo bardaği **komoiği** do **Nandidik** çai **dolobasen**."-ya uʒu.

(Yuksel-Sokmen & Wei, 2014, p. 14)

IPA Transcript

P'ap'ulik Motas "**Handğa** Mota **çkimik** çai **dovu**! Hayde Mota **çkimi**, otxo bardaği **komoiği** do **Nandidik** çai **dolobasen**."-ya uʦ'u.

Excerpt 4 (translation into the Ardeşen dialect)

P̌ap̌u Monta "**Andğa** Monta **şǩimi** çai **dou**! Hayde Monta **şǩimi**, otxo bardaği **komoği** do **Nandidi** çai **dolvobasen**."-ya užu.

(Yuksel-Sokmen & Wei, p. 15)

IPA Transript

P'ap'u Monta "**Andğa** Monta **şk'imi** çai **dou**! Hayde Monta **şk'imi**, otxo bardaği **komoği** do **Nandidi** çai **dolvobasen**."-ya uʦ'u.

Turning to Mota, Grandpa said, "Today my dear Mota [grandson] did [prepared] the tea. Darling Mota, go fetch four cups and Nandidi will poor the tea.

Table 5.2 below lists all the observed variations between the two dialects illustrated in the four excerpts above. A rich variation in pronounciation (e.g., kožiru vs. kaziru) and lexical differences (e.g., k'ai vs. vorsi) are apparent. Observed is also the missing ergative case into the Ardeşen dialect from the original text written in the Findikli dialect. Although the Caucasus region is known to host a high concentration of ergative languages, the Ardeşen dialect has lots its marking for the ergative and the dative case (Kutscher, 2001).

Table 5.2 - Morphological and Lexical Differences between two Lazuri Dialects (Viçe, Ardeşen) and their Equivalent IPA transcription

Type	Change	Viçe	Ardeşen	Turkish	English
Lative case	şen> şa	pencereşen	pencereşa	pencereden	out of the window
Vocabulary	ʦ'k'> ʦ'	oʦ'k'es	gamaʦ'es	bakıyor	he looks
Vocabulary	lexical	çumers	uondray	bekliyor	he waits
Pronounciation	-s> 0	mundes	munde	ne zaman	when
Pronounciation	n> r	mulunun	muluran	geliyorlar	they are coming
Pronounciation	ʤ> z	koʤiru	kaziru	gördü	he saw
Pronounciation	t> t'	komoxtu	komoxt'u	geldi	she came
Pronounciation	ç> ʧ	domaʧk'indu	domanʧinu	yoruldum	I am tired
Pronounciation	s> te	oʦ'ilus	oʦ'ilute	toplamaktan	from plucking

Pronounciation	t͡s'k'> t͡s'	mat͡s'k'unu	mat͡s'unu	ağrıdı	it hurts
Vocabulary	lexical	hat͡s'i	huy	şimdi	now
Vocabulary	lexical	k'ai	vorsi	iyi	good
Ergative case	-k> 0	p'ap'ulik Motas	p'ap'u Monta	dede torununa	grandpa him Mota
Pronounciation	çk> şk'	çkimi	şk'imi	benim	my dear, darling
Pronounciation	h> 0	handğa	andğa	bugün	today
Pronounciation	-v> 0	dovu	dou	yaptı	did
Pronounciation	-i> 0	komoiği	komoği	getir	fetch
Pronounciation	v>` 0	dolobasen	dolvobasen	dolduracak	will poor

The following sections report results of the content-analysis for the characteristics of the Laz authors' books and the authors' language-use, type of genre, and style of expression.

6. Results of Content-analysis

6.1. Characteristics of the Laz authors

These fifty-eight literary Lazuri books were produced by twenty-nine individual authors and/or translators. 72.24% of the authors are above the age of 45. While the majority of the authors did not live among the linguistic community of concern, only one-third (31.03%) lived in Lazona, meaning within the concentrated Laz settlements in Turkey from Pazar (Rize) to Hopa (Artvin). Table 5.3 below shows which regional Lazuri dialect the authors represent based on their biological sketches provided either in the published book itself or via interviews published in the media. Most authors were regionally affiliated with the Ardeşen dialect spoken in Ardeşen (41.38%), followed by the Xopa dialect spoken in Hopa (17.24%), the Arkabi dialect spoken in Arhavi (13.79%), the Viçe dialect spoken in Fındıklı (13.79%), the Atina dialect spoken in Pazar (6.90%), and finally the Çxala dialect spoken in Borçka (6.90%).

Table 5.3 - *Regional Lazuri Dialect-affiliation of the Literary Book Authors/Translators (N=29)*

Lazuri Dialect (N=29)	%
Ardeşen	41.38%
Hopa	17.24%
Arhavi	13.79%
Viçe	13.79%

Atina	6.90%
Çxala	6.90%

6.2. Published Lazuri Books by Dialect

The authors of the literary books were likely to use and write in their native dialect of Lazuri: a quarter of the books were written in the Ardeşen dialect (25.9%) or in combination with the Arkabi dialect (13.8%) or in the Viçe dialect (5.2%). The second most used dialect was the Arkabi dialect (20.7%), followed by the dialect of Xopa (19.0%), which was also used with other dialects (1.7%). The Viçe dialect was the least used (8.6%) and sometimes in combination with the Ardeşen dialect (5.2%). In our book-review, we also encountered instances where the authors were alternating between dialects, but this was rare (8.6%). Besides the variety in dialects, almost half of the books (or 41.4%) included Turkish translations. Some even had English abstracts or translations into other non-Turkish languages, whereas 55.2% were written only in Lazuri. We could not analyse the rest of the books (2 in total, 3.4%) since the books were not in our possession during the analysis.

6.3. Writing-proficiency of the Lazuri Authors

Almost every author used Feurstein's roman alphabet to express their literary work in Lazuri; the exceptions were four books written in the Turkish alphabet (Kabaoğlu, 2018; 2019; Özşahin, 2010; Şeşenoğlu, 2003). To assess the author's written language-proficiency as attested in the published books, a Lazuri writing rubric was developed (see Table 5.3). The second author of the current chapter read in its entirety the books that were in his possession and followed the said rubric. Upon completing the language coding within the select sample of books, both authors of the current chapter discussed the coding and resolved disagreements. A score of 5 indicated that the author's work is free of any language-alteration between Lazuri or Turkish or dialect-mixing or of loanwords from Turkish. A score of 4 was given when the text had few dialect-alterations or included very few neologisms. A score of 3 showed more dialect-alteration and indicated a mixing of grammatical structures from other dialects. A score of 2 signalled dialect-alterations and grammatical structure-mixing across dialects as well as heavy usage of loanwords across various dialects and languages. A score of 1 was given when the text was hard to understand due to heavy mixing of dialects, grammatical errors, the inclusion of neologisms or the invention of new words.

We found a significant association between the style of language-use (i.e., modern vs. classic) and Lazuri language writing-proficiency, $r(56) = -.690$,

$p<.001$ meant that traditional literature (e.g., collections of poems, folktales, fairy-tales, and memoirs) was more likely to achieve higher scores in written Lazuri language-proficiency than more modern work (e.g., novels, essays, and translations of classic works). 64.3% of the Lazuri books achieved a high score above 4 for the language-proficiency scoring, while a quarter of the books (25.0%) were mediocre, 10.8% receiving scores lower than 3. Out of the six Lazuri-translated works, which received a score lower than 4, only one translation into Lazuri (Steinbeck, 2018) was robust and received a score of 5.

Table 5.4 - Lazuri Writing Rubric with Scoring Outcomes (N=56)

Score	Description	Frequency	%
5	No presence of foreign dialectic elements, words, phrases, etc.	17	30.4%
4	A small number of words were taken from other dialects, or a small number of neologisms were produced.	19	33.9%
3	In addition to the above, grammatical structures were taken from other dialects.	14	25.0%
2	Grammatical structures, neologisms and borrowed words have been moved away from the underlying dialect.	3	5.4%
1	The above features were more widely in evidence, and in addition to grammatical errors, the text is beyond comprehension	3	5.4%

6.4. Published Lazuri Literary Books by Genre

Table 5.4 shows an extensive range of literary works. While 32.8% of the authors utilized a traditional style, 60.3% experimented with a modern style, and 6.9% used a combination of traditional and contemporary styles. The most popular genre is poetry (37.9%) and was used in the very first Lazuri book ever published with the Feurstein alphabet in Turkey by a female author (Koçiva, 1997). However, to date, only eight books have been authored by female Laz writers, including the translation of *The Little Prince* (Saint-Exupéry, 2014), while 47 books (81.0%) were produced by male Laz writers. Three Lazuri books (5.2%) had no available authors, such as the Biblical translation *Luǩa Lazuri*, and two children's books. The report displayed in Table 5.5 below also revealed that the books predominantly target adults (87.9%) and children (12.1%).

Table 5.5 - Lazuri Books by Genre Printed in Turkey from 1997 to 2021 (N=58)

Genre	Frequency	%
Poetry	22	37.9
Fairy-tales & Stories for Children	7	12.1
Translation of World Literature	7	12.1
Drama	6	10.3
Memoir/Autobiography	5	8.6
Essay	2	3.4
Short Stories	2	3.4
Wisdom-literature	2	3.4
Compilation	1	1.7
Cookbook	1	1.7
Interview	1	1.7
Political Fiction	1	1.7
Theatre	1	1.7

Next, we grouped the above-mentioned genres to better organize the broad spectrum of literary creation through various genres, such as poesy, fiction, memoir, or translations of acclaimed classical world-literature. Each book-description starts with a title marked in italics translated into English from the original Lazuri book-title. Due to limited space, we have divided the books into the following genres and presented them in a tabular format: poetry (Table 5.6), translations, references, political fiction, and wisdom-literature (Table 5.7), novels, essays, short stories, and theatre (Table 5.8), memories, autobiographies, and interviews (Table 5.9), and finally fairy-tales and folktales (Table 5.10). Tables 5.6 through 5.9 include each reference of the sampled book with a short description.

Table 5.6 - Lazuri Poetry

Book (*n*=22)	Description
Abaşişi, N. D. (2011). *Tu şkurna gale*. *Lazuri şiirepe*. Lazika Yayın Kollektifi	"*Out of Fear*" is a collection of marvellous poems written in the Viçe dialect. In addition to freely written poems, there are also traditionally composed poems. The work contains one of the best examples of poetry ever produced in Lazuri.

	The author also portrays Laz village-life and discusses current political issues in connection with past social events.
Albayrakoğlu. S. (2014). *İzmoce.* Lazi Kültür Yayınları	"*Dream*" contains lyrical and modern poems by the author in the Xopa dialect.
Amaťinaşi, S. A. (2015). *Gurişi çilambri ğvanduri şiirepe.* Lazika Yayın Kollektifi	"*Poems from The Tear of The Heart*" includes poems by the Ardeşen poet narrating his village-life, nature, and the highland. The language is quite simple and natural. It is written in a traditional style.
Ançaşi, R. Ö. (2011). *Çona.* Lazi Kültür Yayınları	"*Ray*" is a compilation of poems written in the Ardeşen dialect and connects humans to fundamental needs, such as longing for nature, love, and ancestral roots.
Avcı, Y. (1999). *Şurimşine lazca / türkçe.* Kurye	"*Sweetheart*" is a collection of Lazuri love-poems written in the Xopa dialect with Turkish translations. The book ends with a bilingual story about a court-case and some popular poems. Some of the poems are the most distinguished examples of Lazuri poetry developed in the 1990s and are written in a traditional style but with modern expressions and images. Free-verse poems are also numerous.
Bucaklişi, I. (2006). *Mu pat e skiri.* Helimişi Xasani yaşamı ve şiirleri. Chiviyazıları	"*What Shall We Do?*" is a poetry-collection by the Laz poet Hasani Helimişi from Xopa which were transcribed from audio-recordings of Helimişi's work. The self-voiced autobiography of Helimişi in Lazuri is also included in the book with Turkish translation. Turkish abstract-translations of the poems are also included. In 2015, it was republished by the Lazika Yayın Kollektifi and used the Feurstein alphabet.
Bucaklişi, I. A. (2014). *Laz destanları.* Lazika Yayın Kollektifi	"*Lazuri Destans*" is a traditional type of ornate form of story-telling called *destan*. The orally-transmitted poems were compiled from various places and written across Lazuri dialects.
Çakırusta, M. (2010). *Dutxuri palikari. Dutxe, dutxurepe, lazuri meseli do şiirepe.* Lazika Yayın Kollektifi	"*The Led of Dutxe. Dutxe, the People of Dutxe, Lazuri Tales and Poems*" has two distinct parts and is written in the Ardeşen dialect. The first part focuses on the author's early life and community in Dutxe and discusses the early years of the Laz cultural movement in Turkey. The second part includes a collection of poems and folktales. The poems are written in a traditional, indigenous manner.

Çupinaşi, M. (2016). *Samarile*. Lazika Yayın Kollektifi	"*Meadow*", written in the Ardeşen dialect, is a good example of modern Lazuri poetry and demonstrates intricate language and style. The themes of the poems include romance, love, Lazuri ethnic awareness, and societal change. The foreword is written in Turkish, followed by Lazuri poems and ending with a set of Turkish poems by the author.
Kabaoğlu, M. (Laz Osman) (2018). *Çoyişkimişi şura*. M*emleketimin kokusu*	"*The Scent of the Homeland*" includes Lazuri poems in the Ardeşen dialect with Turkish translations. The poems are crafted in the traditional style, and the language is natural and understandable. The authors use the Turkish alphabet.
Kabaoğlu, M. (Laz Osman). (2019). *Pavrepe goyiğfasi. Yapraklar döküliince*. Mamur Ajans	"*Leaf Fall*" is a collection of poems about change and continuity written in the Ardeşen dialect with Turkish translations. The language is natural and understandable. The authors use the Turkish alphabet.
Koçiva, S. (1997). *Nena murunʒxi*. Kurye	"*Stellar Tongue*", written in the Ardeşen dialect, is a collection of the poet's early poems on socio-political issues written both in free and traditional style. Koçiva's work is the first book entirely ever written in Lazuri in the Republican period.
Koçiva, S. *Guri parpali - Kelebek yürek*. Lazi Kültür Yayınları	"*The Butterfly Heart*" includes social and socio-political poems depicting the perspective of the author. Next to modern poems, there is also traditional poesy written in the Ardeşen dialect with Turkish translations.
Murğulişi, M. (2014). *Sum şoroni*. Lazika Yayın Kollektifi	"*The Three Goats*" comprises poems written in both free and traditional style to entertain and amuse the reader. The work is a mixture of the Ardeşen dialect and the Arkabi dialect.
Odabaş, R. (2018). *Bere do daçxiri*. Aydili Sanat Derneği Yayınları	"*The Child and The Fire*", written in the Xopa dialect, contains poems in the traditional and modern style. The language is very easy to follow, understandable, and natural.
Özkurt, R. (2014). *Mendra*. --	"*Far*", written in the Ardeşen dialect, is a collection of poems about love typical of traditional Laz poetry. It also includes free-range poems that can be called modern. The language is quite fluent and natural, making it easy to follow.
Özşahin, Ş. (2010). *Vibir türkçe ve lazca şiirler*. --	"*I Write Poems in Turkish and Lazuri*" is a privately printed reproduction of the author's 19 Lazuri poems, written in a very traditional style and the Xopa dialect. Other parts of the book are in Turkish.

	The book does not include page-numbers and is estimated to be around 150 pages. The author uses the Turkish alphabet.
Saidişi, Ö. E. (2013). *Oxoşkva*. Lazika Yayın Kollektifi	In "*Freedom*", the poet analyses his mother-tongue through poesy and illustrates the unique love between humans for nature and their quest for freedom in an endangered language. The work is a mixture of the Viçe and Ardeşen dialects.
Şeşenoğlu, M. (2003). *Arkabili lazların ayak izleri*. --	"*The Footprints of Arhavi Lazi*" is written in Turkish and portrays studies of music from Arhavi and features many traditional Laz poems, lyrics and musical notes. Biographical sketches of local singers and poets are also provided. The authors use the Turkish alphabet.
Turna, I. D. (2015). *Tzuťa oxori*. Lazika Yayın Kollektifi	"*Little House*" is a collection of poems about romance, love, and life written in traditional style and the Arkabi dialect.
Yılmaz, I. G. (2019). *Şinaxeri*. Laz Kültür Derneği	"*Tucked Away*" are poems written in a modern style. The language is intricate and entertaining and in the Arkabi dialect.
Yılmaz, I. G. (2014). *Zemsku*. Lazi Kültür Yayınları	"*Black Chicken*" is a collection of the author's poems in the Arkabi dialect. Being in a modern style, the language is quite intricate and inviting.

Table 5.7 - Translations, References, Political Fiction, and Wisdom-literature in Lazuri

Book (*n*=11)	Description
--. (2020). *Luka Lazuri*. Kitabı Mukaddes Şirketi	"*Gospel of Luke*" is a Lazuri translation into the Ardeşen dialect.
Aksamaz, A. I. (2013). *Lazlar, lazca, laz kimliği*. Sorun Yayınları	"*The Lazi, Lazuri, Laz Identity*" is a collection of the author's socio-political essays on identity and language translated into the Xopa dialect.
Saint-Exupéry, A. de (2014). *Žulu prensina* (M. Ö. Durmaz, Trans.). Lazi Kültür Yayınları	"*Little Prince*" is a translation into the Ardeşen dialect. The language is cumbersome.
Behrengi, S. (2014). *Uça çxomina* (I. Çagatay Aleksiva, Trans.). Lazi Kültür Yayınları	"*The Little Black Fish*" is a translation into the Ardeşen dialect of the author's famous book. The language is natural and understandable.
Dostoyevski, F. (2015). *Kabaeťi do ceza*.	"*Crime and Punishment*" is an abbreviated translation of the famous novel, written in a mixture of the Ardeşen and Arkabi dialects.

(M. Ş. Uzunalişi, Trans.). Lazika Yayın Kollektifi	
Kal, P. A. (2006). *Paponi.* Çiviyazıları	"*Laz Patty*" is a cookbook in which dishes of traditional Lazuri cuisine are described in Lazuri, Turkish, and English. It includes over 100 ethnic recipes and a description of indigenous ingredients and cooking tools.
London, J. (2016). *K̆ibir k̆çe* (O. Ş. Buyuklişi, Trans.). Lazika Yayın Kollektifi	"*White Fang*" is the translation of the author's famous novel into the Arkabi dialect.
Saint-Exupéry, A. de (2011). *Çit̆a mapaskiri.* (S. Albayrakoğlu, Trans.). Lazika Yayın Kollektifi	"*Little Prince*" is a translation of the author's famous work into the Çxala dialect, some of which are more liberal. The language is cumbersome and difficult to use at for beginners. Some elements differ from the Çxala dialect.
Shakespeare. W. (2014). *Romeo do Juliethi* (M. Murğulişi, Trans.). Lazika Yayın Kolektifi	"*Romeo and Juliet*" is an abbreviated translation into a mixture of Ardeşen and Arkabi dialects.
Steinbeck, J. (2018). *Mtugepe do k̆oçepe* (H. Uzunhasanoğlu, Trans.). Lazi Kültür Yayınları	"*Of Mice and Men*" is the translator's rendition of the famous novel into the Viçe dialect. Although it is a translation, its language is quite understandable and natural. It is one of the best among works translated into Lazuri.
Uzunhasanoğlu, H. (2018). *Nemazi dobiguram.* Lazi Kültür Yayınları	"*I am Learning to Pray*" is a pocket-size guide for prayer in the Viçe dialect.

Table 5.8 - Novels, Essays, Short Stories, and Theatre in Lazuri

Book (*n*=11)	Description
Abaşiş, N. (2013). *Kançoba p̌aramitepe.* Lazika Yayın Kollektifi	This book, which contains sexually explicit jokes and events, is very successful in terms of language. It uses language as we encounter it in natural, everyday life.
Avci, M. Y. (2013. *Aleynas mu ağodu? Aleyna'ya ne oldu?* Sorun Yayınları	"*What Happened to Aleyna*" is a crime-novel about the mysterious death of a girl named Aleyna. This is a bilingual novel in Lazuri and Turkish and is suitable for language-learners.
Buyuklişi, O. Ş. (2011). *Si giçkin.* Lazika Yayın Kollektifi	"*It's Up to You*" is a mixture of the author's short stories and poetry, as well as his personal view on the preservation-efforts for the Laz language and the dynamics amongst Laz activists.

Buyuklişi, O. Ş. (2013). *Ucoxe. goşağeri lazuri metsadupe.* Lazika Yayın Kollektifi	It is a continuation of his previous book with updated developments on the efforts to preserve Lazuri.
Murğulişi, M. E. (2011). *Daçxuri.* Lazika Yayın Kollektifi	"*Fire*" is a mystical village-novel about a supernatural event written under the influence of Stephen King novels. The language is clear, fluent, and easy to follow. It can be recommended for those who want to improve their Lazuri language-skills.
Murğulişi, M. E. (2013). *Çinka do moni bozo.* Lazika Yayın Kollektifi	"*The Genie and the Beaded Girl*" is written for children and includes 16 short stories about supernatural creatures. It is written in the Ardeşen dialect, yet grammatical structures that are not specific to this dialect are apparent, drawing attention to syntactic errors.
Murğulişi, M. E. (2013). *Didamangisa* Lazika Yayın Kollektifi	"*The Bugaboo*" is written in diary-form. Like the novels by Stephen King, the work describes supernatural events and features heroes speaking in both the Arhavi and the Ardeşen dialect. Unfortunately, the language of the work, which combines indigenous horror-elements with modern fiction, is not always clear to follow.
*Murğulişi, M. E. (2014). *Tzitzepe.* Lazika Yayın Kollektifi	A thriller.
Murğulişi, M. E. (2015). *Xami do xortzi.* Lazika Yayın Kollektifi	"*The Knife and the Meat*" is a thriller and depicts the redemption of a psychopath. The work uses a mixture of the Ardeşen and Arhavi dialects.
*Uzunalişi, M. Ş. (2015). *Gza.* Lazika Yayın Kollektifi	
Xasan Helimişi, X. (2019). *Çandaş gverdi (Jur perdoni lazuri piesi).* Laz Kültür Derneği	"*The Unfinished Wedding*" depicts a love-story during World War I within two acts. Written in 1945 by the infamous and controversial Laz poet and writer Xasan Helimişi, this is the only play ever written in Lazuri. The prologue is in German, Turkish and Laz.

*No book-description is available since the books were not in possession of the authors at the time of the content-analysis.

Table 5.9 - Memoirs, Autobiographies, and Interviews in Lazuri

Book (*n*=7)	Description
Aleksishi, I. Ç. (2014). *Lazuri texts artaşeni dialect.* Lazi Kültür Yayınları	"*Lazuri Texts in the Ardeşen Dialect*" are transcripts of conversations with native Lazuri speakers compiled from various villages of Ardeşen.
Arslan, O. (2013). *Tutaste. Hayat hikayesi ve bütün şiirleri.* İyi Yayınlar	"*Moonshine. Life Events and Entire Poems*" is an autobiography in which the author discusses his village-life and childhood, including 15 poems in Turkish and Lazuri. The introduction to the book is bilingual, with predominantly Turkish poems. Traditional poems are also incorporated.
Arslan, O. (2017). *Ognit herkes duysun noğaşen yaylaşaki.* ıslu Kitaplığı	"*Everyone Listen from the Town to the Village*" is a book narrated in alternating languages between Lazuri and Turkish. The author describes his village-life, the highlands, the people he met, the horticulture and the traditions of his childhood and youth.
Koçiva. S. (2012). *Guroni ar lazi oxorca- Yürekli bir laz kadını bedia xala.* Kaldıraç Yayınları	"*A Brave Laz Woman. Aunt Bedia*" is a biography of a woman named Bedia from the Azlaga village in Hopa, narrating her childhood throughout her adult-life. The reader is invited to an intimate conversation between the author and the Laz woman Bedia who lived through the Turkification-campaign in Turkey in the 1930s, "Vatandaş Türkçe konuş!" [Citizen Speak Turkish!].
Murğulişi, M. (2016). *Terzoğlipxe Heva.* Lazika Yayın Kollektifi	"*Heva Terzoğlipxe*" is an interview, in which an ethnic Laz woman, called Heva, tells her life-story in her mother-tongue.
Özşahin, B. (2020). *Sarpi moleni. Lazuri şiirepe do çarape.* Laz Enstitüsü Derneği	"*Beyond Sarpi. Lazuri Poems and Stories*" is a book of writings about the author's poems and village-life in Sarpi, childhood and different memories of growing up at the eastern Black Sea between the border of Turkey and the former Soviet Union (modern-day Georgia).
Şanaşi, Ç. & Francişi, H. (2021). *Tolikçeturi faik dai. Lazuri heçaepe.* Laz Kültür Derneği.	"*Uncle Faik of Tolikçeti*" is a compilation of orally transmitted stories and jokes about real and funny events of a charismatic person called Faik. In this humorous memoir, the reader meets Faik's (extended) family-members and neighbours and learns about life in a typical Laz village called Tolikçeti, in Ardeşen.

Table 5.10 - Lazuri Fairy Tales and Folk Tales

Book (n=7)	Description
Avcı, M. Y. (2005). *Laz masalları. Lazuri p'arametepe.* Sorun Yayınları	"*The Laz Fairy-tales*" contains folktales adapted from the Soviet authors such as K'art'ozia, Zhghent'i, Kutelia, Çikobava and translated into the Hopa dialect. The author also added a few original tales and provided Turkish translations for each fantasy-story. It is a linguistically successful work. The Laz language alphabet is not used, and the ejectives are marked with the sign 'subjective sounds'. Some arbitrary additions were made to the alphabet.
Abaşişi, N. (2005). *Lazuri p̌aramitepe – Laz halk masalları.* Akyüz Yayın Grubu Kolkhis	"*Laz Folk-tales*", taken from some of the textbooks published in Georgia and arranged by the author with the addition of new ones. The fairy-tales include Turkish translations and English abstracts. About ten fairy-tales were read on CD by the author and given as a book-supplement. A few fairy-tales have been written as prose. Consisting of 3 poems and 49 fairy tales, the book is a linguistically very successful work. Although neologisms are sometimes used, there is no difficulty due to a fluid and natural expression style. It can be used in the teaching of the Viʒe dialect.
—. (2010). *En didi mtugi.* Lazika Yayın Kolektifi	"*The Biggest Mouse*" is a picture-book for little ones about a brave mouse. The text was used in afterschool programs for teaching Lazuri.
—. (2010). *Mamuli do mkyapu.* Lazika Yayın Kolektifi	"*The Rooster and the Jackal*" is a picture book for little ones and narrates a journey through the forest with various animals. The text was used in after-school programmes for teaching Lazuri.
Yuksel-Sokmen, P. O. & Wei, S. (2014). *Çai pşvat.* Lazi Kültür Yayınları	"*Let's Drink Tea*" is an original picture-book story for pre-schoolers to learn how to boil tea. The short story is written in the Viʒe and Ardeşen dialects and includes text-translations into Turkish, German, English, and Mingrelian.
Yuksel-Sokmen, P. O. & Wei, S. (2014). *Porçoni katu.* Lazi Kültür Yayınları	"*Dressed-up Kitten*" is an original picture-book story for pre-schoolers portraying a little girl and her kitten. The short story is written in the Viʒe and Ardeşen dialects and includes text translations into Turkish, German, English, and Mingrelian.
Çupinaşi, M (2014). *Mtuti kuťavi.* Lazika Yayın Kollektifi.	"*The Bear Cub*" is a story about the friendship between a little boy and a bear-cub, written for children to respect nature and animals.

7. Summary and Outlook

In the current chapter, we sought to quantify literary books written in Lazuri and describe the early and contemporary efforts in the development and employment of the Lazuri Alboni. The analysis has shown that since 1997 fifty-eight literary books were published in Turkey by fourteen different publishers and written by a broad range of writers in their native dialects within the contact-induced linguistic community in Lazona and beyond. The work attests to a collective effort to document and preserve Lazuri thoughts and expressions in the digital era and provides a window into the endangered language-community's sense of identity and history. However, our discussion of the initiatives for developing a Lazuri orthography throughout historical times has shown how arduous, complex, and even fatal language-maintenance efforts can be.

In the current chapter, the presented Lazuri literary authors have used the newly invented Laz script (Lazoğlu & Feurstein, 1984) in creative and experimental ways to respond to the approaching linguicide of all currently endangered languages of the 21st century. The question remains: Will the newly emerging Lazuri literary genres encourage a new generation of speakers to read and write in their mother-tongue in order to preserve it in the era of globalization? No doubt the newly developed Lazuri Alboni provides a collectively constructed and diverse Lazuri voice to awaken an ancestral language partially silenced due to linguicide. Access and usage of a Lazuri literacy may be a sign of language-valorisation and pride and, thus, bolster the status of this indigenous language not only within the Laz community at the plateaus and foothills of the Caucasian mountains but also also within the wider society in Turkey.

8. Conclusion

Oral languages are vanishing at an alarming rate, and many leave no traces due to the lack of a writing system. Linguistic diversity is a precious repository of human wealth and an invaluable resource to understand the unique history and environmental changes of local communities (Crystal, 2000). Just like any other human cognitive skill, becoming multilingual and multiliterate require dedication, time, language-planning, and the support of a linguistic community to offer many opportunities for daily social interactions. The local community's commitment to their cultural preservation also requires the support of formal education for literacy funded by governmental pathways through explicit language-policies (Brenzinger et al., 2003; Crystal, 2000; Fishman, 1991). Societal ideologies and beliefs on the development of an orthography for the transmission and teaching of an endangered language shape language-policy and allocation of public funding (Grenoble & Whalen, 2006; Wiertlewska, 2012) [3]. The fate of all endangered languages of the 21st century is that they are not likely to survive into the next century unless the contact-induced speech-community sees meaning in the oral and written transmission of their ancestral tongue and receives adequate, sustainable resources coupled with unbiased socio-cultural support. As of now, prior to the last breath of the last Lazuri voice, plenty of imagination, dreaming, and improvisation has been consigned to writing with the aid of the Lazuri Alboni. Hopefully, this human intellectual wealth will be passed on through transliteracy across time and contexts.

Declaration of Statement of Interest

The authors of the current paper declare no conflict of interest in the preparation of the present chapter.

Acknowledgment

We extend our gratitude not only to all Lazuri writers, their publishers, proof-readers, funders, and editors but also their literary inspirations (protagonists, antagonists), contributing to the diverse linguistic expressions of unique human experiences.

References

Adjarian, M. H. (1899). *Étude sur la langue laze. Extrait des Mémoires de la Société de linguistique de Paris*, x.t.

Andrews, P. A., & Benninghaus, R. (1989). *Ethnic groups in the Republic of Turkey*. Reichert.

Ascherson, N. (1996). *The Black Sea*. Hill & Wang.

Ascherson, N. (2007). *Black Sea: The birthplace of civilization and barbarism*. Random House.

Bellér-Hann, I. (1995). The 'Laz songs' revisited: oral tradition in North-east Turkey. *Acta Orientalia Academiae Scientiarum Hungaricae, 48*(3), 291-311. http://www.jstor.org/stable/43391226

Berelson, B. (1952). *Content analysis in communication research*. Free Press.

Bernard, C., Chapel, L., Deffuant, G., Martin, S., & San-Miguel, M. (2008). Maintaining viability and resilience of endangered languages. *Working paper-European project PATRES*. https://www.researchgate.net/profile/Claire-Bernard2/publication/265006701_Maintaining_viability_and_resilience_of_endangered_languages/links/5502b07b0cf231de076f470f/Maintaining-viability-and-resilience-of-endangered-languages.pdf

Braund, D. (2003). *Georgia in antiquity.* Clarendon Press.

Brenzinger, M., Yamamoto, A., Aikawa, N., Koundiouba, D., Minasyan, A., Dwyer, A., ... & Zepeda, O. (2003). Language vitality and endangerment. *Paris: UNESCO Intangible Cultural Unit, Safeguarding Endangered Languages.* http://www.unesco.org/culture/ich/doc/src/00120-en. Pdf

Catford, J. (1977). Mountain of tongues: The languages of the Caucasus. *Annual Review of Anthropology, 6,* 283-314. http://www.jstor.org/stable/2949334.

Çolak, Y. (2004) Language policy and official ideology in early Republican Turkey, *Middle Eastern Studies, 40*(6), 67-91. https://doi.org/10.1080/002632 0042000282883.

Crystal, D. (2000). *Language death.* Cambridge University Press.

Davis, W. (2009). *The wayfinders: Why ancient wisdom matters in the modern world.* House of Anansi. Devlet İstatistik Enstitüsü (Turkey) (1968). Genel nüfus sayımı: idari bölünüş: il, ilçe, bucak ve köy (muhtarlık) nüfusları, 24.10.1965: Census of the population by administrative division: province, district, sub-district, and village (muhtarlık) population. Ankara: T.C. Başbakanlık Devlet İstatistik Enstitüsü.

Dobrushina, N., Daniel, M., & Koryakov, Y. (2020). Languages and sociolinguistics of the Caucasus. In M. Polinski (Ed.), *The oxford handbook of languages of the Caucasus* (pp. 1-50). DOI: 10.1093/oxfordhb/9780190690694. 013.30

Dumézil, G. (1937). *Contes lazes.* Institut d'ethnologie, Paris.

Erckert, R. (1895). *Die sprachen des kaukasischen stammes* (Vol. 1). Hölder.

Feurstein, W. (1983). *Untersuchungen zur materiellen Kultur der Lazen.* (Unpublished MA Thesis). Freiburg University.

Fillmore, L. W. (1991). When learning a second language means losing the first. *Early Childhood Research Quarterly, 6*(3), 323-346. https://doi.org/10.1016/S0885-2006(05)80059-6.

Fishman, J. A. (1991). *Reversing language shift.* Multilingual Matters.

Grenoble, L. A., & Whaley, L. J. (2006). *Saving languages: An introduction to language revitalization.* Cambridge University Press.

Guérin, V. (2008). Writing an endangered language. *Language Documentation and Conservation, 2*(1), 47-67.

Hann, C. (1997). Ethnicity, language and politics in north-east Turkey. In C. Govers, & H. Vermeulen (Eds.), *The politics of ethnic consciousness* (pp. 121-156). Palgrave Macmillan.

Hervás, L. (1787). Articolo VIII - Lingua Lesga, detta ancora Laza, e Lassa, Vocabolariopoligloto con prolegomeni sopra più di CL. lingue Dove sono delle scoperte nuove, ed utili all'antica storia dell'uman genere, ed alla cognizione del meccanismo delle parole. Cesena: Insegna di Pallade.

Hewitt, B. G. (1990). Aspects of language planning in Georgia (Georgian and Abkhaz). In M. Kirkwood (Ed.), *Language planning in the Soviet Union* (pp. 123-144). Palgrave Macmillan. https://doi.org/10.1007/978-1-349-20301-7_7

Hinton, L. & Hale, K. (2001). *The green book of language revitalization in practice*. San Diego: CA: Academic Press.

Holisky, D. A. (1991). Laz. In A. C. Harris (Ed.), *The indigenous languages of the Caucasus, Vol. 1: The Kartvelian languages* (pp. 395-472). Caravan.

Karpat, K. H., & Karpat, K. H. (1976). *The Gecekondu: Rural migration and urbanisation*. Cambridge University Press.

Klaproth, H. J. (1827). *Vocabulaire et Grammaire de la Langue Georgienne:* Part 1. University of Michigan Library.

Krauss, M. (1992). The world's languages in crisis. *Language (Baltimore), 68*(1), 4-10.

Kutscher, S. (2001). *Nomen und nominales syntagma im Lasischen. Eine deskriptive analyse des dialekts von Ardeşen*. Lincom Europa (Lincom Studies in Caucasian Linguistics 17).

Kutscher, S. (2008). The language of the Laz in Turkey: Contact-induced change or gradual language loss? *Turkic Languages, 12*, 82-102.

Lazoğlu, F. & Feurstein, W. (1984). *Lazuri alfabe. Lazca alfabe. Entwurf eines lazischen Alphabetes.* (Parpali 1. Lazuri Carelepe. Laz dili ve kültürü yaymlari. Schriftenreihe zur lazischen Kultur.) Freiburg i. Br. (privately printed).

Marr, N. (1910). *Grammatika čanskago (lazskago) jazyka s xrestomatieju i slovarem. Sankt*-Peterburg.

Moseley, C. (2012). *The UNESCO atlas of the world's languages in danger: Context and process*. World Oral Literature Project.

Peacock, D. R. (1887). Original vocabularies of five west Caucasian languages (Georgian, Mingrelian, Lazian, Svanetian, and Abkhazian). *Journal of the Royal Asiatic Society of Great Britain and Ireland, 19*(1), 145-156. https://doi.org/10.1017/S0035869X00019298

Schieffelin, B. & Ochs, E. (1986). *Language socialization across cultures*. Cambridge University Press.

Slavs and Tatars (2009). *Kidnapping mountains*. Book Works. https://www.slavsandtatars.com/site/assets/files/1236/kidnapping_mountains_slavs_and_tatars.pdf

Tuite, K. (2008). The rise and fall and revival of the Ibero-Caucasian hypothesis. *Historiographia Linguistica, 35*(1-2), 23-82. https://doi.org/10.1075/hl.35.1-2.05tui.

Turin, M. (2012). Voices of vanishing worlds: Endangered languages, orality, and cognition. *Análise Social, 47*(205), 846-869. http://www.jstor.org/stable/41959837.

Weber, R. P. (1990). *Basic content analysis* (No. 49). Sage.

Wiertlewska, J. (2012). Language planning and language policy in the ecological perspective. Glottodidactica. In *International Journal of Applied Linguistics, 39*(1), 117-126. https://doi.org/10.14746/gl.2012.39.1.11

Yuksel, P., & Brooks, P. J. (2017). Encouraging usage of an endangered ancestral language: A supportive role for caregivers deictic gestures. *First Language, 37*(6), 561-582. https://doi.org/10.1177/0142723717713502

Yuksel, P., Lowry, C., & Brooks, P. J. (2020). Laz caregivers talk to their young children: The importance of context and utterance type in eliciting ancestral language use. *First Language,4*(3), 268-293. https://doi.org/10.1177/0142723720970004.

Yuksel-Sokmen, P. O., & Wei, S. (2014). *Çai pşvat/ Çay içelim/ Let's drink tea/ Lasst uns tee trinken.* Lazi Kultur Yayinlari.

Chapter 6

Principles of Designing a New Dictionary Model for Endangered Languages: The Case of Laz

Fahrettin Şirin
Bielefeld University, Germany

Hanife Yaman
Tokat Gaziosmanpaşa University, Turkey

Abstract

Scientific studies, written works of any type and other reliable materials are relatively new on the Laz language although promising works, including various types of dictionaries, are emerging in recent years. However, the existing Laz dictionaries fail to meet many lexicographic requirements and industry standards in terms of their usability and reliability, lexicographic standards, structural organization, content, design and corpus usage. Therefore, after a detailed analysis and criticism of the existing Laz dictionaries, this chapter aims to develop a formal description of the procedures of forming modern Laz dictionaries of any type to enable and ease the design and production of a new model for future Laz dictionaries. If carefully designed and implemented, any database of such a Laz dictionary will have the benefit of generating various other products ranging from pocket dictionaries to mobile apps.

Keywords: *Revitalization lexicography, dictionary making, endangered languages' lexicography, Lazuri dictionaries*

***

1. Introduction

Laz, a South Caucasian language from the Black Sea region of Turkey, is an endangered language of Turkey. Scholarly studies, written works of any type and other reliable materials, are relatively new to it. However, promising works have been emerging on Laz only recently (For a detailed list of resources and publications, please see Yaman, 2019). It has been classified by SIL (Summer Institute of Linguistics) as a 6b threatened language, which means that "intergenerational transmission is in the process of being broken, but the child-bearing generation can still use the language so it is possible that revitalization efforts could restore transmission of the language in the home" (Richardson, 2019, p. 3).

Laz is a member of the South Caucasian Language Family together with Mingrelian, Svan and Georgian. Laz is spoken by the Laz people who live in Pazar (Atina), Ardeşen (Ardaşeni), Çamlıhemşin (Vica) and Fındıklı (Vitze) towns of Rize, Arhavi (Arkabi), Hopa (Xopa), Kemalpaşa (Noğedi) and Borçka (Boçxa) towns of Artvin in Eastern Blacksea region in Turkey. There are not many people who speak Laz around Batumi today although the Laz are the local people in this district. Laz is also spoken in small Laz towns and villages in İzmit, Sapanca, Düzce, Akçakoca, Bolu, Karamürsel, Yalova and the districts around them as a result of the migration of the 1877-78 Ottoman-Russian War. Two Laz dialects are foregrounded in the literature. The first is the eastern dialect which is spoken in Fındıklı, Arhavi, Hopa and Borçka, and the second is the western dialect which is spoken in Pazar, Ardeşen and Çamlıhemşin. The Hopa dialect, which is one of the eastern dialects, is popular among the Laz living in the Marmara Region. The dialect differences are not so great as to prevent communication (Özkurt et al., 2018). However, this dialect classification and its suggested sub-divisions are not a generally accepted and agreed concept in Laz studies since different scholars / specialists make different classifications for different reasons. For example, (Kutscher, 2010, p. 253) states that "Laz as spoken in Turkey is divided into four dialectal variants (Pazar, Ardeşen, Vitse-Arhavi, Hopa), all of equal sociolinguistic status, since a standard variety of Laz has not been established". Further, (Kutscher, 2011, p. 49) states that they are "named after the urban centers around which the variant is spoken. The dialects are named either after the Turkish or the Laz name of the corresponding city (Turkish/Laz: Pazar/Atina, Ardeşen/Arťaşeni, Fındıklı-Arhavi/Vitse-Arǩabi, Hopa/Xopa)". However, in an earlier 'draft' study the same author states that "Laz consists of three main dialects: Hopan (spoken in Hopa), Vitse-Arkabian (spoken in Arhavi and Fındıklı) and Atinan, whereby Atinan is subdivided into Atinan (spoken in Pazar) and Ardeshenian (spoken in

Ardeşen). This fairly rough division is based exclusively on phonological features" (Kutscher, p. 7). On the other hand, (Aksoylu, 2016, p. 47) claims that, Laz language has three dialects according to the geographical positions of the dialects spoken: 1. Eastern group dialects (Hopa, Borçka and surroundings), 2. Central/Middle group dialects (Arhavi, Fındıklı and surroundings), 3. Western group dialects (Ardeşen, Çamlıhemşin, Pazar). But he doesn't mention about the Laz dialects spoken in İzmit, Sapanca, Düzce, Akçakoca, Bolu, Karamürsel, Yalova and the districts around them as a result of the migrations in different times.

The Laz language already has some dictionaries published in print and online. The Laz dictionaries produced so far are unsatisfactory for many reasons: for their usability and reliability, their lexicographic standards, structural organization, content, design and corpus-usage, while also failing to provide many lexicographic requirements and industry-standards. The dictionaries of all types – bilingual (Bucaklişi, Uzunhasanoğlu, & Aleksiva, 2007), and multilingual (Kurdadze, Shonia, Tandilava & Nizharadze, 2015; Kabadayı, 2001) –produced for different purposes at different times and platforms (Laz-Enstitüsü, 2020) for the Laz language so far are no exception.

Each single dictionary-entry and dictionaries, in general, are highly structured objects with many recurring elements and require a proper, well-formed, proven set of rules and standards defined at the beginning of any dictionary project. The use of metadata and language, treatments of M-Structure elements, data-selection and collection, document-type definition (DTD), XML schema, database-planning and the overall rules and principles of the dictionary must be well-planned, consistent, accurate and explicit throughout the entire dictionary-project before implementation, testing, compiling and following-up the dictionary.

2. Objectives: Theoretical Goals and Practical Aims

Bearing in mind that studies related to the Laz language and lexicography are very new and limited, the motivation of this chapter is the relative lack of precedents. Therefore, this chapter aims to develop a formal description of the procedures of forming modern Laz dictionaries of any type that will enable and be easy to design, produce and hopefully provide a new model for future Laz dictionaries. If carefully designed and implemented, any database of such a Laz dictionary will have the benefit of generating from the same database and based on the same material a great variety of other products (e.g., pocket-dictionaries, dialect-dictionaries, thesauruses, whether in print or as mobile apps) as well.

Such a study will also enrich and contribute to the Laz language's revitalization, scholarly documentation, data-collection, and formation of a standard dialect. Additionally, the dictionaries formed according to this new model will be a great cultural heritage for future generations.

3. The Scope of This Study

In this chapter, information about data-collection and the tools necessary to make and compile a dictionary of Laz or any endangered language or any language, in general, is briefly presented. The assumptions are usually detailed, but the implementation-parts are general information, since any detailed and practical work for endangered languages requires fieldwork. Also, the whole dictionary-making process is so complicated and detailed that describing the entire process is beyond the scope of this study.

4. The Architecture of a Dictionary: Organisation of Lexical Information

The practice of dictionary-making (i.e., lexicography) is a long, tiring, often tedious, time-consuming and multifaceted process, and it includes at least the following aspects as described in Coward and Grimes (2000). Each of these steps, especially the dictionary-making part, is related to the 'M-Structures' of the dictionary, which are detailed in Section 5.

1. Understanding the language(s) structurally, functionally, semantically and socio-culturally.
2. Structuring the information (e.g., kinds of information in an entry, codecs, ordering of information in an entry)
3. Inputting the information (i.e., compiling the lexical database) normally over a period of years.
4. Testing, checking and refining information in the lexical database.
5. Manipulating the data for analytic or other purposes (e.g., extracting semantic domains, doing reversals).
6. Output; deciding the format and making necessary changes.
7. Printing or presenting the dictionary online, in a smartphone-application or any other type electronically.
8. Marketing and distribution.

5. Structural Parts of a Dictionary: M-Structures

Well-planned dictionaries have specific structures, and these structures are not arbitrary. 'M-Structures' (e.g., *megastructure, macrostructure, microstructure* and *mesostructure*) or the lexicon resource-structures constitute the overall structure of a dictionary according to the planned use of the dictionary. Also, every structure requires a unique combination of resources. The example of the semasiological alphabetic dictionary may help outline those structures as follows:

> In generic terms, any dictionary is a set of *lemmas* (singular: 'lemma'; alternative plural: 'lemmata') organised in a specific well-defined *macrostructure* such as a list or a tree hierarchy, the lemmas each being associated with a well-defined *microstructure* of *data categories*. Additionally, lemmas may be interlinked with cross-references and additional explanations; the cross-references constitute the *mesostructure*. The overall structure of the dictionary, together with its published metadata and perhaps also any additional explanatory information is sometimes referred to as the *megastructure*. (Gibbon, 2012, p. 242)

5.1. Macrostructure

The macrostructure of a dictionary or a lexicon is the organization of the lexical entries in the body of a dictionary into lists, tree-structures and networks (Gibbon, 2007). The most prominent concern of macrostructure in a dictionary is the order of headwords or lemmas. In a broader sense, it is the arrangement of lexical entries in the lexicon. For example, the alphabetic order may be suitable for most languages with alphabetic orthography but may not be suitable for syllabic scripts, right-to-left alphabets or for languages having large sets of prefixes (Gibbon, 2012). Moreover, some procedural or operational determining factors may affect the arrangement in the lexicon, like the medium of the dictionary. Presumably, the arrangement or sort-order in a print, electronic and multimedia lexicon would be different from each other for obvious reasons. Likewise, arrangements of an alphabetic dictionary and a thesaurus would be different.

Regarding navigation of the dictionary or organisation of lexical information, we might differentiate two types of macrostructure; *semasiological* and *onomasiological*. A form is mapped on semantics in a semasiological dictionary (i.e., reader's dictionary *or* decoding dictionary) and asks what a word means. In an onomasiological dictionary (i.e., a writer's dictionary *or* an encoding dictionary), a meaning is mapped on form and asks for names of these forms.

The semasiological (from Greek *semasia* 'meaning') approach moves through forms (terms, words) to meanings or concepts, and it leads to traditional, alphabetically ordered dictionaries. The onomasiological (from Greek *onomasia* 'term') approach moves from concepts to terms, and it leads to works of the thesaurus-type, organised by theme or topic (Jackson, 2002).

Thus, regular, standard monolingual alphabetic dictionaries providing descriptive definitions are expected to be *semasiological* dictionaries and dictionaries such as having concept-orientated terminological entries like term-bases, thesauri, WordNet, thematic, bilingual and terminological are *onomasiological* dictionaries. In some dictionaries, the two approaches are or might be combined and used together in a single entry.

Considerations about the relative arrangement of dictionary-entries in macrostructure, 'how and by which criteria' the entries are ordered, are important factors in most cases, and there should be linearity in the entry arrangements among monolingual dictionaries. '*Letter by letter* or *word by word?*' or '*Should the run-on derivatives be listed as (sub)entries* or *identified as separate entries?*' or similar arrangements should always be clear according to the structure of the language. For example, in a print-dictionary, when no proper syllabication or alphabetical order is used or when there is usage of nonlinear placement of entries and their related derived subentries, another problem of listing run-on derivatives as (main) entries may emerge as the alphabetical order since another type of word entry will interfere between the run-on derivatives. In most cases, it means that the derived form is not in proper alphabetical order or listing, and the user must either recognize the derivation and look under the base-entry or be prepared to hunt around for the derived word. The Turkish example from *TDK – Türkçe Sözlük* shows this problem. (First-level indentations are the derivatives of the first entry, the italics indicate the derivations. Bolds in the second-level indentations are different entries) (TDK, 2011, pp. 1893-1894):

- parti
- part*ici*
- part*icilik, -ği*
  - **partikül**
  - **partiküllü**
- parti*lerüstü*
- parti*leşme*

Principles of Designing a New Dictionary Model for Endangered Languages

- parti*leşmek*
- parti*leştirme*
- parti*leştirmek*
- parti*li*
- part*ililik*
- parti *ocağı*
  - **partisip**
- parti*siz*

Here the problem of the listing is that the first level in the tree-structure belongs to the headword 'parti' (*political* party). Still, when listed with the run-on derivatives as (main) entries in a tree-structure, the emerging alphabetical order becomes useless since other types of totally different entries (*partikül* = particle / *partisip* = participle) are interfering between the run-on derivatives.

Likewise, in Laz, different approaches are applied in various Laz dictionaries. In print-dictionaries (e.g., Bucaklişi et al., 2007), some verbs are listed with their base-forms as main entries, and related personal pronoun-inflections are listed as sub-entries as their derivatives though this is not consistent.

- Dobalu [to spill something liquid]
  - dobams [s/he is spilling something liquid]
  - dubams [s/he is spilling something liquid for someone]
  - dibams [s/he is spilling something liquid for herself/himself]
  - dvaben [s/he can spill something liquid for herself/himself]
  - dubapun [s/he has the experience of spilling something liquid]
- dodvalu [to place something on the ground]
  - dodums [s/he is placing something on the ground]
  - dudums [to place something somewhere for someone]
  - didven [to lay herself/himself something on the ground]
  - dodvalapams [s/he is making someone place something on the ground]

- doberi [the liquid is spilt]
- dodveri [something placed on the ground]
- dodvaloni [what needs to / can be placed on the ground]
- udodu [without placing]

In another (draft-) dictionary, based on hypertext though not an electronic dictionary (Kojima, 2021), synonym-entries in different Laz dialects are listed alphabetically, thus providing similar results in the Turkish examples above. Thus, for example, *ağani* (i.e., *new*) in Pazar (Atina) and Ardeşen (Ardaşeni) dialect is listed with its synonyms as *yengi* in Arhavi (Arǩabi) and Borçka-İçkale (Çxala) dialect as *ağne* under the same entry with a cross-reference but also listed as separate entries in the dictionary.

Depending on some procedural or operational determining factors, the arrangement in the lexicon might be different according to the medium of the dictionary for the end-user. Atkins (1996) states this new phenomenon as 'and now at least we are liberated from the straitjacket of the printed page and alphabetical order.' Nowadays, modern and electronic dictionaries are offering mostly the so-called 'Search Autocomplete' feature; thus, the search-field will be expanded and offer a list of suggestions as the user starting to type for the word 'look up' and this feature is virtually presenting the results for the entries from a network for the end-user.

One final remark concerning the macrostructure of dictionaries is the 'syntagmatic' and 'paradigmatic' relations and definitions. Syntagmatic relations (i.e., co-occurrences in some contexts, collocations) in lexicography are combinatory relations that create larger signs from smaller signs. Paradigmatic relations (i.e., synonymy, antonymy, hyponymy, meronymy), which are widely used in thesauri or WordNet-like systems, on the other hand are classificatory relations of similarity and difference between signs like internal and external structures, meaning and appearance. In this context, syntagmatic definitions are 'contextual definitions and definitions by text examples' in semasiological dictionaries. Paradigmatic definitions, on the contrary, are word fields as in thesauri having semantic relations such as hyponyms, hyperonyms, synonyms and antonyms.

5.2. Microstructure

The microstructure of a lexicon or a dictionary is the consistent organization of lexical information within lexical entries in the dictionary (Gibbon, 2007). In other words, its main concern is to describe the types of lexicon-information and its arrangement in lexical entries. Still, it is the most complicated part of structure since it is a conceptual whole made up of complicated, and too many interconnected but related parts.

> These types of lexical information (also known among computational lexicographers as '*data-categories*') concern the following main properties of words:
>
> a. Word-*form* (spelling and hyphenation; pronunciation and prosody, e.g. stress or tone).
> b. Word-*structure* (internal: prefixes, suffixes, constituent words in compounds; external: part of speech, grammatical restrictions).
> c. Word-*meaning* (descriptive components such as abstractness, animacy, pragmatic components such as style, taboo).
> d. Inter-article *cross-references* (to synonyms, antonyms, examples, sources, etc.).
> e. In a *lexical database*, also *metadata* about the lexicographer, date of processing, comments).
> f. *Hierarchical information*: in more complex cases, the microstructure can be hierarchical, organised as a set of related sub-entries, typically words derived or compounded from the same root.
>
> (Gibbon, 2012, p. 247)

The main problem for available Laz dictionaries is that there are so many missing components in entries that it is not even possible to find some information to criticise. The dictionaries are mostly compiled as *onomasiological* dictionaries, so they only provide L2 (mostly Turkish) equivalents of the entry though this is not consistent. Some dictionaries seem to be *semasiological* dictionaries and expected to provide descriptive definitions for entries, but this is not true for the whole entries in dictionaries. Most of the time, they use the two approaches combined and use together in a single entry. However, most of the time this approach produces many problems throughout the dictionary.

Thus, we see inadequate and incomplete definitions in the entries. For example, a "standard definition method" (such as *X is a Y kind of Z*) is not followed throughout the whole dictionary. Therefore, we rarely see such definitions as "abaza şuroni: Çok süt veren bir keçi cinsi" (a type of goat that gives much more milk) (Bucaklişi et al., 2007) in Laz dictionaries. Moreover, definition types of "contextual definition", "recursive definition" or "circular definition" or many others are not clear or intersecting each other incorrectly, thus resulting in various false and defective entries and definitions in Laz dictionaries.

Entries such as "abca" provides only some equivalents in L2 language as "Çay, nehir, ırmak; dere" (Bucaklişi et al., 2007) and it reflects an *onomasiological* dictionary entry type in nature but it does not provide any other hierarchical information as to distinguish between them as "river, stream, brook, watercourse" etc. or is it a "type of" river? Moreover, it is shown as "Çay, nehir, ırmak; dere", so ";" punctuation gives the impression that "dere" is listed as the sum of "Çay, nehir, ırmak".

There are also entries that provide definitions that do not fit in any definition or dictionary type. For example, '**açaminen:** Kaşıntısı vardır, kaşıntılıdır' (he/she has some itching) (Bucaklişi et al., 2007). Thus, the entry does not provide any information about the part-of-speech and what actually 'itching' means. Or in entries such as '**abaia:** ihtimal bildirir' (shows possibility) (Bucaklişi et al., 2007) does not provide any information about 'who/what shows a kind of possibility to whom/what?' and what is a 'possibility' means?

There are also severe 'sense order problems' because Laz dictionaries do not rely on a modern and well-designed corpus and 'Tagged Corpus,' and 'Word Frequency Dictionary Studies' are missing for Laz dictionaries. Examples and sense orders are provided according to the native speaker dictionary compiler's intuition only, but this approach does not provide valid results in all entries. Thus, there are problems in the method of ordering senses and this ordering is not based, for example, on the frequency of occurrences in Laz dictionaries.

'Syntactic and Morphological Problems,' 'Inflexion Problems,' 'Phonology & Phonetic Description Problems,' 'Orthography Problems' are just a few of the problems to name, but criticising them and many others will be beyond the scope of this chapter.

5.3. Mesostructure

The mesostructure of a dictionary is the set of relations between lexical entries and other entities such as other parts of a dictionary or a text-corpus (Gibbon, 2007). The mesostructure of a lexicon implicitly interconnects the lexical entries to the mini-grammar (sketch grammar; see below for the explanation of this term) in the 'front matter' in the megastructure of the dictionary. The category-names in the entries, such as the names for different parts of speech (e.g., 'noun', 'verb', different pronunciations, transcriptions or other abbreviations for those categories) are not explained for each entry in the microstructure, but a reference is given to the sketch grammar in the front matter in the megastructure of the dictionary. Thus, an abbreviation like '*n.*' refers to the grammatical category '*noun*', and a '*v.*' refers to '*verb*' (e.g., in the front matter in the megastructure of the lexicon).

Likewise, the mesostructure also regulates the relations between lexical entries to text-corpora in the lexicon. Thus, any 'example' given for the entry or for each sense or more 'Examples of -the entry- in a sentence' or 'Quotations' (i.e., contextual usage, generally extracted from a large corpus automatically) are parts of the mesostructure.

Another important feature of the mesostructure in the lexicon is the cross-reference network-relationships between words. These are usually cross-referenced relationships between related entries, such as the relationships between synonyms and antonyms (co-hyponyms) in the dictionary. Another detailed example of the mesostructure are the systems whose main macrostructure is in a lexical database of semantic relations between words through synsets such as WordNet.

One final prominent feature of the mesostructure, though usually unintended, is the 'cyclicity' in cross-references. 'The "cross-reference depth" of the mesostructure of a dictionary could contain, for example, the following: the word "thing" is defined in terms of the nearest kind "object," the word "object" is defined in terms of the nearest kind "entity," and the word "entity" is defined in terms of the nearest kind "thing." Without references to external examples, this cyclicity is inevitable' (Gibbon, 2012). If this formal feature of the mesostructure usually between synonyms is not carefully considered, this will lead to a 'circular definition' type (i.e., the definition-chain into a circle in terms of synonyms) in the entries in the dictionary.

In Laz dictionaries, all dialect-differences and synonyms and other differences are shown (Bucaklişi et al., 2007) as a 'general' → (or similar) sign in the dictionary, not providing any other specific differences, thus breaking the mesostructure of the dictionary, for example.

Other mesostructure information is also poor in Laz dictionaries. For example, there are either no POS (part-of-speech) information or wrong categories or missing categories in POS. Although it was stated in the front matter of the dictionary (Bucaklişi et al., 2007, p. 13) that Latin names are provided for plant and animal names, this is not consistent throughout the dictionary. 'Heteronyms and homonyms listing problems,' 'etymology' or the 'source language problems' are just a few to name for other problems.

5.4. Megastructure

The megastructure of a dictionary is the entire structure of the dictionary, including the front matter abbreviations and explanations of grammar (sketch grammar), the body of the dictionary and the back matter (Gibbon, 2007). This structure defines the real organization of the 'metainformation' (i.e., metadata, front matter, back matter) in the lexicon either in a print-dictionary, a database or a website. The typical case is the print-dictionary in a book-format. In such a dictionary, front matter includes the title-page, publication-information (e.g., author, date, publisher, copyright, volume, edition), followed by some introductory texts (e.g., dedication, foreword, preface), abbreviations, the sketch grammar and some explanatory examples from the dictionary. The front matter part is followed by the actual body of the lexicon and finally the back matter of the dictionary, usually some appendixes and supplementary materials such as maps, list of (ir)regular or exceptional structures of the language, affixes or even some advertising of the publisher.

In most published dictionaries or even in any kind of electronic dictionaries providing the following information in the front matter of the megastructure is very useful for the end-user of the dictionary for many reasons as described in detail in Coward and Grimes (2000):

1. Identifying the primary audience and purpose of the dictionary as well as explaining the overall organization of the dictionary-information.
2. Briefly describing the location of the language and the number of speakers.
3. Briefly describing any historical events (war, migration, forced settlement.).
4. Brief information about the language-name and alternate names (e.g. Laz / Lazuri).
5. Mentioning the 'linguistic classification' and ISO 639-3 code with some explanatory information.[1]

---

[1] Information about the Laz language please see, https://www.ethnologue.com/language/lzz

6. Listing relevant previously published works, especially dictionaries on the language.
7. Providing brief information about the 'dialects' and 'sociolinguistic profile' of the language.
8. Providing maps (though usually put in the back matter) where the language or dialects are spoken.
9. Providing a 'sketch of the phonology' for guiding the pronunciation and the orthography used in the dictionary.[2]
10. Providing a brief 'sketch grammar' of the language, focusing particularly on how various 'parts of speech' are defined and their distributional behaviour.[3]
11. Providing a table for 'abbreviations' and 'labels' used in the dictionary.
12. Providing a specific section describing 'how to read a dictionary entry' in the dictionary.

In Laz dictionaries, megastructure is not also well-designed and formed. Some dictionaries (Kurdadze, Shonia, Tandilava, & Nizharadze, 2015) for example) even do not provide any front matter or back matter information. In (Bucaklişi et al., 2007) for example, although poor and missing, some abbreviations and 'how to read a dictionary entry' information are added, a

---

[2] There is no agreed a standard and widely used 'phonology sketch', 'alphabet', 'Laz phonemes' and 'the grapheme system' for the Laz Language. All sources firstly refer to a journal called '*Mçita Murunʒxi*' which uses a Laz alphabet in Latin scripts for the first time by İskender Ӡitaşi in 1929, in Sokhumi/Sukhum(i), former USSR. Another Laz alphabet called *Alboni* is published by the same author in 1935 in Sokhumi/Sukhum(i), consisting of 34 letters which is re-published in 1994 in Turkey. Later, Georges Dumézil used a transcription in Latin consisting of 36 letters in 1937. In 1984, another Laz alphabet was used and proposed by F. Kahraman / W. Feurstein (widely known as "Lazoğlu Alfabesi") consisting of 35 letters. It seems this 'Lazoğlu Alfabesi' is widely used today. Lastly, another Laz alphabet was proposed by Gôichi Kojima consisting of 38 letters (For more information please see (Aksoylu, 2016, pp. 29-32)). As it can be seen from these sources there is not a standard alphabet and phonology sketch used by the Laz language and the authors of this chapter are unable to propose a new Laz alphabet and phonology sketch since it is beyond the scope of this chapter, unfortunately.

[3] The same statements for footnote 2 above are also valid here although some extra information is provided in section 8 below.

reliable 'sketch grammar', 'alphabet', 'phonemes and grapheme system' are missing.

6. Data Collection for Dictionary Making

One of the essential parts of dictionary-making is data collection first. When compiling or making a dictionary, generally, one of the following methods or a combination of them are used as data-sources:

6.1. Primary Resources

These are any and as much as spoken (transcriptions of oral, audio or multimedia recordings of any type) and written corpus-material of any type of language. Any good dictionary-project must be based on a corpus that makes it possible to discover new words, senses, collocations, word-frequencies and a relevancy-index based on the language's real use in situations of real communication as examples of usage. The corpora make it possible to discover a number of these combinations as well as collect wordlists to be used as lemmata, of-which the benefits are cruelly lacking in the majority of the dictionaries. If there are not enough corpora to be used, one of the most important tasks should firstly be collecting corpus material.

For corpus-studies, there are a number of free and commercially available products on the market. For example, *WordSmith Tools*[4] (commercial) by Scott (2020) as software for finding patterns in texts, keywords, word-lists or for use as a concordancer, or *AntConc*[5] (freeware) by Anthony (2020) both as a corpus-analysis toolkit for concordancing and for text-analysis can be used. For parallel (Laz and Turkish or Laz and any other language) corpus-analysis and example-usage, there is even software called *AntPConc*[6] by Anthony (2017). A better solution, which may also work for Laz language, as a 'Corpus Query' and 'Concordance Software' is *tlCorpus* (commercial) (Joffe, 2021a). It is the appropriate software for corpus-query and example-usage for Laz language. This software also works well especially when used as a 'TLex Suite: Dictionary Compilation Software'. The choice is up to the needs and budget of the compiler of the dictionary.

---

[4] For more information, please see, https://lexically.net/wordsmith/index.html
[5] For more information, please see, https://www.laurenceanthony.net/software/antconc/
[6] For more information, please see, https://www.laurenceanthony.net/software/antpconc/

6.2. Secondary Resources

These are available dictionaries of any type so far in any format. A good and reliable dictionary-project always must benefit from existing dictionaries, which most of the time constitute a priceless mine of rough material. The primary data-source suggested here is mainly the previous and currently used Laz dictionaries of any type, especially '*Büyük Lazca Sözlük, Didi Lazuri Nenapuna, Lazca-Türkçe / Türkçe-Lazca*' by (Bucaklişi et al., 2007), but other similar sources and other dictionaries can also be taken into consideration.

Incorporating the material of such previous dictionaries into a new dictionary-format or database, most of the time, is tedious. Often, the whole dictionary needs to be scanned first if there is not an electronic format for such dictionaries. If there is an electronic copy, conversion from a legacy-first (*MS Word* or *Adobe Acrobat PDF* files) to encode the dictionary into a standard format, preferably in XML encoding using some XSL or similar scripts or through some regular expression-operations, to be used by others is necessary. Similar studies by Thieberger (2011), and Warner, Butler, and Luna-Costillas (2006) give some ideas for implementing the whole process. In case a conversion of the previous dictionary is not possible for any reason, then, the crowd-sourcing method, which needs a collaborative work of retyping the whole material into a working format (preferably into a database or XML structure), is the only solution. Of course, any type of issues of copyright should carefully be taken into consideration in such works.

6.3. Word-collection

This type of data-acquisition is mostly done in three ways:

6.3.1. Translating Wordlists from L2 into L1 (e.g., Turkish into Laz language)

This method is generally used if the above methods do not work, or otherwise require great effort and much work when time is limited. The fallacy of this type of data-collection lies in the assumption that the translation-equivalents of L2 match exactly the vocabulary of L1. Since the two languages are totally different languages, so the vocabulary-coverages and concepts would be very different, and it would not discover and document the target language's vocabulary exactly. Although this method works for some basic vocabulary, it will not work for discovering and describing the target language's vocabulary as a whole.

6.3.2. Compiling Thematic Word-lists with Native Speakers (e.g., animal-, plant-names and so forth)

The so-called Rapid Word Collection method. 'Ron Moe of SIL International pioneered a technique called the Dictionary Development Process (DDP), of which the first phase is Rapid Word Collection'[7] (Moe, Simons, Warfel, Higby, & Cooper, 2010). It is a 'process to quickly develop a semantically categorized glossary that can be used as a thesaurus and later developed into a dictionary.'[8] In this method, a pre-defined semantics domain-list[9] of more than 1800, which are organized in a hierarchy under nine major headings so that similar domains can be found together, is given to the native speakers. They form groups / teams of four or more people, and each group writes the words in a topic and submits the words to the glossator, who is a native speaker of the language trained and able to speak a national language. The glossator adds a national language gloss with one or two words to each of the words and submits the material to the typists, and the typist writes the words into the computer. There are special templates for this kind of word-collection in software tools such as *FLEx (FieldWorks Language Explorer)*,[10] but any other similar software can be used to process this activity. At the end of this process, approximately 15,000 words can be collected and made into a basic dictionary for any language just in two weeks or so, the SIL International Rapid Word Collection coordinators claim.

6.3.3. Word-submission through Online-forms

This type of word-collection is rare but serves as a very useful and practical method. When compiling new dictionaries or writing the first dictionary of an endangered language, many native speakers or language-specialists contribute to its vocabulary in certain ways, as mentioned above. For the Laz language, for example, a name-list of the contributors is provided in the front matter as above of '*Büyük Lazca Sözlük, Didi Lazuri Nenapuna, Lazca-Türkçe / Türkçe-Lazca*' by (Bucaklişi et al., 2007) under the heading 'Thanks to' on pages 11-12. These people are volunteers, and their contribution to the dictionary is either via face-to-face meetings, phone-calls, sending and replying e-mails, posting some word-lists via the postal service or through individual visits to record some audio-visual materials. One of the difficult parts of these efforts is that the

---

[7] For more information, please see, http://rapidwords.net/
[8] Please see, https://software.sil.org/fieldworks/
[9] For a complete list, please see, http://semdom.org/
[10] For more information, please see, https://software.sil.org/fieldworks/

compilers of the dictionary must find or know and reach those people because, for in a language like Laz the speakers of different dialects are in totally different places, and most of the time, data-collectors reach a very limited number of native speakers. This is often a very time-consuming and costly method for collecting words and slows down the whole process of compiling and/or writing the dictionary. In recent years, however, a better, more reliable and practical method has been in use even by famous and large dictionary-publishers. The online-version of the 'Oxford English Dictionary,' for example, uses a 'submission-form'[11] to collect new material and provides some basic instructions[12] for submission. In this way, new words, senses, usages, examples, spelling, pronunciation, POS-information (where POS = part of speech), idioms, proverbs and many other new and useful data can be collected from a larger number of contributors from all over the world and at any time. The only thing required for this method is designing such functional and useful data-submission forms through a website or even via a smart mobile app to submit raw but new data to the dictionary-editors or compilers. This saves a lot of time, effort, and money; it is also very practical and returns more reliable and a greater amount of data as well as increasing the quantity of the material and quality of the work done.

7. Data-bases for Dictionaries

Prior to databases becoming a modern solution, the traditional solution was creating card-indexes. With the start of using computers, dictionaries began to be compiled in text-editors, mainly in word-processors such as MS Word using some templates or tables. Only large dictionary publishing-houses used certain types of customized software of their own. The product of text-editors was an advance on card-indexes, but the outcome still remained texts, providing little scope for re-use and was only slightly more enhanced in comparison with plain texts lacking all the benefits of a database of any type.

Using a database for creating any type of dictionary-project has numerous benefits. It records the data to be re-used in future studies. It is especially crucial since 'for lexicographers building dictionaries of endangered languages, the challenge is to create lexical databases that can be reused to allow new versions of dictionaries to be created with minimal work, and to allow enrichment of the content over time' (Thieberger, 2011, p. 464). The use

---

[11] For more information, please see, https://public.oed.com/contribute-to-the-oed/submission-form/
[12] For more information, please see, https://public.oed.com/contribute-to-the-oed/

of a database makes it possible to use any type of data, including multimedia objects, hyperlinks, data-sets and many others and makes it possible to create different products using the same material over and over again. With the help of a well-constructed data-base, the textual outputs can be properly organized, 'including various arrangements of the lexical database (e.g., dictionary, topical list, reversal, and so on) and these can be rendered as printed documents or created as stand-alone dictionaries or as web-pages' (Thieberger, 2011, p. 465). Thus, the idea of creating data-bases 'illustrates the underlying principle of creating the data once and then allowing it to be used in multiple outputs' (Thieberger, 2011, p. 466). This roadmap-principle is also true for the Laz language since it lacks a well-constructed database for language-revitalization and dictionary-studies.

8. Sketch grammar

A sketch grammar in lexicography is the complete and consistent set of rules written to regulate how the grammar of the language-elements should be represented in every single entry in microstructure and differs from fully-fledged reference-grammars. The output is displayed in the dictionary mostly as POS-tags or labels and other grammatical notes and relations in each single entry. In an XML-based dictionary, on the other hand, it is the customizable dictionary-grammar, and a 'Document Type Definition' (DTD) is used to define the structure and the legal elements and attributes of the dictionary. In traditional print-dictionaries, the sketch grammar is provided in the front matter of the dictionary, usually together with some lists (e.g., abbreviations, proper-names and so forth), tables, figures, or sample dictionary-entries. Mosel (2006) lists at least five different types of sketch grammars, two of them, 'the grammar in the front matter of a dictionary (dictionary grammar)' and 'the sketch grammar of a language documentation,' are directly related to dictionary-making and language-documentation.

The Laz language lacks a proper, complete grammar at the moment for any of the dialects. Accordingly, current Laz dictionaries also lack a well-defined sketch grammar. In '*Büyük Lazca Sözlük, Didi Lazuri Nenapuna, Lazca-Türkçe / Türkçe-Lazca*' by (Bucaklişi et al., 2007), for example, there is a part called '*Sözlükle İlgili Açıklamalar – Goknapa*' (pp. 13 – 22) which makes quite general statements and explanations about Laz grammar rather than being a sketch grammar. Thus, a consistent representation of Laz grammar in entries is not observed. Nor to be found is any information of the parts of speech, plural forms, affixes and their representations in the dictionary. Thus, one of the most essential but cruelly lacking studies for current and any Laz dictionaries of the future is a well-prepared sketch grammar, but this is not within the scope of this study.

9. Dictionary-writing Systems

Current Laz dictionaries and many other dictionaries of other languages are the products of old, traditional, general-purpose tools and methods such as word-processors like MS Word or some customized generic XML tools. They are mostly print dictionaries. This makes it very hard to plan, design and compile the dictionary; it is very time-consuming and costly, and the outputs produced are limited and cannot be used in different formats for different purposes since the data are unsuitable for easy re-use and are very hard to update. Also, many useful lexical data are omitted for publication because there is not enough space when publishing, and the data are not very suitable for multimedia-integration.

Instead of using such outdated tools and methods, employing dedicated lexical data and dictionary-compilation software provide significant benefits in terms of both dictionary-development time and output-quality either for individual lexicographers or for teams.

Such software and tools provide:

- increased consistency for the structure of lemmata,
- various levels of automation for organizing the data,
- unlimited filtering/sorting options of the data,
- controlling various tasks such as cross-reference tracking/updating and error checking,
- balanced treatment of all languages in a bilingual or multilingual dictionary,
- improved teamwork to save time, reduced project completion time,
- proper and easy usage of corpora,
- generating a great variety of other products (e.g., dictionaries of pocket, dialects, thesaurus, print, mobile apps) from the same database and based on the same material and many others.

Below are described leading software and tools on the market available both as freeware and commercial. All are suitable for any type of Laz dictionaries or any other language's dictionary, but the choice is up to the user's needs, planning and budget.

9.1. Lexonomy

Lexonomy[13] is a 'cloud-based, open-source platform for writing and publishing dictionaries online' (Měchura, 2017). It is also an XML-based 'highly scalable system to adapt to large dictionary projects as well as small lexicographic works such as editing and online publishing of domain-specific glossaries or terminology resources'[14] and it is very suitable to create mono-, bi- or multilingual Laz dictionaries online without any technical skills and financial cost (Měchura, 2017). The only minor difficulty at the beginning might be that the user should be familiar with, or should quickly develop skills into, hierarchical and XML data-structures and parsing.

9.2. FLEx (FieldWorks Language Explorer)

Another dictionary-writing system which is used worldwide especially for endangered languages or for language-revitalization purposes is SIL International's famous freeware 'FLEx (FieldWorks Language Explorer)'[15] or for short 'FieldWorks' software (SIL-International, 2021). This software is like a 'Swiss army knife' for field linguists. It helps field-linguists, with a set of supporting software-tools, manage linguistic, ethnographic and cultural data to document and analyse. It can also maintain lexical data and pars and inter-linearize texts in multiple languages. It is especially useful and supports various tasks from the initial entry of collected data to the preparation of data for publication, including dictionary-development, morphological analysis, and many other publications. Moreover, it can handle large corpora of over a million words and a very large dictionary-project. Another significant feature of FLEx is the support for Rapid Word Collection mentioned in section 6.3.2.

FLEx has also a built-in support for 'Grammar Sketch' tool and can "generate an HTML document which gathers grammatical data from the complete Language Project in one place, which lacks for all Laz dictionaries. Then 'this document can be either the basis for another, hand-edited document, or used as-is as a quick way to share information with, for example, a grammar consultant.'[16] Likewise, FLEx has a built-in 'Grammar Categories' support which 'not only do they fill the traditional "Part of Speech" tagging role,' but

---

[13] For details, please see, https://www.lexonomy.eu/

[14] For Lexonomy and many other open-source tools, please see, https://elex.is/tools-and-services/

[15] For details, please see, https://software.sil.org/fieldworks/

[16] For details, please see, https://software.sil.org/fieldworks/resources/tutorial/grammar/sketch/

they also help 'how words are put together (e.g., which affixes may or must appear, and in what order), inflection classes (e.g., gender and noun classes), what features are born by morphemes of the category (e.g., person and number).'[17]. This catalogue is based on the GOLD ontology of EMELD[18]. This feature also provides 'A Conceptual Morphological Parsing'[19] to describe and create an outline of the grammar of the language processed.

FLEx supports hierarchical XML data-structures, especially for importing and exporting of the data. It is simple to learn the software and SIL International provides a detailed manual and many video tutorials as for self-paced individual learning. Users can work simultaneously in different locations and can share and merge their data. The software also has a concordance feature.

As can be easily seen, among others, FLEx has all the solutions for the problems of the Laz language and dictionaries, namely, language-documentation, corpus- and data-creation and management, morphological issues, grammar-sketch, XML like hierarchical structures of the language, word-collection, multimedia and multilingual support, dialectal differences support, compiling dictionaries of any type and many others. This has great potential for the Laz language-community to use in order to derive the benefits of such a great product for their endangered language.

9.3. TLex (TshwaneLex) Suite

Another piece of software suitable for Laz or the compilation of any dictionary is 'TLex (TshwaneLex) Suite' (Joffe, 2021b). 'TLex (TshwaneLex) is a professional, feature-rich, fully internationalised, off-the-shelf software application suite for compiling dictionaries or terminology lists'[20]. Unlike 'Lexonomy' or 'FLEx', it is commercial software but offers an 'Academic and Endangered Language' licence also.

TLex is actually an XML based dictionary-compiling editor which is very flexible and highly customizable by the user for any intended dictionary-project including many different types of built-in sample dictionary-projects. 'TLex contains many specialized features that allow to dramatically reduce dictionary production time and costs while increasing the quality and

---

[17] For details, please see, https://software.sil.org/fieldworks/resources/tutorial/grammar/categories/
[18] For details, please see, http://emeld.org/tools/ontology.cfm
[19] See, http://downloads.sil.org/FieldWorks/WW-ConceptualIntro/ConceptualIntroduction.htm
[20] For details, please see, https://tshwanedje.com/tshwanelex/

consistency of dictionaries (from single-user projects to large teams). These include an integrated Corpus Query System, real-time preview, full customisability, advanced styles system, "smart cross-references" with tracking and auto-updating, automated lemma reversal, automated numbering and sorting, export to MS Word and typesetting systems (e.g., InDesign, Quark and XPP), multi-user support for managing teams, and much more.'[21] It supports all languages (including 'right-to-left languages') and can handle massive multi-GB dictionary-data-bases. It has also a built-in ODBC (Object Database Connectivity) support to connect and store data into an SQL (or MySQL) database. It is used mainly by dictionary publishing-houses, individual dictionary-compilers, dictionary-development teams, terminology-managers and practitioners, to compile and produce mono-, bi- or multilingual dictionaries (paper, electronic, online/intranet), multilingual terminology-lists, term-dictionaries, thesauri and many others. It is also very suitable for endangered languages, documenting linguistic and lexical data for dictionary-projects or for any other language-revitalisation works. It also offers professional support for any lexical data- or dictionary-project and offers a detailed manual for the software and many free video-tutorials. If used as a bundle as 'TLex Suite,' the integrated corpus-query software 'tlCorpus' can handle Laz language (or any other) corpora very efficiently.

9.4. Customized Software

Apart from the above-software, one can create a unique, customized piece of software for personal or institutional use as stand-alone software, or a web-page application suitable for personal or teamwork-use. Many major dictionary publishing-houses use their own in-house, customized software for publishing electronically and printing, but creating and maintaining such software are very expensive and require the employment of many other people. In most cases, such efforts for creating customized software are not needed, and any of the above tools will do the job.

10. Lexical Metadata

In simplest terms, metadata is 'data about data.' In this chapter's scope and in the context of lexica, it is the schema-description and descriptive information about a lexical resource with its own unique lexicon-objects (i.e., common data-categories) and metadata-elements (i.e., data-descriptors). This schema

---

[21] For a complete list of features, please see, https://tshwanedje.com/tshwanelex/overview.html

itself describes its linguistic and lexical content at a high level of detail (Wittenburg, Gibbon, & Peters, 2001). Additionally, the metadata-elements for lexicon-descriptions used for discovery of the lexical resource as well as providing catalogue-information about the production of the dictionary, are intended for describing the data-fields as metadata-sets in dictionary-making and identification of the characteristics of the dictionary itself.

For any new dictionary-project, one of the tasks that should be completed first is to develop a metadata-set as required by the project. The methods, ways, and principles for metadata and sub-categorial information for representation and depiction can be quite different for the various lexica. User- and requirements-specifications, editor's choice, usage, needs for different purposes can be quite different as well. Additionally, 'in field-linguistics, it can be seen that the language under investigation influences the structural choices and the complexity". Thus, in languages such as Laz, most utterances can be lexical entries bearing a rich internal structure. Also, different formats such as XML-structures, typed-feature structures, relational structures or project-idiosyncratic structures can be the features of lexica (Wittenburg et al., 2001).

The lexical metadata-elements (both lexicon object-elements and lexicon entry-elements) serve the functions as data-entry fields when they are converted into a real dictionary database for collecting the dictionary entry-data in a hierarchy. Thus, every metadata-element actually is an entry-field to be filled in the database to produce the dictionary at a later stage.

Both the lexicon object elements and lexical entry elements are still suggestions and in the form of proposals due to the observation 'that the grouping of data categories (i.e., the primitive elements found in lexica) is also very heterogeneous. This leads to the assumption that differences in linguistic theory and languages influence the structural choices' (Wittenburg et al., 2001, p. 9) for the reasons mentioned above.

However, for clarity and purposes of exemplification, Gibbon's proposal will be followed here. Gibbon suggests 'a layered approach to the problem of defining a metadata set for lexica' and 'distinguishes two levels of lexical objects: (1) The Lexicon Object covering general information about the lexicon as a whole. (2) Information about the Lexical Entries which describe the content.' He then distinguishes three further categories for Lexicon Object Elements as '(1) bibliographical data such as creator, publisher, title, date, and so forth. (2) Medium and format aspects; (3) macrostructure type of information such as languages involved, lexicon type (taxonomy).' According to the Gibbon's proposal, Lexicon Entry Elements are also composed of 'a type description' and mainly as a 'microstructure description' which for the most part provides 'information about the underlying structure of the entries and the enclosed data category groups each having their special list of data categories defined by some user groups or standardization bodies' (Wittenburg et al., 2001).

The classification-proposal below is an exemplification and approach to mentioning the main categories and elements of lexical data to allow the field-linguists and lexicographers to add values to the categories they specify according to their needs and requirement-specifications and to prevent over-specifications during the course of a real project. In the related literature and proposals, the status of the elements is categorized as 'expired, approved or candidate' although there is no fully agreed specific consensus on them. The following skeleton of proposals and content is largely borrowed from CLARIN (2021), Wittenburg et al. (2001) and Coward and Grimes (2000) with some minor modifications and additions.

10.1. Lexicon Object elements

The list can be extended or narrowed down according to the choice of the lexicographer or the needs of the project.

Table 6.1 - Lexicon Object Elements

Name	A short human understandable label name which identifies the Lexicon, e.g. '*Laz Multilingual Dictionary Project*'
Title	A descriptive and more elaborated title of the Lexicon, e.g., '*Laz-Turkish Bilingual Dictionary*'
Date+	Date of the creation and major modifications or the date of the last edition. Can be extended or sub-categorized as '*creation-date, dateBegin, dateEnd, FormationDate, etc.*'
Version	A number that identifies the indication of the version of the metadata-description of the Lexicon
LexiconType	A description of the type of the lexicon or taxonomy such as a *dictionary, word-list, glossary, concordance, terminology list* or *data-base* etc.

Creator+		Writer, generator or producer of the resource or the project described by the metadata. Can be sub-categorized as '*Name, Contact+, Description, Role*, etc.'
Project		A block to describe the project.
	Name	A short name or abbreviation of the project that led to the creation of the resource or tool/service.
	ID	A unique identifier identifying the project
	Description	Description in detail, the aim or purpose of the project.
	Status	An indication of the status of the represented project, such as 'completed'.
Object Languages		A block to describe the languages included in the lexicon.
	Multilinguality Type	languages can occur in different flavours in lexica, they can occur as multilingual entries in ML lexica, but they also can occur as translations of, for example, sense-descriptions; this difference can be indicated with the help of a controlled vocabulary
	Language+	A list of languages included; each language be described in a substructure
Meta Languages		A block to describe the languages which are used to define terms, to describe meaning and similarity.
	Language+	A list of languages included, each language being described in a substructure.
Format		A rough indication of the format the lexicon is in, such as relational table, structured plain text, some XML format, Html-format, etc. or tradition (books, physical representation of content).
Access		The description of the medium in which the lexicon can be accessed.
	Tool	Any concrete access-tools such as FLEX, TLex, MySQL, MS Access, Web Browser, etc.
	ResourceLink	URL pointing to the resource if it is directly accessible.
	Protocol	Indication of the name of a protocol that is required to access a resource or a tool.
	Permission	Any type of permission to access the lexicon or lexical database.
Media		Information about whether the lexicon includes audio- or video-samples or graphics.

Character Encoding+		The type of fonts needed to render all data included, such as UTF-8, ISO-latin etc.
Source+		Any sources which were used to build the lexicon, such as a written or spoken corpus, previous dictionaries, etc.
Reference		Block to give references to publications used etc.
Schema		The name of or reference to the documented structure which could be a DTD, Schema or similar.
Keys		Any possibility to add feature/value pairs to define new keywords.
Language		
	Name	The name(s) of the language(s) involved in the project.
	Language ID	Formal language specifier from ISO or SIL lists
	Language Identification	Information concerning the identification and identity of a language. Name, the geographical area where it is spoken, etc. Properties that are not part of the synchronous description of its system.
	Language Script	Indication of the writing-system used to represent the language in the form of a four-letter code as it is defined in ISO-15924.
	Primary Language	The language that is used most in the Lexicon if it is a multilingual project expressed as an ISO-639-3 language-code.
	Secondary Language	The language that is used together as an equivalent or in translation in the Lexicon if it is a multilingual project expressed as an ISO-639-3 language-code.
	Source Language	Indicates if a language is a source-language in the project.
	Target Language	Indicates if a language is the target-language in the project.
	Language Status	Indication of the status of a language in the project, such as dead, endangered language.
	Language Family	Group of language that is genetically related, i.e. can be traced to a common proto-language.
	Language Subfamily	Group of language within a language-family which is more closely related to each other than to other languages of that family.

	Language Variety	Any form of the primary language seen as systematically different from others in the community.

10.2. Lexicon entry Elements: The Organisation of the Dictionary entry

The following 13 main lexicon-entry elements categories describe the linguistic content covered by the lexicon and have been distinguished as a proposal for implementation (Wittenburg et al., 2001). Any modification, addition or extraction is possible according to the choice of the dictionary writer/editor or according to the needs of the project. The lexicon-entry elements are microstructure data-models in a dictionary. The form and content of the proposal below are largely borrowed from Wittenburg et al. (2001), CLARIN (2021) and Coward and Grimes (2000) with some minor modifications and additions. (Also, please see similar elements with detailed examples in Roberts, Hedinger, and Gravina (2014, pp. 34-39).

Table 6.2 – Lexicon entry Elements

Modality		Indicates which mode of communication is captured in the lexicon. Possible values are:
	Written	Pertaining to the modality of a resource as being written. Distinct from spoken language.
	Spoken	Pertaining to the modality of a resource as being spoken. Medium of transmission for language; the spoken medium or phonic substance of language (as opposed to writing or signing).
	Sign	A visual language used by a deaf community or written word from and/or a spoken language that is used to represent a lexical item in sign-language.
Date		A dictionary-making software book-keeping field to help keep track of the last time an entry was edited. One per record (usually the last field) is adequate. Usually inserted automatically by the software.
Headword type		A word or an entity that serves as the heading for an entry in a dictionary. It is an indication of the linguistic nature of the entry in the lexicon. **Possible values are:**
	Lemma	Any entry conforming to the unmarked word form or base-form a word or term that is used as the formal entry in a dictionary. (e.g. infinitive for verbs). Also known as 'lexeme', 'headword' or 'article'. Generally, bound morphemes are listed with a preceding or following hyphen. For some languages, it may be acceptable to give an inflecting citation-form.

	Abstract Lemma	Any entry not conforming to any word-form of the group subsumed by the lemma.
	WordForm	A form-subclass represents a form that a lexeme can take when used in a sentence or a phrase. So, the Word Form class can manage simple lexemes, compounds and multi-word expressions.
	Stem	Abstract form of a word that is obtained by removing its inflectional endings and that functions as the base form for morphological processes or for an entry.
	Affix	A bound morpheme with an abstract meaning that can only be used when combined with another word or root but also can be used as an entry in a dictionary.
	Phrase	A group of words (or possibly a single word) forming a syntactic constituent with a single grammatical function.
Orthography		Representing a language or the sounds of language by written symbols in a dictionary. **Possible values are:**
	Spelling Variants	Orthographic variations with or without preferred spelling-information.
	Hyphenated Spelling	Any spelling-variation that is divided or connected with a hyphen.
	Syllabified Spelling	An analytical procedure for dividing a phonological representation into a well-defined sequence of syllables.
	Citation-form	Also known as 'lexical-citation', the form of a word that heads a lexical entry and is alphabetized in a dictionary. This gives a complete surface-form of bound roots that will be printed as the head-word in the final printout.
Phonology		The patterns and principles behind the sound-system of the project-language. **Possible values are:**
	Transcription	Rules for mapping spoken words onto written forms as prescribed by the orthography of the given language.
	IPA Transcription	Transcription in the International Phonetic Alphabet.
	CV pattern	Transcription in terms of consonant-vowel combinations.
	Constituent Structure	Segmentation into phonetic constituents.
	Intonation	Stress-marking, constituent-length etc.

Morphology		Studies of the rules for forming admissible individual words in a dictionary. **Possible values are:**
	Stem	Deep or surface stem to be included in the dictionary.
	Stem Allomorphy	Allomorphy in which the variation in the phonological shape of a stem is conditioned by non-phonological factors.
	Segmentation	Analysis into morphological constituents such as affixes.
	Production rules	Governing the production of surface-forms on the basis of stems.
	Typology	Any classification of entries or morphological entities.
Morphosyntax		Any grammatical categories or linguistic units that have both morphological and syntactic properties. **Possible values are:**
	Part of Speech (POS)	A category assigned to a word based on its grammatical and semantic properties; syntactic class of the entry such as nouns, verbs, adjectives, etc.
	Inflection	Any inflectional or conjugational information for the entry.
	Countability	Pluralization properties of the entry and refers to the property of nouns, i.e. whether they have plural forms or not and whether they refer to countable or uncountable concepts.
	Gradability	Any comparative/superlative constructions of the entry. e.g. adjectival comparative / superlative constructions.
	Gender	Any morphosyntactic entity (depending on languages) to describe morphological forms that could be either masculine, feminine or neuter in an entry.
Syntax		The systematic, orderly arrangement of entries. **Possible values are:**
	Complementation	Syntactic subcategorization or the selection of obligatory arguments by a lexical head.
	Alternation	Alternative complementation-patterns or variations in the forms that realize linguistic units.
	Modification	Structural dependence of one grammatical unit upon another. e.g. adjectival modification patterns.
	Shallow Parsing	Segmentation into chunks.
	Deep Parsing	Finer grained analysis below chunk-level.
	Functional Parsing	Syntactic functions such as subject.
	Collocations	Significant juxtaposed entries/word-forms.
	Typology	Any classification, e.g. prepositional/phrasal verb.

Semantics		Elements related to the meaning of words, phrases etc. **Possible values are:**
	Sense distinction	One of zero to many meanings or concepts associated with a given head-word in a lexical entry such as polysemy and/or homonymy.
	Sense number	Where a lexeme has more than one sense, this code is used to mark, and number marks the beginning of each section that discusses a new sense. A sense-number to mark that a different part of speech is not used, and it is only used within a given part of speech (in this hierarchy).
	Ontological classification	Related concepts and conceptual relations.
	Gloss/Gloss (vernacular)	Informal description of the sense in natural language. This field is primarily for a monolingual dictionary. It can be used as a temporary place to record succinct glosses provided by native speakers.
	Definition	Representation of a concept by a descriptive statement which serves to differentiate it from related concepts, i.e., a formal description of the sense, e.g. as a 1st-order logic formula.
	Connotation	Any subjective cultural or emotional association that some word or phrase carries, in addition to the word's or phrase's explicit or literal meaning; non-denotational information such as pejorative.
	Idiom	Any set-expression in which two or more words are syntactically related but with a meaning like that of a single lexical unit; idiosyncratic use.
	Componential Features	Any formula or list containing a finite set of meaning-attributes.
	Cross-references	Any entry whose content links to other entries/word-forms to another entry in a lexical data-base.
	Semantic relations	Relations between entries or associated concepts.
	Preference	Characterization of the arguments in the semantic predicate.
Etymology		The word or words from which a head-word is derived, or to which it is related, and any information about the historical context (morphological, phonological, syntactic, semantic) of a lexical entry or word-form.
Usage		Pragmatic/sociolinguistic information and use of the head-word. **Possible values are:**
	Region	The region or sub-region where the resource was created, originated or used; e.g. dialect.

Style	Any particular use of the head-word or word-forms, e.g. slang.
Frequency	The virtual frequency of occurrence for the given tag and lemma for the given token in the current lexicon-entry.
GeoLocation	Defines any type of location information associated with the head-word such as location-data as postal code, country, village, town, city, region name or latitude, the longitude of the location, especially when the lexical data is first collected to form dialect- or language-maps. **Possible values/outputs are:**
Source	Used to indicate the name and village of the informant who provided the data in the current entry.
Language/Dialect Maps	Any display or projection of the lexical data on a map to form maps such as dialect-maps.

11. Conclusion

This brief overview of the study about designing a new dictionary model is intended to show that a modern dictionary for endangered languages in general and in Laz in specific is possible and necessary according to the new developments in Lexicology and Lexicography of the endangered languages and such a general new model of dictionary-making is also applicable to other endangered languages.

General but specifically important information about data-collection and tools necessary to be used in the making and compilation of a dictionary of Laz or any endangered language, or any language in general, is discussed. It is hoped that languages such as Laz can make use of these data and information for making a modern dictionary to serve its own community and the linguistic society and to revitalize the language better.

References

Aksoylu, K. (Ed.) (2016) *Lazca Deyimler ve Atasözleri Sözlüğü - Laz Dili ve Alfabesi, Alfabe Kullanımı ve Diyalektolojik Özelliklerle* (Genişletilmiş 2. Baskı ed.). Phoenix.

Anthony, L. (2017). AntPConc (Version 1.2.1) [Computer Software]. Tokyo, Japan: Waseda University. Retrieved from https://www.laurenceanthony.net/software/antpconc/

Anthony, L. (2020). AntConc (Version 3.5.9) [Computer Software]. Tokyo, Japan: Waseda University. Retrieved from https://www.laurenceanthony.net/software/antconc/

Atkins, B. T. S. (1996). *Bilingual Dictionaries: Past, Present and Future.* Paper presented at the EURALEX '96 International Congress on Lexicography, Göteborg University, Göteborg, Sweden.

Bucaklişi, İ. A., Uzunhasanoğlu, H., & Aleksiva, İ. (Eds.). (2007) Büyük Lazca Sözlük, Didi Lazuri Nenapuna, Lazca-Türkçe / Türkçe-Lazca (Vols. I). İstanbul: Çiviyazıları.

CLARIN. (2021). Common Language Resources and Technology Infrastructure (CLARIN), Concept Registry Browser. Retrieved from https://concepts.clarin.eu/ccr/browser/index.php

Coward, D. F., & Grimes, C. E. (2000). *Making Dictionaries, A Guide to Lexicography and the Multi-Dictionary Formatter.* Waxhaw, North Carolina: SIL International.

Gibbon, D. (2007). *How to Make a Dictionary: The architecture of a dictionary.* Unpublished Lecture Notes. B.A. British and American Studies / Basic Module 2 / Winter Semester 2007/2008. Bielefeld University. Bielefeld.

Gibbon, D. (2012). Resources for Technical Communication Systems. In A. Mehler, L. Romary, & D. Gibbon (Eds.), *Handbook of Technical Communication* (Vol. 8, pp. 255-285). Göttingen: De Gruyter Mouton.

Jackson, H. (2002). *Lexicography: An Introduction.* London: Routledge.

Joffe, D. (2021a). tlCorpus - Concordance Software (Version 2020 - 12.1.0.2968) [Computer Software]. Gordon's Bay, South Africa: TshwaneDJe Human Language Technology. Retrieved from https://tshwanedje.com/corpus/

Joffe, D. (2021b). TLex Suite: Dictionary Compilation Software (Version 2020 - 12.1.0.2968) [Computer Software]. Gordon's Bay, South Africa: TshwaneDJe Human Language Technology. Retrieved from https://tshwanedje.com/tshwanelex/

Kabadayı, M. (Ed.) (2001) Doğu Karadeniz Lehçeleri Karşılaştırmalı Sözlüğü (Deneme). İstanbul: Gelenek Yayınları.

Kojima, G. (2021). Temel Lazca-Türkçe Sözlük Taslağı. Retrieved from http://ayla7.free.fr/laz/

Kurdadze, R., Shonia, D., Tandilava, L., & Nizharadze, L. (Eds.). (2015) Georgian-Megrelian-Laz-Svan-English Dictionary. South Caucasus: Swiss Cooperation Office.

Kutscher, S. Lazuri Nena - The Language of the Laz. In (Draft) To appear in Rüdiger Benninghaus (ed.) (The Laz people).

Kutscher, S. (2010). When 'towards' means 'away from': the case of directional-ablative syncretism in the Ardeşen variety of Laz (South-Caucasian). *STUF - Language Typology and Universals, 63*(3), 252-271. doi:10.1524/stuf.2010.0021

Kutscher, S. (2011). On the Expression of Spatial Relations in Ardeşen-Laz. *Linguistic Discovery, 9*(2), 49-77. doi:http://dx.doi.org/10.1349/PS1.1537-0852.A.394

Laz-Enstitüsü. (2020). Lazca Sözlük. Retrieved from https://www.lazcasozluk.org/

Měchura, M. (2017, 19-21 September). Introducing Lexonomy: An Open-source Dictionary Writing and Publishing System. Paper presented at the Electronic Lexicography in the 21st Century: Lexicography from Scratch, Leiden, The Netherlands.

Moe, R., Simons, G., Warfel, K., Higby, D., & Cooper, A. (2010). Rapid Word Collection. Retrieved from http://rapidwords.net/

Mosel, U. (2006). Sketch Grammar. In J. Gippert, N. P. Himmelmann, & U. Mosel (Eds.), Essentials of Language Documentation (pp. 301 - 209). Berlin: Mouton de Gruyter.

Özkurt, M., Büyüklü, O., Alper, M., Demirok, Ö., Eren, Ö., Bakay, Ö., & Balcı, S. (2018). Lazuri Doviguram/ Lazca Öğreniyorum: Yeni Başlayanlar İçin Lazca Ders Kitabı (İ. A. Bucaklişi Ed.). Istanbul: Laz Enstitüsü.

Richardson, A. L. (2019). Developing a Talking Dictionary for a Morphologically Complex Language: The Case of Laz. (MA). Boğaziçi University, Istanbul.

Roberts, J. R., Hedinger, R., & Gravina, R. (2014). Dictionary Making: European Training Programme, ART - Dictionary.

Scott, M. (2020). WordSmith Tools (Version 8.0) [Computer Software]. Stroud: Lexical Analysis Software. Retrieved from https://lexically.net/Lexical AnalysisSoftware/index.html

SIL-International. (2021). FLEx (FieldWorks Language Explorer) (Version 9.0.16 / Version Date: March 3, 2021) [Computer Software]. Dallas, USA: SIL International. Retrieved from https://software.sil.org/fieldworks/

TDK. (Ed.) (2011) Türk Dil Kurumu - Türkçe Sözlük (11th ed.). Ankara: TDK - Türk Dil Kurumu.

Thieberger, N. (2011). Building a Lexical Database with Multiple Outputs: Examples from Legacy Data and from Multimodal Fieldwork. International Journal of Lexicography, 24(4), 463-472. doi:10.1093/ijl/ecr027

Warner, N., Butler, L., & Luna-Costillas, Q. (2006). Making a Dictionary for Community Use in Language Revitalization: The Case of Mutsun. International Journal of Lexicography, 19(3), 257-285. doi:10.1093/ijl/ecl014

Wittenburg, P., Gibbon, D., & Peters, W. (2001). Metadata Elements for Lexicon Descriptions. ISLE Metadata Initiative (IMDI), PART 1 C, Metadata Elements for Lexicon Descriptions, Draft Proposal Version 1.0, IMDI Technical Report. Retrieved from MPI, Nijmegen: https://www.mpi.nl/ISLE/documents/draft/ISLE_Lexicon_1.0.pdf

Yaman, H. (2019). Lazca Ürünler ve Lazca Üzerine Yapılan Çalışmalar Bibliyografyası. Tehlikedeki Diller Dergisi / Journal of Endangered Languages (15 / Summer).

Měchura, M. (2017, 19-21 September). Introducing Lexonomy: An Open-source Dictionary Writing and Publishing System. Paper presented at the Electronic Lexicography in the 21st Century: Lexicography from Scratch, Leiden, The Netherlands.

Moe, R., Simons, G., Warfel, K., Higby, D., & Cooper, A. (2010). Rapid Word Collection. Retrieved from http://rapidwords.net/

Mosel, U. (2006). Sketch Grammar. In J. Gippert, N. P. Himmelmann, & U. Mosel (Eds.), Essentials of Language Documentation (pp. 301 - 209). Berlin: Mouton de Gruyter.

Özkurt, M., Büyüklü, O., Alper, M., Demirok, Ö., Eren, Ö., Bakay, Ö., & Balcı, S. (2018). Lazuri Doviguram/ Lazca Öğreniyorum: Yeni Başlayanlar İçin Lazca Ders Kitabı (İ. A. Bucaklişi Ed.). Istanbul: Laz Enstitüsü.

Richardson, A. L. (2019). Developing a Talking Dictionary for a Morphologically Complex Language: The Case of Laz. (MA). Boğaziçi University, Istanbul.

Roberts, J. R., Hedinger, R., & Gravina, R. (2014). Dictionary Making: European Training Programme, ART - Dictionary.

Scott, M. (2020). WordSmith Tools (Version 8.0) [Computer Software]. Stroud: Lexical Analysis Software. Retrieved from https://lexically.net/Lexical AnalysisSoftware/index.html

SIL-International. (2021). FLEx (FieldWorks Language Explorer) (Version 9.0.16 / Version Date: March 3, 2021) [Computer Software]. Dallas, USA: SIL International. Retrieved from https://software.sil.org/fieldworks/

TDK. (Ed.) (2011) Türk Dil Kurumu - Türkçe Sözlük (11th ed.). Ankara: TDK - Türk Dil Kurumu.

Thieberger, N. (2011). Building a Lexical Database with Multiple Outputs: Examples from Legacy Data and from Multimodal Fieldwork. International Journal of Lexicography, 24(4), 463-472. doi:10.1093/ijl/ecr027

Warner, N., Butler, L., & Luna-Costillas, Q. (2006). Making a Dictionary for Community Use in Language Revitalization: The Case of Mutsun. International Journal of Lexicography, 19(3), 257-285. doi:10.1093/ijl/ecl014

Wittenburg, P., Gibbon, D., & Peters, W. (2001). Metadata Elements for Lexicon Descriptions. ISLE Metadata Initiative (IMDI), PART 1 C, Metadata Elements for Lexicon Descriptions, Draft Proposal Version 1.0, IMDI Technical Report. Retrieved from MPI, Nijmegen: https://www.mpi.nl/ISLE/documents/draft/ISLE_Lexicon_1.0.pdf

Yaman, H. (2019). Lazca Ürünler ve Lazca Üzerine Yapılan Çalışmalar Bibliyografyası. Tehlikedeki Diller Dergisi / Journal of Endangered Languages (15 / Summer).

Chapter 7

Speaking Lazuri Beautifully: Discourses on Lazuri as an Endangered Language

Gülşah Türk-Yiğitalp
Universitat Autònoma de Barcelona, Spain

Abstract

While the role of material factors, including language-policies, migration, or urbanisation, is often scrutinised to understand phenomena such as language-shift and language-endangerment, the discourse around languages and how this shapes speaker-agency receives less focus, which is also the case with Lazuri. The analysis of material factors alone is not sufficient for a full grasp of the language-behaviour of Lazuri speakers. For a better understanding, the conceptual framework of language-ideologies (i.e., beliefs about a language and its speakers which rationalise and legitimise certain linguistic practices; Schieffelin et al., 1998; Kroskrity, 2000) proves useful for its focus on discourse and how it could shape social reality. Ideologies of language in language-loss and endangerment-discourses deserve particular attention to understand how people make sense of the changes in language-use. Through interviews with individuals from Lazuri speaking families and observations in Istanbul, Rize and Artvin between December 2016 and March 2017, I explored what it means to speak Lazuri, Turkish and other languages and how people responded to the phenomenon of language-endangerment. This chapter mainly focuses on the notions of authenticity, purism, and monolingualism. I claim that these notions, often reproduced in public and scholarly discourse, negatively influence linguistic practices and attitudes toward Lazuri and may even discourage language-use. This chapter does not try to depict an 'objective' sociolinguistic reality detached from people's perceptions and their narratives. On the contrary, it approaches the study of language in society 'not only as what people [do] with language, but also what they believe[d] and [feel] about language, and how both are part of larger structures of power' (Cavanaugh, 2020, p. 51). While tangible factors such as oppressive language policies, migration and urbanization have been shown to shape language use, beliefs about what it means to be competent in a language and speak a language well, and whose responsibility it is to transmit a language influence linguistic practices as well. These ideologies of language oftentimes stem from the same sociopolitical power dynamics that also introduce the oppressive language policies. While it is more common to investigate the way language policies have influenced language use, fewer studies analyze how such ideologies of language have been internalized by minoritized language speakers and how they shape evaluations of linguistic behavior. After introducing the topic and laying out its conceptual basis, the chapter will paint a picture of the fieldwork-experience, which has provided the narratives from which this chapter benefits. By presenting examples of narratives and observations from the fieldwork, the following sections will discuss how the beliefs about what a language is and who counts as a speaker inform linguistic practices and attitudes towards language-use. The chapter will conclude with suggestions for a more constructive discourse on linguistic practices.

Keywords: *Language ideologies, authenticity, discourse of language endangerment, agency*

***

1. Introduction

Language-endangerment discourse has recently been criticised for its essentialising approach to communication among people and the dynamics of change in such communication (Duchêne & Heller, 2007; Hill, 2002; Koreinik, 2011; Moore, Pietikäinen & Blommaert, 2010). The criticism is directed at adopting a metaphor of the ecosystem and referring to languages as endangered or extinct. Such discourse masks sociopolitical processes through which linguistic hierarchies are (re)produced and presents the issue as a natural phenomenon without much emphasis on the structures in place and on the agency of speakers. Due to the danger of language-extinction, preservation and protection of languages are expected, which necessitates defining the contours of a language and what counts as the real and 'authentic'. This approach to language, then, assumes it to be a static and bounded entity in itself. However, the recent scholarship on language-use points out the dynamism in people's linguistic practices. Instead of treating languages as separate objects and something people 'have', they treat it as an act, something people 'do'. Therefore, concepts such as linguistic repertoire (Busch, 2012), languaging (Makoni & Pennycook, 2007) and translanguaging (Wei, 2018) are commonly used in the literature to refer to how people communicate instead of the more limiting terms such as mother-tongue, bilingualism or multilingualism.

Various studies have reported that Lazuri use is declining (Hann & Bellér-Hann, 2000; Haznedar, 2018; Kutscher, 2008). Furthermore, the UNESCO Atlas of the World's Languages in Danger designated Lazuri as an endangered language (Moseley, 2010). In such a context and in light of the above-critique of endangerment-discourse, this chapter questions what it means for its speakers that Lazuri is an endangered language and how they make sense of the process of 'language-loss' or 'language-endangerment.' The following section will provide a conceptual framework in which I lay out the common conceptions about language-use that shape language-endangerment discourse. Then, I will present information about the data-collection methods and the resulting corpus of data informing this chapter. Finally, I offer an analysis of the data through the concepts laid out in the section on theory. Here I try to demonstrate that internalised beliefs beneath the common discourses of language-loss and endangerment neither sufficiently reflect the complex reality of linguistic practices of Lazuri speakers nor encourage the younger speakers to make use of their diverse linguistic resources. I conclude with final remarks about the study and suggestions on how to approach linguistic practices, particularly in the context of minoritised languages.

2. Ideologies of language

The framework I adopt to analyse the narratives in this study is that of language-ideologies (i.e., socially embedded ideas or beliefs about language(s), their speakers, and communication in general; Schieffelin, Woolard, & Kroskrity, 1998). These ideologies include ways of thinking about the meaning and value of linguistic and communicative acts, thus forming a hierarchy of languages (Blommaert & Jie, 2010). This process also leads to a ranking of the speakers with whom languages are 'indexed' (Silverstein, 2003). While language-ideologies are a basis, 'underlying conceptual frames,' (Woolard, 2016, p. 16) to think about and evaluate linguistic practices, they materialise in discourse when an account or a representation of linguistic practices is provided. As conceptual frameworks about language, these beliefs can influence individuals' and/or communities' linguistic practices (Howard, 2012).

Discourses of language-shift or change in the context of minoritised languages, particularly the discourse of endangerment (Duchêne & Heller, 2007), are based on specific ideologies of language. Language-endangerment discourse, for instance, legitimises itself through the counting of languages and speakers (Hill, 2002; Moore et al., 2010). Therefore, it is based on an ideology of languages as 'separate and enumerable categories' (Makoni & Pennycook, 2007, p. 2) and the taken-for-granted notion of the native or the authentic speaker.

For a language to be named and delimited as a category, it needs to have established boundaries, rendering more complex and 'mixed' linguistic practices as 'non-languages' (Makoni & Pennycook, 2007). Similarly, determining whether a person is a speaker of a language requires defining a category of native or authentic speaker. Nativeness and authenticity depend on perceived links to a community and a territory. Therefore, an authentic speaker is understood to be local and natural, and thus representative of a community (Woolard, 2016). This ideal image of the authentic speaker also involves a 'high' or 'complete' proficiency in the language which is not 'contaminated' (O'Rourke & Ramallo, 2011), that is, not influenced by other, possibly dominant, languages. Therefore, particularly in the context of minoritised languages, ideologies of purism (Dorian, 1994; Jaffe, 2007; Woolard, 2016) and correctness define who the legitimate native speaker of the language is.

Along with being authentic and speaking a pure form of the language, an ideal speaker of an endangered/minoritised language is imagined as monolingual. This is both because of the notion discussed above suggesting that one language corresponds to one community and one territory, and also because monolingualism possibly implies a 'pre-language-contact' (Moore et al., 2010) speaker, who, for the reasons above, has a pure, unmixed language-use. Finding a monolingual speaker of a minoritised language is indeed ever harder, and more diverse linguistic repertoires are the current reality. However, even bi/multilingualism in its dominant conceptualisation is determined by the 'monolingual norm' (Jaffe, 2007), leading bilingualism to be understood as 'parallel monolingualisms' (Heller, 2006). Quite often, however, real-life bilingualism is not 'balanced' and involves an 'uneven mixture of codes, practices and competencies' (Jaffe, 2007, p. 51). This leads to a common understanding of bilingualism as a deficit, which leads to the conviction that the first language is an obstacle to learning (usually) the dominant language or vice versa (p. 52).

In short, ideologies of authenticity, purism, and monolingualism (or bilingualism as separate monolingualisms) are commonly (re)produced in discourses of endangerment and revitalisation-movements in the context of minoritised languages. Consequently, these ideologies do not only shape interpretations and evaluations of linguistic practices but could also direct the practices themselves. While this paper will not expand on the roots of these ideologies, they have been shown to take hold in modernity and thrived with nationalism (Bauman & Briggs, 2003). The role of the ideology of purism in Turkish modernization and nationalism has also been discussed before (Bayar, 2011; Çolak, 2004).

3. Data and methods

The data analysed in this chapter comprise 16 hours of recorded semi-structured in-depth interviews, field-notes from observations, and informal exchanges collected in various locations in Istanbul, in Pazar, Ardeşen and Fındıklı towns of Rize, and in Arhavi and Hopa towns of Artvin between December 2016 and March 2017. I conducted the study as part of my Master's thesis. For the data-analysis, I initially took note of any themes and patterns that I recognised across all data-sets including interviews, informal exchanges, and field-notes. For instance, Lazuri was often associated with the villages, the elderly, and the past in the interviews, thus discursively being distanced from everyday life. Similarly, field-notes of observations and informal exchanges during fieldwork pointed to the relative absence of Lazuri in public sphere and constant advice from locals about where to find genuine speakers of the language. Once I finished transcribing the interviews, I coded them with these themes using MAXQDA. After finalising the initial coding, I went through the interviews again to find examples falling into one of these established codes. I used the field-notes and informal exchanges to contextualise and support the findings from the interview-data.

I met my first informants through acquaintances who are Laz activists, and I was introduced to the following participants of the study through a snowball-technique. A few interviews in Istanbul were with single individuals introduced to me by acquaintances, and the rest volunteered during my regular visits to an association for a Laz town. During my visits to this association, I had informal exchanges with those attending events there. I was also invited to some of the music and dance-events they organised. For the interviews in Pazar, Ardeşen, Fındıklı, Arhavi, and Hopa, I stayed in each town for a few days spending the time left from the interviews walking around and having informal chats with the locals. I recorded a total of 22 interviews with individuals from various backgrounds who were all raised in Lazuri-speaking families. Lazuri-proficiency was not a criterion for participation in the study.

The interviews were predominantly in Turkish. Using the dominant language as the medium of interviews in the context of such a minoritised language runs the risk of reproducing the power-relations in society that led to the current language-situation. However, apart from two female participants in their eighties, all others interviewed stated that they were more comfortable explaining themselves in Turkish. The Lazuri classes for beginners that I had taken before the fieldwork helped me follow when people mentioned a phrase or a word in the language. When talking to those participants who casually expressed themselves through one or the other language, I asked for clarifications, or others present with us assisted in translation. Despite all, I acknowledge that my assumed position as an 'outsider' researcher might have duplicated inevitable tensions regarding language-use for some of the informants.

One challenge of the research, which is closely related to the topic of this chapter, was how people perceived its purpose. Retrospectively, I realise that this also connects to how I formulated my research-topic while explaining it to potential participants. Whenever I introduced myself as working on Lazuri or Lazuri-use, people started listing 'experts' or 'better speakers' of the language. They believed I had to go to the villages and talk to old women to learn about Lazuri. Even when I made it clear that I was interested in any narratives regardless of their language-proficiency, interviews started with disclaimers warning me that they might not be the most knowledgeable person to whom I should be talking. The belief that there was some essential knowledge about language that only the 'real native speakers' could provide characterised many interviews.

The overarching questions of the research were as follows: a) how do individuals rationalise their current and past linguistic practices in Lazuri, Turkish, and any other languages they speak? How do they reflect on the places, instances, and people they associate Lazuri and Turkish with? b) what are their thoughts on language-loss in Lazuri and why? c) how do they evaluate the revitalisation-efforts for Lazuri and why? In some interviews, I did not need to ask many detailed questions; specific cues such as "your experiences with Lazuri" led people to construct long narratives and state their opinions on key-issues.

4. Analysis

The rich data from the interviews provided invaluable insight into how people make sense of changing linguistic practices and repertoires, how they remember and interpret the past, how these interpretations shape family language policies and individuals' language-choices in the present, and how these might project into the future. While there were some striking similarities in most narratives, different practices and discourses seemed to be shaped by intersectional factors such as gender, socio-economic status, and world-view, along with various affordances these bring. However, some ideologies of language proved to be pervasive, and thus will be the focus of this chapter. These are the ideologies of authenticity, purism, and monolingualism, as explained above.

While commenting on language-change or 'loss' or evaluating their own or others' language use and proficiency, most interviewees adopted a discourse in which languages are things beyond the agency of their speakers. They also treated phenomena such as language contact, borrowing and mixing as detrimental, assumed linguistic practices to be homogenous within generations, and evaluated language-proficiency against an idealised native speaker. However, everyday language-use depicted in people's stories was much more complex and dynamic than it sounded to be in those evaluations and commentary. This does not necessarily mean that people did not believe in the validity of their claims. On the contrary, these were internalised ideas about how things should be and how people should act, which, in time, shaped people's stances and even behaviour. In the following sections, I will first present a general depiction of language-loss/endangerment provided in the interviews and then analyse the beliefs beneath such evaluations. Even though the perceptions of authenticity, purism, and bi/monolingualism are quite intertwined, I will discuss each separately for the sake of analysis. After this analysis, I will discuss potential reasons for adopting these ideologies and their repercussions for future language-use.

4.1. Explaining language-loss

Language-practices of younger generations, particularly the urban ones, were the usual suspects behind language-loss. The young were claimed to rarely speak, be unable to speak or not know Lazuri. This claim was commonly put forward as a reason that will eventually cause Lazuri to 'disappear' or 'be lost'. Orhan's[1] depiction was one that was typical of what I heard from many others, and an observation referred to in earlier studies (Hann & Bellér-Hann, 2000; Kutscher, 2008) as well:

---

[1] All names are pseudonyms.

Extract 1 O: Orhan (62, Arhavi) G: Gülşah

1	O:	belirli yaşın üstündekiler artık Lazcayı	1	O:	now those over a certain age know
2		biliyor\ gençler Lazcayı bilmiyor\	2		Lazuri\ the young do not know Lazuri\
3	G:	hıhı	3	G:	uhuh
4	O:	şöyle söyleyeyim 40 yaşın altındakiler	4	O:	let me say it this way those under 40
5		köy haricinde yani kent içinde	5		years old except the village I mean
6		yaşayanlar tamamen (.) yani kullanamaz	6		those living in the city are (.) in such a
7		durumda\ anlıyorlar konuşmuyorlar\	7		state I mean that they cannot use it at
			8		all\ they understand it but do not speak
			9		it\

I will analyse what this rural/urban distinction (lines 5 & 6)[2] entails in more detail later, which will be an attempt to understand what Orhan, similar to many others, has in mind when they say Lazuri is not used in the city. However, I first aim to question Orhan's definitive account, which paints quite a homogenous picture. This comment came at the very beginning of our interview when Orhan explains to me the current situation of language-use. He starts by contrasting the older and younger generations and makes a clear-cut distinction between those who know it and those who do not. He then goes on to detail this black and white picture by citing the exception of villages. Even though he says the urban population cannot use the language, he provides a caveat for that as well, namely that they understand the language but do not speak it. Therefore, he contradicts his initial definitive statement, but this is not necessarily a contradiction for him. Only having receptive skills in the language does not amount to the ideal language-proficiency he has in mind.

Most participants depicted the situation similarly, suggesting that Lazuri is not spoken anymore or that the young do not speak the language, more often than not nuancing this claim with the explanation that many actually understand the language. As interviews proceeded, it turned out that everyday linguistic practices were not as homogenous as they sounded to be in participants' comments on language-loss. Then, the reason why this claim remained valid for the participants even though they described to me many instances in which Lazuri is employed in successful communication among interlocutors of all ages, rural and urban alike? I argue that the answer is very much related to how people make sense of these varied linguistic practices, shaped by the ideologies of language analysed in the following sections.

---

[2] The analysis follows the line-numbers from the English version.

4.2. Authentic speakers and where to find them

In most interviews, there were evaluations of one's own or others' Lazuri-proficiency. The proficiency of younger generations was found to be somewhat lacking and weak, as illustrated in Extract 1. Most, though not all, of the younger informants reiterated such evaluations. People were often hesitant to talk to me about Lazuri as they did not consider themselves an authority on such matters; they were just not knowledgeable enough about the language. Aynur, for instance, starts the interview with a disclaimer followed by a burst of nervous laughter:

Extract 2 A: Aynur (28, Istanbul)

1	A:	çok belki bilgilendirme olmaz	1	A:	it may not be that informative maybe but
2		belki ama genç nesilden tecrübe\	2		experience from the young generation\
3		((gergin gülüyor))	3		((laughs nervously))

It has been common, though increasingly questioned, in language-studies to look for informants who can represent the language in its 'purest' form, which is to say the authentic speaker (Bucholtz, 2003; Eckert, 2003). Even though I was not after such language-production for my study, my interest in Lazuri raised questions among participants about who would be the authority to talk about it. Since there was an assumed lack or weakness in how young people used the language, an ideal speaker of Lazuri was usually brought up for comparison. Such evaluations of insufficient proficiency or concerns over linguistic authority seemed to be informed by ideologies of purism and authenticity. This was because those ideal speakers were either old women or those who have always lived in the 'home-town' or in remote villages, all sharing the quality of not having had much 'outside' contact. This had repercussions for discursive tropes of both the authenticity and the purity of language, detailed in the next section.

4.3. Staying local

In her work on linguistic authority, Woolard (2016) differentiates between authenticity and anonymity of languages and argues that the value of national languages is attributed to their anonymity. In other words, one who speaks the national language is expected to sound like 'from nowhere' (p. 25), not including any features in their language that would index locality. Authenticity, on the other hand, she claims, 'has become the special preserve of minority languages and speakers' who attain their value from being 'local' (p. 23). Being local indeed meant better Lazuri-speakerhood in the interviews and imbued people with linguistic authority. In her answer to my question on the future use of Lazuri, Aynur made such a connection:

Extract 3 A: Aynur (28, Istanbul) G: Gülşah

1	G:	peki sence hani bu değişiyor mu/ bu nesil	1	G:	well do you think I mean this is changing/
2		çocuklarına öğretir:: mi/ hani bu değişir	2		would this generation teach:: their kids/ I
3		mi acaba/ yoksa yine ailelerinizin yaptığı	3		mean would this change/ or does it seem like
4		gibi mi/ devam edicek	4		it would go on like your parents did/
5	A:	bence nesil daha kötüye gidiyor gibime	5	A:	I think [this] generation is getting worse I
6		geliyor yani <u>unutma</u> anlamında bir de- he	6		mean in terms of <u>forgetting</u> and- well maybe
7		belki orada memlekette kalanlar hani (.)	7		those who have stayed there in the hometown
8		yaşatabilir ama dışarıya:: giden insan bir	8		I mean (.) could make it live but someone
9		şekilde köreltiyor lazcasını ister ya da	9		who goes outsi::de [leaves] somehow gets
10		istemez o yüzden hmmm bizden sonraki	10		rusty in Lazuri unavoidably that's why umm
11		nesle ne kadar yansır- ki/ bizim mesela	11		how much could it reflect on the generation
12		annemin nes- anne babamın nesline	12		after us- for our [generation] for instance my
13		baktığında dışarda olan kuzenlerimle de	13		mother's gen- when you look at my parents'
14		kıyasladığımda onlarda mesela şu anda	14		generation when I also compare it to my
15		Lazca sıfıra yakın yani ki/ biz de bu sefer	15		cousins who are outside [have left] for them
16		biz de dışarıdayız hani baktığında bize de	16		right now Lazuri is almost zero and/ we are
17		aynı şey olur >belki işte memlekette	17		now also outside so when you look at it
18		kalan kesim için< hani bence devam eder	18		maybe the same thing will happen to us as
19		ama hmm yani (.) dışarıya çıkınca (.)	19		well >maybe for the ones staying in the
20		unutuluyor ister istemez yani Lazca	20		hometown< I think it will go on but hmm I
21		konuşmuyorsun çocuğuna da yansıyor	21		mean (.) when you leave (.) it is forgotten
22		yani	22		unavoidably I mean you don't speak Lazuri
			23		and this is also reflected on your child

For Aynur, the power to make the language live lies with the Lazuri-speakers who have not left their home-town and stayed local. Nevertheless, those who are 'outside' like her are represented as not having agency over their own linguistic practices. The words and phrases she uses such as 'unavoidably' (lines 10 & 22) (the literal translation of the Turkish phrase is 'whether you want it or not'), 'somehow' (line 9) and 'happen to us' (line 18) point to such lack of agency for those who have lost their authenticity for 'wandering beyond [their] natural habitat and being subjected to conscious, therefore unnatural social influences' (Woolard, 2016, p. 23). However, in two instances (lines 6 & 19), she interrupts her line of thought and brings up those who have stayed in their 'natural location' as potential saviours of the language. Her constant comparison and juxtaposition of the urban and rural population shows that she indexes authentic, and thus ideal Lazuri-speakerhood, with staying local.

Speaking Lazuri Beautifully

Besides not having left the geographical location to which the language and the identity seem to belong, the authentic speaker is also the one to whom language comes naturally. When Okan referred to the villages in the highlands, which had been mentioned quite a few times in earlier interviews, I asked him to clarify:

Extract 4 O: Okan (24, Istanbul) G: Gülşah

1	G:	bunu bi' kişiden daha duydum hani daha	1	G:	I heard this from another person as well
2		yukarıki köylerdendi	2		you know s/he was from the upper
3		[o yüzden çok Lazca konuşuyor diye	3		villages
4	O:	[evet ben mesela şimdi alan	4		[so s/he speaks more Lazuri
5		araştırmasına gittiğim için daha iyi	5	O:	[yes I for instance observed that better
6		gözlemledim onu (.) özellikle	6		since I went to a field trip (.) especially in
7		çocuklarda (.) şimdi yaşlılar- yaşlı	7		kids (.) now the elderly- many old people
8		birçok insan biliyor zaten\ ama	8		already know it\ but when we look at kids
9		çocuklara baktığımızda mesela sayı	9		for example counting- counting in Lazuri
10		sayma- Lazca sayı sayma birçok çocuk	10		many kids can't do it you know a Laz kid\
11		yapamaz hani Laz çocuğu\ hani şey şey	11		well well there aren't any in our family
12		bizim ailede falan da yok mesela\ ama	12		for example\ but there is this village
13		işte o ııı *Gvandi* diye bir köy var	13		called umm *Gvandi* in Ardesen\ there I
14		Ardeşen'de\ orda işte karşılaştım	14		came across this the kids were really
15		çocuklar baya Lazca sayı sayıyordu ve	15		counting in Lazuri and it is not that
16		bunu hani bunun bilinci- kimlik	16		someone who has the awareness-
17		meselesinin bilincinde olan birisi sen	17		someone who has the identity awareness
18		bunu öğren diye <u>öğretmemiş</u> yani çocuk	18		<u>taught</u> them like you learn this I mean the
19		zaten öğrenmiş orada\ orada daha çok ııı	19		kid had already learnt it there\ it is
20		kapalı bir toplum olduğundan aslında\	20		because there is more of a umm closed
21		çünkü otuz kırk kilometre şehirden uzak\	21		community actually\ because it is thirty
22		şehre haftada bir kez iniyor belki hiç	22		forty kilometers from the city\ they go
23		inmiyorlar\ çocuklar oradaki okula	23		down to the city once a week maybe
24		gidiyor felan\ ondan kaynaklandığını	24		never\ the kids go to the school there and
25		düşünüyorum\	25		all\ I think it is because of that\

Here Okan not only links the ability of the children to count in Lazuri to their relatively isolated life in the village but offers an interesting explanation about how they are able to do so. Juxtaposing the Lazuri-performance of the kids in those remote villages with those who were deliberately taught with an awareness of a distinct identity, Okan attributed a kind of naturalness and thus authenticity to the Lazuri spoken in the village. From the tone of surprise in his voice, it was clear that he was in awe of such language-use as opposed to the language acquired by other, inauthentic means. These children in the upper villages were praised by others for their natural fluency as well. In a group-interview with several women at a tailor's shop, a young woman also mentioned these villages, which led to the co-construction of the depiction of an ideal speaker:

Extract 5 GK/YW: Young woman (20s, Ardeşen) R: Remziye (39, Ardeşen) Z: Zeliha (80s, Ardeşen)

```
1   GK:   bazı köylerde hiç Türkçe bilmiyorlar\      1    YW:   I mean in some villages they don't know
2         sadece lazca biliyorlar\                    2          any Turkish they only know Lazuri\
3   Z:    [he he köylerde- yüksek köylerde            3    Z:    [yeah yeah in villages- in higher villages
4         türkçe bilmiyolar hep lazca konuşurlar      4          they don't know Turkish they always
5         çocuklar\                                   5          speak Lazuri the kids\
6   R:    [çocuklar bile (.) yani Lazca öyle güzel    6    R:    [even the kids (.) I mean speak Lazuri so
7         konuşuyorlar\                               7          beautifully\
8   GK:   =((hayret içinde)) böyle 5 yaşında          8    YW:   =((amazed)) I mean a 5-year-old kid
9         çocuk bülbül gibi konuşuyor\ çok            9          speaks like a nightingale\ really
10        güzel\ (.) sonra zamanla okula             10          beautiful\ (.) then in time when s/he
11        başlayınca mecbur öğreniyor yani           11          starts school s/he inevitably learns I
12        Türkçeyi de/                               12          mean Turkish/
```

Note the emphasis on not knowing 'any' (line 2) Turkish and the confirmation Zeliha provides by asserting that they always speak the language (line 4 & 5), which clearly shows that the children are imagined to be monolingual. Remziye's use of 'even' (line 6) when the kids are mentioned points to the unexpectedness of such monolingual Lazuri-proficiency in children, which apparently is lost when the kid goes to school and becomes bilingual (lines 11 & 12). A highly positive depiction of these children's proficiency (lines 7, 9 & 10) implies that these women see monolingualism as a prerequisite of desired proficiency. However, the idiom that the young woman uses (line 9) brings about an additional feature of such proficiency. While speaking like a nightingale points to ease of language-use and connotes being beautiful and song-like, this allusion to a bird also invokes perceptions of naturalness. Therefore, quite similar to Okan's juxtaposition (Extract 4) between a kid who is deliberately taught and the one who has acquired the language naturally, the women here also painted a picture of an authentic monolingual villager who is a natural speaker of Lazuri.

4.4. Pure Lazuri

Various references to these apparently 'good' speakers of the language who stayed local, even isolated, and to whom language comes naturally raise the question about what it means to speak Lazuri well. Almost all comments on one's proficiency in Lazuri included references to Turkish, thus showing how beliefs about 'proper' Turkish use have influenced beliefs about 'proper' Lazuri use. These references also represented the ways people made sense of being

Speaking Lazuri Beautifully

bilingual or having a linguistic repertoire made up of elements from more than one named language. Phenomena such as code-switching or language-mixing were cited as signs of assumed weak command of language. While such impure practices pointed to the 'loss of language' at the individual level, there were also references to 'loanwords' from Turkish or probably from Arabic or Persian. These loanwords were believed to prove that the community has already lost some of the language and replaced the original Lazuri ones. For instance, when I asked him whether he prefers to speak to anyone more in Lazuri than Turkish, Ahmet explained:

Extract 6 A: Ahmet (50, Istanbul)

1	A:	bazen Lazca konuşuyoruz tabii\ devamlı	1	A:	sometimes we speak Lazuri of course\
2		konuşmasak bile konuşuyoruz çünkü- (.)	2		even though not all the time because- (.)
3		etrafımızda (.) herkes Laz olsa Lazca	3		around us (.) if everyone were Laz you
4		konuşursun\ ama Lazcanın içinde çok	4		would speak Lazuri\ but there are also
5		Türkçe kelimeler de var\ Lazca Türkçe	5		many Turkish words in Lazuri\ we speak
6		karışık konuşuyoruz\ <u>ful Lazca</u>	6		a mix of Lazuri and Turkish\ a <u>full</u>
7		konuşulmuyor hiçbir zaman\ belli bir	7		<u>Lazuri</u> is never spoken\ you speak to a
8		yere kadar konuşuyorsun\ çünkü çoğu	8		point\ because they don't know the
9		şeylerin Lazcasını bilmiyorlar Türkçeyi	9		Lazuri for many things they (.) include
10		(.) katıp da (.) konuşuyorlar\ onun için	10		Turkish and (.) speak it that way\ that's
11		ful Lazca konuşulmuyor yani\	11		why a full Lazuri is not spoken I mean\

His repeated reference to 'full Lazuri' (lines 6, 7 & 11) shows that he perceives their language-use to be short of ideal performance, and he relates this to the existence of Turkish words in their speech. His explanation for this is that people do not know the corresponding Lazuri words for certain concepts. Putting it this way could mean, indeed, that there exist some original Lazuri words out there, which authentic, natural speakers of the language apparently know, while those like Ahmet do not. This situation is consequently interpreted as evidence that the language is disappearing or being lost.

The widespread use of Turkish words in Lazuri utterances, which many provided as proof that they have limited proficiency, is exemplified by Birol when explaining to me how much Turkish an elderly woman from their village speaks. Even though his purpose here is to prove that the elderly speak very little Turkish and this is comprised chiefly of Turkish-origin words they employ while speaking in Lazuri, he presents an obvious example of how such a phenomenon is evaluated:

Extract 7 B: Birol (56, Istanbul)

1	B:	bu Hatice hala dediğimiz kadın	
2		Türkçe'yi yüzde on yüzde yirmi	
3		konuşabiliyor yani çok az (.) mesela	
4		Türkçe'de ne var/ şey mesela	
5		permatik nedir/ Türkçe\ Lazca'da	
6		permatik yok, şey nedir/ mesela örnek	
7		veriyorum (.) soba/ soba sobadır yani\	
8		o da sobayı biliyor işte (.) tamam mı/	
9		ondan sonra (.) odun farklı, odun	
10		odundur- odun *dişka*dır ama seyde::	
11		ııı Lazcayla Türkçe'nin benzeri >yani	
12		Türkçesi olmayan mesela< araba/	
13		araba arabadır bizde\ Lazca'da da	
14		arabadır\ sandalye:: sandalyedir-	
15		değil pardon sandalye *kuli* (.) derler	
16		ama araba (.) ya Türkçe'ye- şey	
17		Lazca'ya sığdıramazsın ki/ *cexunaşe*	
18		dersin olmaz değil mi/ [...] mesela	
19		Lazcayla benzeşeni söylüyorum	
20		>Türkçeyle Lazca'ya benzeşeni	
21		söylüyorum< mesela kitap kitaptır\	
22		takvim takvimdir\ televizyon	
23		televizyondur\ başka bir Lazcası <u>yok</u>	
24		var mı duydun mu hiç/ <u>yok, asla yok</u>	
25		(.) ama bu tabi az, çoğu değil yani o	
26		az kısım bu yüzde on benzer\	

1	B:	this woman we call aunt Hatice can speak
2		ten per cent twenty per cent Turkish I mean
3		very little (.) for example what do we have
4		in Turkish/ well for example what is
5		*permatik*/ Turkish\ there is no *permatik* in
6		Lazuri, what is/ for instance as an example
7		(.) *soba*/ *soba* is *soba* you know\ so she
8		knows *soba* (.) right/ then (.) *odun* is
9		different, *odun* is *odun*- *odun* is *dişka* but
10		in:: ermm the similar one in Lazuri and
11		Turkish >I mean ones that don't have a
12		Turkish [equivalent] for example< *araba*/
13		*araba* is *araba* for us\ it is *araba* in Lazuri
14		as well\ *sandalye*:: is *sandalye*- not sorry
15		*sandalye kuli* (.) it is called but *araba* (.) I
16		mean you can't fit it into Turkish- I mean
17		Lazuri/ call it *cexunaşe* wouldn't work
18		right/ [...] for example I am saying the
19		ones resembling Lazuri >I am saying the
20		ones resembling each other in Turkish and
21		Lazuri< for example *kitap* is *kitap*\ *takvim*
22		is *takvim*\ *televizyon* is *televizyon*\ there is
23		<u>no</u> other Lazuri word for these is there have
24		you ever heard one/ there is <u>not</u>, <u>definitely</u>
25		<u>not</u> (.) but this is of course a little, not most
26		of it I mean that little part ten per cent that
27		resembles\

Here, Birol lists many words he first describes as similar in Lazuri and Turkish but then rephrases this as words that do not exist in Lazuri (lines 10-12). He claims that *araba* [car] does not fit in Lazuri, meaning you cannot find a Lazuri word for this concept. He later interestingly offers a possible Lazuri word for it that he quickly dismisses as unsuitable (lines 17 & 18). Birol's reasoning here is quite hard to follow as he first defines these concepts as non-existent in the Lazuri lexicon and thus 'loanwords' from Turkish. However, he goes on to reject the word he coins instead of the word *araba* and argues that it is *araba* in Lazuri as well. This discursive move leads us to think he does not deem the existence of these 'loanwords' as an impurity. The following comment also shows he is indeed aware that such a phenomenon is common in Turkish as well and, thus, not necessarily a sign of limited proficiency in Lazuri. However, his final remarks contradict such an explanation:

Extract 8 B: Birol (56, Istanbul)

1	B:	nasıl ki Fransızca'da bazı kelimeleri biz	1	B:	just like some words in French we stole
2		ordan çaldık Türkçede götürüyoruz\ ama	2		them from there and are using in Turkish\
3		Fransızca o/ kelime, ama biz Türkçe diye	3		but that is French/ the word, but we have
4		yıllarca onu öyle götürdük\ Lazca'da da	4		used it like that for years as Turkish\ in
5		<u>Lazca</u> (.) çok az mm Türkçeyle karışan şey	5		Lazuri as well <u>Lazuri</u> (.) there are very
6		var (.) nesne veya vesaire işte\ Lazca <u>çok</u>	6		few erm things mixing with Turkish (.)
7		<u>derin</u> şarkılarımız var, ağıtlar var <u>tamamen</u>	7		objects or whatever\ in Lazuri we have
8		<u>Lazca</u>, Türkçe karışmadan\	8		such deep songs, elegies <u>completely in</u>
			9		<u>Lazuri</u>, without mixing any Turkish\

He compares the use of 'Turkish-origin' words while speaking Lazuri to using 'French-origin' words in Turkish. Despite the ambiguity of his position at first, these last remarks seem to indicate that he perceives the 'borrowing' to be a negative practice as he calls it 'stealing' (line 1) and then presents this all-too familiar argument on pure Lazuri (line 9). As an example of this pure Lazuri, Lazuri without any Turkish interference, he refers to elegies, traditional songs.

4.5. Mixing languages

Along with frequent references to loanwords as negative indicators of language-proficiency, depictions of bilingual practices as primarily subtractive pointed to a monolingual perception of language-use and the ideal speaker being monolingual. One common belief about bilingual proficiency was the inevitability of one language interfering with or even damaging the other. This belief has been one of the most cited reasons why families tend to avoid speaking Lazuri around their children. Remziye's narration of her experiences and her following comments on her family language policy illustrate such reasoning. She tells me they struggle when they go somewhere public, so I ask her to explain:

Extract 9 R: Remziye (39, Ardeşen) G: Gülşah

1	G:	nasıl bir zorlanma/		1	G:	what kind of struggle/
2	R:	ha Türkçe konuşurken/ yani takılıyorsun		2	R:	oh speaking Turkish/ I mean you get
3		işte:: Türkçeyi tam (.) olarak- Lazca alıştı		3		stuck you kno::w Turkish fully- (.) you
4		ya/ dil\ Türkçe zorlanıyorsun telaffuz		4		know the tongue is used to Lazuri/ you
5		açısından\ cümle kurmakta zorlanıyorsun\		5		struggle in Turkish in terms of
6		çok güzel Türkçe konuşamıyorsun-		6		pronunciation\ you struggle in forming
7		konuşuyorsun da/ güzel konuşamıyoruz		7		sentences\ you cannot speak a beautiful
8		yani ille ki Laz olduğumuz belli oluyor		8		Turkish- I mean you speak it/ but we
9		((gülüyor))		9		cannot speak it beautifully I mean in any
10	G:	olumsuz bir şey duyduğunuz ya da		10		case it is clear we are Laz ((laughs))
11		hissettiğiniz oldu mu/		11	G:	have you ever heard or felt something
12	R:	yok\ yok\ öyle bir şey\		12		negative/
				13	R:	no\ no\ nothing like that\

Even though she denies receiving any negative comments on her language-skills, in Remziye's evaluations of her Turkish proficiency, we find an image of a legitimate speaker whose Turkish is 'beautiful', a word that she also used to describe the pure Lazuri of the children in the remote village in Extract 5 (lines 6 & 7). While she attributes such beauty in language-performance to an imagined monolingual, her language-use falls short of it because she is 'used to' speaking another language (line 4), which, she believes, prevents her from pronouncing Turkish correctly or producing proper sentences. Consequently, this leads parents like Remziye to prefer their children remain monolingual in Turkish just as they praise the monolingual Lazuri-speaking children. There is a similar line of reasoning here, which argues that learning and habitually speaking one language will 'corrupt' the other. This belief led Remziye to refrain from talking to her children in Lazuri.

Extract 10 R: Remziye (39, Ardeşen) G: Gülşah

1	G:	peki siz onlarla niye Lazca konuşmayı tercih		1	G:	then why didn't you prefer talking to
2		etmediniz/		2		them in Lazuri/
3	R:	ya onlar alışmasınlar diye\ şimdiki gençler		3	R:	I mean so that they do not get used to it\
4		zaten çok ender konuşuyorlar\ anlasınlar		4		the young today already speak it rarely\ it
5		da:: Lazca konuşmasınlar\ çünkü		5		is better that they understand it but:: do
6		Türkçeleri bozuluyor\		6		not speak Lazuri\ because their Turkish
				7		gets corrupted\

While the earlier framing of the decrease in Lazuri-use through the assumed weakness in younger and urban generations' proficiency seems unrelated to this concern about Turkish proficiency, these two discourses indeed feed on the same perception of bilingualism. Bilingualism is understood as 'separate monolingualisms' (Jaffe, 2007), each having clearly demarcated boundaries. Therefore, any linguistic practice in which both Lazuri and Turkish are used interchangeably indicates inadequacy or even indexes other negative qualities. Irfan's comments are a case in point:

Extract 11 I: Irfan (47, Istanbul) G: Gülşah

1	I:	şimdi bizde Lazca Türkçe sahillerde
2		karışık konuşuluyor\ hani Türkçe
3		kelimeyi tam olarak öğrenemiyorlar\
4		Türkçe öğreneyim derken Lazcayı da
5		öğrenemiyorlar bu sefer\ ikisi de
6		yarım yamalak gidiyorlar\ doğru
7		dürüst ikisini de bilmiyor\ sahil
8		kesimine gittiğin zamanki konuşulan
9		Türkçe çok kaba\ Lazca da kaba\
10		Lazcanın o tatlı dili mesela yüksek
11		kesimlerde konuşuluyor\
12	G:	kabalık derken/ hani iyi konuşmamak
13		gibi mi nasıl bi' kabalık/
14	I:	=geldum diyo yani\ rizeye tseleyrum
15		diyo\ ha o zaten öyle öğrenmiş\
16		düzeltemiyor\ şimdi ne kadar- hiç-
17		kendi ailesinden koparıp farklı yerde
18		yaşaması lazım ki- ailede bu adam
19		anasıylan öyle konuşuyor ne bilsin ki/
20		bizde mesela oradan gelenler dikkat
21		ediyorsun hepsi (.) üniversite okusa
22		bile bazı kelimeleri- az kelime
23		biliyorlar\ bi' bölümü Türkçe
24		konuşuyor (.) bi' bölümü Lazca
25		konuşuyor\ Lazcanın tıkandığı yerde
26		Türkçeye çeviriyor\ Türkçe tıkandığı
27		yerde bilmediği kelimeleri Lazcaya
28		çeviriyor herkes her şeyi anladığı için\
29		bu sefer ikisinin karmasından bir dil
30		ortaya çıkmış gibi bişi oluyor\

1	I:	now Lazuri and Turkish is mixed when
2		speaking in the coast\ I mean they cannot
3		learn a Turkish word properly\ when they
4		try to learn Turkish then they cannot learn
5		Lazuri either\ they just go on partially in
6		both\ they don't know either properly\ when
7		you go to the coastal towns the Turkish
8		spoken there is really rough\ Lazuri is also
9		rough\ the sweet language of Lazuri is for
10		instance spoken in the higher lands\
11	G:	rough/ you mean like not speaking well or
12		what kind of rough/
13	I:	=s/he says 'geldum' you know\ says 'rizeye
14		tseleyrum' ((impersonates a stereotypical
15		pronunciation)) I mean s/he has already
16		learnt it that way\ cannot correct it\ now
17		how much- s/he has never- s/he has to be
18		separated from family and live somewhere
19		else so that- this man talks to his mother like
20		that how could he know/ for example those
21		coming from there you realize all (.) even if
22		they had university education some words-
23		they know few words\ some speak Turkish
24		(.) some speak Lazuri (.) when they get
25		stuck in Lazuri they switch to Turkish\
26		when they get stuck in Turkish they
27		translate the words they don't know into
28		Lazuri since everyone understands
29		everything\ then it is like a language out of
30		the mixture of both\

Irfan comments here on the linguistic competence of those living on the coast. Coastal towns are where speakers of languages other than Lazuri would also reside. Turkish has long been a *lingua franca* and has also been required in various public institutions such as schools, hospitals, courts, and any other place where public officials or dominant Turkish speakers would be encountered. Therefore, Irfan highlights the assumed negative impact of language-contact and bilingualism by referring to the linguistic practices there. Mixing both languages, that is, employing elements from both Lazuri and

Turkish, is proof of partial competence (lines 5 & 6) for Irfan and this sounds 'rough'. He clearly contrasts this impure, mixed language-use, which sounds rough, with the 'sweet' Lazuri of the higher villages (lines 8-10). It was these villages that others also referred to in the earlier examples in which the monolingual pure Lazuri speakers were described to be natural and their Lazuri to be beautiful. It is worth noting that neither Irfan nor others claim that such mixed language-use hinders communication. Irfan points out that such 'mixed' practices are indeed understood by all parties involved in communication (lines 28 & 29). However, it is rather the impurity and hybrid identification that such mixing connotes that Irfan finds problematic.

5. Discussion

Numerous quotes like those discussed above depicted similar beliefs about what features a language and a native/legitimate speaker of that language should have. The authentic or genuine Lazuri-speaker is understood to be either an elder or a villager who naturally has the full knowledge of a pure language without loanwords. Their language-use does not show signs of language-contact, and they do not switch to Turkish or mix languages. Common references to Turkish and other languages indicate that these ideologies of authenticity, purism and monolingualism are indeed shaped both by individuals' social experiences of language-use and the public discourse in Turkey on language-use and language-learning. To put it differently, by socialising in the linguistic *habitus* (Bourdieu, 1991) in Turkey, Lazuri-speakers develop certain 'dispositions' regarding languages, which lead to quite similar beliefs about both Lazuri- and Turkish-use. This is a process that prompts many minority movements to adopt the discourse of the nation-state on language and identity (Jaffe, 1999; 2007). We see this, for instance, when the ideal speakers of Lazuri, depicted above, are monolingual, since a community is deemed to have a single language representing their identity. This is the Herderian understanding of the *Volk* with its single language being its natural expression (Bauman & Briggs, 2000, 2003), one of the basic premises of nationalist thought. Just as speaking Turkish has been equated with a legitimate Turkish identity, an authentic Laz identity corresponds to a natural Lazuri-monolingualism, a romantic ideal. Purism has a similar basis as well with the ever-present discussions on pure Turkish, purged of Arabic and Persian origin words in the earlier years of the Republic (Bayar, 2011; Çolak, 2004) to more recent panic on the corruption of the language through the use of primarily words of English origin.

The reproduction of the dominant discourse on languages in Turkey by the speakers of the minoritised languages, while evaluating their linguistic practices, is an intriguing process that this chapter illustrated. However, such deep-seated beliefs and the resulting discourse have the potential to discourage those with a limited repertoire in Lazuri, particularly younger speakers, from classifying themselves as legitimate speakers of the language. These also inhibit their attempts at communication because such discourse 'devalue[s] language contact phenomena, mixed usage and partial competencies' (Jaffe, 2007, p. 56; Woolard, 2016). Therefore, even in the absence of overt bans on minoritised languages and the encouragement by language-revitalisation movements, internalised beliefs and evaluations about proper language-use persist and inform linguistic practices not only in Turkish but in Lazuri as well. Not considering themselves Lazuri speakers, most of the younger people I interviewed devalued their partial and mixed Lazuri-use compared to the ideal proficiency of the elderly or the rural native speakers. The narrative of Yeliz, an 18-year-old high-school student, illustrates how this process might unfold and result in the familiar story of the youngster who 'understands but cannot speak':

Extract 12 Y: Yeliz (18, Ardeşen)

```
1   Y:  çocuk-ken mesela ben de Lazca        1   Y:  as a ch-ild for instance I also spoke
2       konuşuyordum\ kötü bir anı diye       2       Lazuri\ so you asked about a bad
3       sordunuz ya/ mesela ben (.) çocukken (.) 3       memory/ for example when I (.) was a
4       karşımdaki büyükler mesela Türkçe     4       child (.) when the adults in front of me
5       konuşuyorken (.) ben Lazca kelimeler  5       for example were speaking Turkish (.)
6       söylemeye çalışıyorken gülüyorlardı\  6       when I was trying to say Lazuri words
7       tam da konuşamadığım için gülüyorlardı 7       they were laughing\ they laughed
8       zaten\ orada kendimi kötü hissettim ve 8       because I couldn't speak it fully\ I felt
9       ondan sonra hiç Lazca konuşmayı       9       bad there and after that I never wanted
10      istemedim açıkçası |...| mesela ben  10       to speak Lazuri to be honest\ |...| I do
11      arkadaşımla konuşurken kelime- cümle 11       not form many words- sentences when
12      çok kullanmam sadece kelime olarak   12       talking to my friends I only use word[s]\
13      kullanırım\ dışarda da::- yok ya çok 13       and outsi::de- no actually I do not use it
14      kullanmıyorum\ ama çok iyi anlarım\ iç 14       much\ but I understand it really well\ I
15      ses olarak çok iyi konuşurum ama::   15       speak it really well internally bu::t there
16      dışarı vurma da bir sıkıntı var\      16       is a problem expressing it\
17  G:  kelime olarak genelde Lazca bildiğin 17   G:  what Lazuri words are there you usually
18      söylediğin ne var/                    18       know and say/
19  Y:  [çoğu kelimeyi biliyorum              19   Y:  [I know most words
20  G:  [sık kullandığın belki                20   G:  [you use often maybe
```

21	Y:	*mu ikum* napıyorsun *hay vore* buradayım	21	Y:	*mu ikum* how are you *hay vore* I'm here
22		falan\ ama çok cümle olmuyor\ benim	22		like that\ but not many sentences\ most
23		çoğu arkadaşım daha çok Lazca	23		of my friends speak more Lazuri bu::t
24		konuşuyor ama:: onlar hani- onlar	24		they you know- I don't speak it for they
25		konuşuyor diye ben konuşmam\ ben yine	25		speak it\ I still speak Turkish\ I want to
26		Türkçeyi konuşurum\ Türkçeyi daha iyi	26		know Turkish better but I think I also
27		bilmek isterim ama Lazcayı da	27		know how to speak Lazuri bu::t I just
28		konuşmayı bildiğimi düşünüyorum	28		think I cannot speak it\
29		ama:: sadece konuşamadığımı			
30		düşünüyorum\			

From the beginning of the interview, Yeliz depicted herself as a non-speaker. Therefore, it was a surprise to learn towards the end of the interview that she, in fact, had Lazuri in her repertoire. She remembers being laughed at while trying to speak Lazuri as a child and has come to believe that her incompetence made the adults laugh. While we may not know why the adults had laughed - adults might laugh at children's production of the minoritised language as it is usually not expected that the young speak the language (Jaffe, 1999), Yeliz interpreted this as proof that she could not speak correctly and that this was a laughing-matter (lines 7 & 8). Even though it is highly probable that there have been other reasons alienating her from Lazuri, she constructs her narrative around this memory, which she believes to be a legitimate reason for her reluctance. The following self-evaluation also indicates that what keeps her from speaking is less a matter of incompetence (lines 14 & 15) than of the anxiety of not meeting a standard. Here, what Yeliz is experiencing could be referred to as "linguistic insecurity" (Jaffe, 2007; Sallabank, 2013) or what has also been conceptualised as "heritage language anxiety" (Braun, 2012; Sevinç & Dewaele, 2018), which refers to the negative evaluations one has of their language-use particularly in the context of minoritised languages. Young people like Yeliz and many others in this study indeed had elements from more than one named language in their repertoire, mainly Turkish and Lazuri. However, in the contexts of such a minoritised language where the languages have long been oppressed and negative attitudes towards them have also been internalised, it is unrealistic to expect 'balanced' bilingualism. While many, in fact, have receptive bilingualism and would even be able to employ elements from both Lazuri and Turkish in communication, they instead tend not to speak the language at all as they fall short of the ideal of full competence in Laz(uri).

6. Conclusion

This chapter started with a critique of the discourse on endangered languages and questioned the ideologies of language feeding such discourse. Based on the premise that languages have clear boundaries overlapping with communities and that a particular authentic speaker of a language is the ideal speaker, discourse about endangerment does not help individuals, and communities for that matter, acknowledge their highly varied linguistic practices as valid. As I have portrayed in this chapter, ideologies of authenticity, purity, and monolingualism dominate the ways people make sense of their own and others' language-behaviour. These, in turn, discourage, rather than encourage, people to employ Lazuri in their communication.

Approaching languages from this perspective, deconstructing the notion of language as a bounded entity, surely does not mean that we ignore the effects of structural acts of domination on the speakers of specific languages, in this context, the speakers of Lazuri. Language-policy and planning indeed interferes with individuals' and communities' repertoires, forces them into monolingualism or a clearly separated bilingualism in politically defined language(s), harms communication between generations, and disadvantages individuals by devaluing or even banning their ways of using language. Since these have already been discussed by scholars before, this chapter has not focused on such aspects. Instead, this chapter has aimed to show that how people use language is not only determined by such material factors but also through internalised notions about what language is and how it should be used.

As a final note, I believe it is worth considering for both researchers and activists alike what the use of essentialism is for their work. 'Strategic essentialism' (Bucholtz, 2003; Guha & Spivak, 1988), that is, essentialising communities and languages for that matter to be able to form a common ground for social action, could be a tool to mobilise for advocacy and to address policy-makers to make structural changes. However, assumptions of such discourse do not correspond with the lived reality of people. Instead of reproducing the ideologies of purism and authenticity, which alienates mostly younger generations, acknowledging the more diverse uses of Lazuri along with other languages in one's repertoire would be a more productive path forward.

Symbols used in transcripts

ital	words/phrases in Lazuri	<u>word</u>	speaker emphasis
(.)	short pause	e::	lengthening of the preceding sound
[	overlap	((laughter))	non-verbal actions
=	quick change of turn	-	self interruption
/	rising intonation	> <	quick speech
\	falling intonation		

References

Bauman, R., & Briggs, C. L. (2000). Language philosophy as language ideology: John Locke and Johann Gottfried Herder. In P. V. Kroskrity (Ed.), *Regimes of language: Ideologies, polities, and identities* (pp. 139–204). School of American Research Press.

Bauman, R., & Briggs, C. L. (2003). *Voices of modernity: Language-ideologies and the politics of inequality*. New York: Cambridge University Press.

Bayar, Y. (2011). The trajectory of nation-building through language policies: The case of Turkey during the early Republic (1920-38). *Nations and Nationalism*, *17*(1), 108–128. https://doi.org/10.1111/j.1469-8129.2010.00484.x

Blommaert, J., & Jie, D. (2010). *Ethnographic fieldwork: A beginner's guide*. Bristol: Multilingual Matters.

Bourdieu, P. (1991). *Language and symbolic power*. Cambridge: Polity Press.

Braun, A. (2012). Language maintenance in trilingual families – a focus on grandparents. *International Journal of Multilingualism*, *9*(4), 423–436. https://doi.org/10.1080/14790718.2012.714384

Bucholtz, M. (2003). Sociolinguistic nostalgia and the authentication of identity. *Journal of Sociolinguistics*, *7*(3), 398–416. https://doi.org/10.1111/1467-9481.00232

Busch, B. (2012). The linguistic repertoire revisited. *Applied Linguistics*, *33*(5), 503–523. https://doi.org/10.1093/applin/ams056

Cavanaugh, J. R. (2020). Language ideology revisited. *International Journal of the Sociology of Language*, *2020*(263), 51–57. https://doi.org/10.1515/ijsl-2020-2082

Çolak, Y. (2004). Language policy and official ideology in early Republican Turkey. *Middle Eastern Studies*, *40*(6), 67–91.

Dorian, N. C. (1994). Purism vs. Compromise in language revitalization and language revival. *Language in Society*, *23*(4), 479–494.

Duchêne, A., & Heller, M. (Eds.). (2007). *Discourses of endangerment: Ideology and interest in the defence of languages*. London: Continuum.

Eckert, P. (2003). Elephants in the room. *Journal of Sociolinguistics*, *7*(3), 392–397. https://doi.org/10.1111/1467-9481.00231

Guha, R., & Spivak, G. C. (Eds.). (1988). *Selected Subaltern studies*. New York: Oxford University Press.

Hann, C., & Bellér-Hann, I. (2000). *Turkish region: State, market & social identities on the East Black Sea coast*. Oxford: Currey.

Haznedar, B. (2018). *Türkiye'de Lazcanın mevcut durumu*. Istanbul: Laz Enstitüsü.

Heller, M. (2006). *Linguistic minorities and modernity: A sociolinguistic ethnography*. London: Continuum.

Hill, J. H. (2002). 'Expert rhetorics' in advocacy for endangered languages: Who is listening, and what do they hear? *Journal of Linguistic Anthropology, 12*(2), 119-133. https://doi.org/10.1525/jlin.2002.12.2.119

Howard, K. M. (2012). 'I will be a person of two generations': Temporal perspectives on sociolinguistic change in Northern Thailand. *International Multilingual Research Journal, 6*(1), 64-78. https://doi.org/10.1080/19313 152.2012.639249

Jaffe, A. (1999). *Ideologies in action: Language politics on Corsica*. New York: Mouton de Gruyter.

Jaffe, A. (2007). Minority language movements. In M. Heller (Ed.), *Bilingualism: A social approach* (pp. 50-70). London: Palgrave Macmillan UK.

Koreinik, K. (2011). Agency lost in the discourse of language endangerment: Nominalisation in discourse about South Estonian. *Eesti Rakenduslingvistika Ühingu Aastaraamat. Estonian Papers in Applied Linguistics, 7*, 77-94. https://doi.org/10.5128/ERYa7.05

Kutscher, S. (2008). The language of the Laz in Turkey: Contact-induced change or gradual language loss? *Turkic Languages, 12*, 82-102.

Makoni, S., & Pennycook, A. (Eds.). (2007). *Disinventing and reconstituting languages*. Clevedon: Multilingual Matters.

Moore, R. E., Pietikäinen, S., & Blommaert, J. (2010). Numbers as the language of language endangerment. *Sociolinguistic Studies, 4*(1), 1-26. https://doi.org/10.1558/sols.v4i1.1

Moseley, C. (Ed.). (2010). *Atlas of the world's languages in danger* (3rd ed.). Paris: UNESCO Publishing. Retrieved from http://www.unesco.org/languages-atlas/

O'Rourke, B., & Ramallo, F. F. (2011). The native-non-native dichotomy in minority language contexts: Comparisons between Irish and Galician. *Language Problems and Language Planning, 35*(2), 139-159. https://doi.org/10.1075/lplp.35.2.03oro

Sallabank, J. (2013). *Attitudes to endangered languages: Identities and policies*. Cambridge: Cambridge University Press. https://doi.org/10.1017/CBO97811 39344166

Schieffelin, B. B., Woolard, K. A., & Kroskrity, P. V. (1998). *Language-ideologies: Practice and theory*. Oxford University Press.

Sevinç, Y., & Dewaele, J. M. (2018). Heritage language anxiety and majority language anxiety among Turkish immigrants in the Netherlands. *International Journal of Bilingualism, 22*(2), 159-179. https://doi.org/10.1177/1367006916661635

Silverstein, M. (2003). Indexical order and the dialectics of sociolinguistic life. *Language & Communication, 23*(3-4), 193–229. https://doi.org/10.1016/S0271-5309(03)00013-2

Wei, L. (2018). Translanguaging as a practical theory of language. *Applied Linguistics, 39*(1), 9–30. https://doi.org/10.1093/applin/amx039

Woolard, K. A. (2016). *Singular and plural: Ideologies of linguistic authority in 21st century Catalonia.* Oxford University Press.

Chapter 8

An Applied Linguistics Perspective on the Preservation of the Laz Language

Züleyha Ünlü
Tokat Gaziosmanpaşa University, Turkey

Abstract

The introduction to this edited volume has described the invaluable contributions made by distinguished scholars on the Laz language. Through the chapters, this book has presented the current status of Laz, documentation of the Laz language, linguistic variation of Laz, and literature and culture of Laz as well as discourses around the use of Laz. All these studies are essential in understanding the direction of the studies that have been undertaken around the Laz language as well as revealing what research-gaps exist to be filled by future studies. More importantly, all these studies contain invaluable findings for the education of Laz, on which this concluding section focuses. The current study conducted a small-scale, systematic review to reveal the lines of studies that have been conducted on the Laz language from an educational perspective in Turkey. This study investigated research on the Laz language from an educational perspective. The main purpose of the study is to identify 'critical points and also provide a wider perspective to the researchers in the field', particularly those who work in the field of applied linguistics (Lawson, Çakmak, Gündüz & Busher, 2015, p. 3).

To this end, this study utilized the method of systematic review in the collection of data. Systematic review examines literature to answer the specific research-questions (Turan & Akdağ-Çimen, 2019). As has been indicated by several others, systematic reviews aim to present what has been achieved by previous studies as well as to reveal points of conflict (Lawson et al., 2015; Turan & Akdağ-Çimen, 2019). The review showed that a variety of research on the Laz language has been conducted while, however, there is a lack of research on the pedagogy for the Laz language as well as the needs and experiences of the Laz community members within the mainstream educational contexts.

Keywords: *Lazuri, the education of Lazuri, educational needs, applied linguistics*

* * *

1. Introduction

The introduction to this edited volume has described the invaluable contributions made by distinguished scholars on the Laz language. Through the chapters, this book has presented the *current status of Laz, documentation of the Laz language, linguistic variation of Laz, and literature and culture of Laz as well as discourses around the use of Laz.*

The chapter by Haznedar and Bucaklişi on 'The c*urrent Status of the Laz Language'* presented findings from a large-scale study on the status of Laz. Using the data collected through 450 participants; the study examined the language-competence of participants, the use of Laz both at home and in the wider community and the extent to which Laz is transmitted from generation to generation. The findings showed the alarming extent to which Laz is endangered, which indicated the necessity of taking immediate action to preserve the Laz language.

The chapter by Demirok and Öztürk *'On the Significance of Laz for Theoretical Research in Linguistics"* focused on the case- and agreement-system, the classification-system for verbs, and the verbal spatial-marking system of the Laz language to present the genuine status of Laz in having typologically rare linguistic features, and the sheer number of notions it grammaticalizes.

The chapter by Kikvidze and Pachulia *'A Spotlight on the 'Lazian' Lexis: Evidence from a 19th-century Lexicographic Resource'* presented Demetrius Rudolph Peacock's "Vocabularies of Five West Caucasian Languages" collection to call for its evaluation within the new trends. This collection, being the first to present the vocabularies of five languages, is particularly important as it paves the way to compare and contrast the word structure of the Kartvelian languages.

The chapter by Eren examined the synchronic and dialectal variation in Laz from the perspective of language-complexity. Through a detailed analysis of reflexive constructions, the study showed that even though Laz is starting to display a decrease in morphological complexity, its syntactic complexity counterbalances this decrease.

The chapter by Şirin and Yaman *'Principles of Designing a New Dictionary Model for Endangered Languages: The case of Laz'* analysed and critiqued the existing dictionaries on Laz and presented the procedures to form a suitable

Laz dictionary for a variety of purposes. Through the description of such dictionary-making procedures, this chapter underlined the fact that dictionary-production is a significant component of language-revitalisation.

The chapter by Yüksel and Aleksiyeva *'Stories of Perseverance: Using the Lazuri Alboni for the Emergence of Literary Genres in a South Caucasian Endangered Language'* examined the Lazuri alphabet as well as existing literary work. The examination showed that there is a variety of written genres in Laz, which represents different dialectics of Laz as well as language-fluency and stylistic expressions. Additionally, the existing literary genres cast light on the Laz community's sense of cultural identity and consciousness.

The chapter by Türk-Yiğitalp on '*Discourses on Lazuri as an Endangered Language*' presented how perceptions of the speakers of endangered languages are shaped. The chapter showed how the community perceptions shaped the use of the endangered language in daily life, which clearly created a vicious circle for the speakers of Laz. Avoiding being perceived as incompetent in the Standard Language, Turkish, the chapter highlighted the fact that Laz people avoid(ed) speaking in Laz to the upcoming generations.

All these studies are essential in understanding the direction of the studies that have been undertaken around the Laz language as well as revealing what research-gaps exist to be filled by future studies. More importantly, all these studies contain invaluable findings for the education of Laz, on which this concluding section focuses.

2. Applied Linguistics in the Picture

The Lahey Agreement (2021) recommends that education is the ultimate way to sustain and protect any languages. Basing their arguments on such international agreements, studies on the role of education in maintaining the endangered/heritage- or minority languages in Turkey have usually concentrated on the rights to education for the speakers of those languages, and the policies on this matter mainly due to the fact that providing education in these languages is the most immediate need. More specifically, the studies on the educational rights move from arguments on the rights of minorities while also underlining that distributing equal educational rights is necessary to 'prevent language assimilation and protect the languages of minorities', which are a source of richness' (Erdem & Öngüç, 2021). Although important in terms of revealing why it is necessary to design a more inclusive educational system, existing studies on endangered languages in Turkey still stay at an abstract level. This is mainly because there is a lack of practical findings on the learning and teaching of endangered languages as well as the experiences of students with heritage-backgrounds in the mainstream educational system. Understanding the experiences, needs and perceptions of teachers and students in relation to the heritage-/minority languages in mainstream education is necessary to develop more inclusive educational systems and policies. Thus, there is 'a lack of applied linguistics as a potential missing link in endangered language work' in Turkey (Pennfield & Tucker, 2011, p. 291). Scholars often highlight the critical role of a collaboration between applied linguistics, and linguistics in language-revitalisation. Penfield and Tucker (2011) and Anderson (2011, p. 282) underline that 'the implementation of best practice in second-language instruction and culturally mediated or otherwise appropriate pedagogies is often not possible with input coming only from academic linguists.' More specifically, the expertise of applied linguists and specialists in second-language education is vital in the field of language-revitalisation. This is mainly due to the fact that the teaching and learning of endangered languages have 'features and needs that are different from the teaching and learning of majority or foreign languages', 'teaching goals, student motivations, and future relationship between the learners and the language' being the major ones (Hammine, 2020, p. 5). With these considerations in mind, the current study conducted a small-scale, systematic review to reveal the lines of studies that have been conducted on the Laz language from an educational perspective in Turkey.

3. Methodology

3.1. Research-design and publication-ethics

This study complied with all research- and publications ethics. Since no data-collection methods with participants (e.g., interviews or experiments) were used in the study, no approval was sought from any ethics' committee.

3.2. Data-collection and analysis

This study investigated research on the Laz language from an educational perspective. The main purpose of the study is to identify 'critical points and also provide a wider perspective to the researchers in the field', particularly those who work in the field of applied linguistics (Lawson, Çakmak, Gündüz & Busher, 2015, p. 3).

To this end, this study utilized the method of systematic review in the collection of data. Systematic review examines literature to answer the specific research-questions (Turan & Akdağ-Çimen, 2020). As has been indicated by several others, systematic reviews aim to present what has been achieved by previous studies as well as to reveal points of conflict (Lawson et al., 2015; Turan & Akdağ-Çimen, 2020).

3.3. Procedure

Systematic review studies move from the point of a clearly defined and systematic approach when examining previous research (Ilgaz, 2018). These clearly-defined steps are significant in increasing the trustworthiness of the study as well as establishing the validity of the findings (Ilgaz, 2018). Five steps are recommended to conduct a systematic review (Khan, Kunz, Kleijnen & Antes, 2003):

a) *Framing the research-question:* In this study, the research-questions listed below were defined at the beginning of the study:
   R1: What were the main lines of research on the Laz language between 2010 and 2021?
   R2: What do existing studies indicate to be the needs of learning and teaching the Laz language?

b) *Identifying relevant work:* Clear inclusion- and exclusion-criteria for the studies to be examined have been determined in this stage. In addition to the time-limit (2010-2021), there was one inclusion-criterion for the studies to be examined. First, these studies had to be related to the Laz language and published in either Turkish or English. As for exclusion-criteria, any studies that did not have the aforementioned features were excluded. The table below further details the inclusion- and exclusion-criteria:

Table 8.1 - Inclusion- and Exclusion-criteria

Inclusion-criteria	Exclusion-criteria
Years of Publication: 2010-2021	**Years of Publication:** Any studies published in other years
Type of Publications: Research Articles, Book Chapters, PhD theses, Master's theses	**Type of Publications:** Review-articles, Encyclopaedia (29), conference-abstracts (2), book-reviews, conference-proceedings, editorials, mini reviews
Descriptors: Laz, Laz language	
Language: Turkish, English	**Language:** Publications in other languages

c) *Assessing the quality of studies:* When assessing the quality of the studies, several criteria were followed. First, inclusion- and exclusion-criteria detailed above were used. Second, as has been recommended by Khan et al. (2003), 'more refined quality assessment' has been conducted on the selected studies. In this review, the selected studies were retrieved from Science Direct, Google Scholar, Eric, and ULAKBILIM. These databases were selected due to practicality in terms of rights of access. Since the studies were published according to quality-assessment procedures (e.g., blind review), selected studies for systematic review were regarded as having acceptable quality.

d) *Summarizing the evidence:* This step 'consists of tabulation of study characteristics' and the exploration of differences between studies (Khan et al., 2003, p. 118). In this study, selected studies for the review were tabulated in a way to show their years of publication as well as their titles to show what each study was about.

e) *Interpreting the findings:* This stage focuses on examining the findings in terms of what they indicate about future lines of research.

4. Findings

4.1. Research on the Laz language between 2010 and 2021

Before detailing the research on the Laz language, it is worth presenting Table 8.2 to illustrate the existing studies on Laz (Table 8.2):

Table 8.2 - List of existing studies on Laz

Type of Publication	Numbers	Title
PhD Theses	1	Mediated identity and memories in virtual spaces: The case of Lazish (Şendeniz, 2019)
Master's Theses	6	Agree as a Unidirectional Operation: Evidence from Laz (Demirok, 2013)
		Spatial prefixes of Pazar Laz: A nano-syntactic approach (Eren, 2016)
		Language-ideologies of Lazuri-speakers in Turkey (Türk, 2019)
		Developing a talking dictionary for a morphologically complex language: The case of Laz (Richardson, 2019)
		A study on the cuisine, traditions and language of the Laz community living in the eastern Black Sea region (Çoşan & Seçim, 2020)
		Transitive unergatives in Pazar Laz (2021)

Research Articles	When 'towards' means 'away from': The case of directional-ablative syncretism in the Ardeşen variety of Laz (South-Caucasian) (Kutscher, 2010)
	Cazi belief in the oral tradition of the Laz (Aleksiva, 2011)
	On the expression of spatial relations in Ardeşen-Laz (Kutscher, 2011)
	Ditransitive constructions in Laz (Lacroix, 2011)
	Intergenerational effects on the development of verbal and non-verbal communication among Lazi toddlers in Lazona (Yuksel-Sokmen & Brooks, 2013)
	Transitivity in Pazar Laz (Taylan & Öztürk, 2014)
	The logophoric complementizer in Laz (Demirok & Öztürk, 2015)
	Novus Ortus: The awakening of Laz language in Turkey (Kavaklı, 2015)
	Tales of language-loss and language-maintenance: Elicited ancestral-language use in Lazuri-Turkish and Turkish-German caregiver-child dyads during structured play (Yuksel-Sokmen, 2015)
	Language-use, Choice and Transmission: Laz at the Crossroads (Kavaklı, 2017)
	İskender Chitaşi in the light of new findings (Aleksiva, 2017)
	Zğemi Lower and Upper Durak Town in 1486 (Aleksiva, 2017)
	Encouraging usage of an endangered ancestral language: A supportive role for caregivers' deictic gestures (Yuksel, 2017)
	Who are the Laz? Cultural identity and the musical public sphere on the Turkish Black Sea Coast (Solomon, 2017)
	The development of a bilingual education-curriculum in Turkey: A mixed method study (Ozfidan, 2017)
	'Speak Lazuri!' Use of Lazuri among caregiver-child dyads (Yuksel, 2018)
	Lazuri Materials in the Multilingual Dictionary of Lorenzo Hervas (Aleksiva, 2018)
	Laz (Lacroix, 2018)
	The Minority-languages Dilemmas in Turkey: A Critical Approach to an Emerging Literature (Ozfidan et al., 2018)
	A note on language-contact: Laz language in Turkey (2019)
	Strategies of making and unmaking ethnic boundaries: Evidence in the Laz of Turkey (Serdar, 2019)
	The loss of the case-system in Ardeshen Laz and its morphosyntactic consequences (Öztürk, 2019)
	Laz caregivers' talk to their young children: The importance of context and utterance-type in eliciting ancestral-language use (Yuksel et al., 2020)

	Parental language, functional utterance type, and play-context impact children's usage of an endangered language (Lowry et al., 2020)
	Pazar Laz as a weak verb-framed language (Öztürk & Eren, 2021)
	Laz caregivers' talk to their young children: The importance of context and utterance-type in eliciting ancestral-language use (Yuksel et al., 2021)
Books	Laz Kültürü Üzerine Notlar (Notes on Laz Culture) (Bucaklişi et al., 2011)
	Pazar Laz (Öztürk & Pöchtrager, 2011)
	'Kimdir Bu Lazlar?': Laz Kimliği ve Sanal Mekanda Lazca ('Now Who are Laz People?' Laz Identity and Lazish in Virtual Spaces) (Şendeniz, 2020)
Book Chapters	Benefactives in Laz (Lacroix, 2010)
	Laz middle voice (Lacroix, 2012)
	The multi-purpose subordinator na in Laz (Lacroix, 2012)
	Low, High and Higher Applicatives: Evidence from Pazar Laz (Öztürk, 2012)

The review showed that a variety of research on the Laz language has been conducted while, however, there is a lack of research on the pedagogy for the Laz language as well as the needs and experiences of the Laz community members within the mainstream educational contexts. The existing studies are essentially on linguistic documentation (e.g., Öztürk, & Eren, 2021) or sociolinguistic descriptions of the Laz language. Both lines of research are vital for the revitalisation-works for Laz as they present an invaluable number of sources for the education of Laz while also establishing the basis on which the education of Laz could be built. However, since studies on the experiences of learners with a Laz background (or any other heritage-languages) in the mainstream education remain thin on the ground, it is also necessary to examine the existing literature on the education of endangered languages to reveal lines of research requiring immediate attention in future studies on Laz.

5. Discussion

5.1. Pedagogy for Endangered Languages

5.1.1. Instruction in endangered languages

Existing studies offer valuable insight into the pedagogy of endangered languages as well as minority languages. The special issue published by *The*

Language Learning and Teaching Journal on endangered-language and minority-language pedagogy reveals theoretical considerations for developing pedagogies for endangered languages. These also offer ways through which applied linguists and general linguists could collaborate, as Hinton (2011, p. 317) states that 'absent from second language pedagogy for endangered languages, in many cases, are applied linguists who specialize in language teaching theory and methodology.'

One key-consideration in designing pedagogies for the teaching of endangered languages is to determine how to present the content. At this point, whether to focus on the individual languages or on the individual linguistic repertoires of learners has a critical role in incorporating the endangered language into the curriculum. Displaying a preference for translanguageing practices, which are defined as the approaches focusing on individual linguistic repertoires of learners, Tarsoly and Valijärvi (2020, p. 254) state that 'translanguageing tasks in teaching endangered or minority languages (EML) have the potential to reframe EMLs as vehicles of knowledge transfer and "useful," "practical" knowledge instead of more widespread associations such as "treasure troves of traditional knowledge" and "repository of community values."' Focusing on individual linguistic repertoires of learners would also reveal 'the languages circulating in one community' as well as 'describing how individuals deploy other modes of communication' (Rymes, 2014, p. 4). More specifically, these linguistic repertoires 'allow educators to focus on the benefits of knowing about the histories and valued practices of cultural groups rather than trying to teach prescriptively according to broad, under-examined generalities about groups' (Rymes, 2014, p. 4).

Another theoretical consideration for the teaching of endangered languages is the teaching-methods to be utilised. The field of applied linguistics offers a variety of methods and techniques as a starting-point while also underlining the need for exploring the community-specific requirements. The study by East (2020) presents an example where task-based language-teaching method is used to teach *te reo* Maori, an endangered language in New Zealand. The findings of the study show that the task-based language-teaching method might actually be 'a tool for language revitalisation' as it revealed useful routes to integrate traditional language-teaching methods into the teaching of endangered languages. Others also introduced models such as bilingual education, immersion, language-nests, and the Master-Apprentice language-learning programme to foster communicative competence of the speakers of endangered languages (Hammine, 2020). Among these models are those which draw immensely from second-language acquisition, namely Total Physical

Response (Asher, 1996; as cited in Hammine, 2020) and situational learning (Hinton, 2017).

Also, the *language-hotspots* model has been recommended by Anderson (2011). In this model, language-hotspots indicate the density of languages and their level of endangerment in one area, which could be utilised as a criterion when integrating one endangered language into the primary, secondary and post-secondary school-curricula. While doing that, determining language-hotspots necessitates the documentation of academic linguists, and incorporating these language-hotspots into school-curricula to generate more speakers for a specific endangered language requires the inclusion of applied linguists into the procedure, which once again underlines the vital role of a collaboration between general linguists and applied linguists.

Both designing the content and choosing the appropriate teaching-methods are key-considerations in teaching endangered languages, and they certainly are for the teaching of Laz. In that regard, documentation-studies could present cues on the language-structure while also presenting implications on how to teach these structures. Similarly, studies on the cultural and social issues in relation to the Laz language could better inform applied linguists about the extent of repertoires that students may bring to the classrooms.

5.1.2. Materia- development

In terms of the material-development for the teaching of endangered languages, applied linguistics needs to examine the community-needs from various perspectives including 'learning-styles, situations, participants and other variables which are the characteristics of the speaking community, and adapt learning-models to the community rather than the other way around' (Pennfield & Tucker, 2011, p. 298). More specifically, applied linguists are required to reveal what is appropriate for the communication in those groups to pave the ways for textbook-adaptations. However, applied linguists need the help from linguists who document and create 'dictionaries, grammars, and narrative collections' to meet the demands for communicatively orientated materials in the teaching of endangered languages (Hammine, 2020, p. 5).

5.1.3. Teacher-training for the Endangered Languages

One of the greatest challenges in the education of endangered languages is inadequate teacher-training due to the lack of training resources (Penfield & Tucker, 2011). Applied Linguistics is usually focused on the training of foreign-language teachers, particularly ELT teachers. However, since the context of endangered languages is different from that of the teaching of English, the needs in the training of the teachers of endangered languages are also different. Therefore, any attempts to train teachers based on the principles of the conventional language-teacher-training programmes would fail, according to Penfield and Tucker (2011). As a result, scholars recommend exploring traditional ways of transferring knowledge inside the communities of endangered languages (Hinton, 2011). It is also underlined that the collaboration between general linguists, applied linguists, and the community members is necessary. This is mainly because the teachers of endangered languages are frequently the elderly members of the community or those who are also in the process of improving their language-skills. In such a field, the contribution of the applied linguists could be to develop training-materials through the existing documentation-work (Warner, Luna & Butler, 2007).

6. Conclusion and Future Implications

The field of Laz language-teaching and learning is vast, as is the case with all other endangered languages. This book has shown the invaluable contribution of the studies conducted in other fields such as linguistics and sociology, while this study has demonstrated that educational aspect of Laz requires further systematic research and collaboration. Understanding the education of Laz from the perspectives of all members of the process, as well as exploring the experiences of the speakers of Laz within mainstream educational contexts could contribute immensely to the revitalization of Laz. Therefore, future studies need to focus on the following issues but should not be limited to only those areas:

- More collaboration between applied linguists and general linguists,
- More empirical studies on the teaching- and learning-practices of Laz,
- Linguistic ethnographies across educational contexts,
- Studies on learners' experiences and perceptions of Laz
- Studies on teachers' challenges when teaching Laz
- Studies on the policies regarding the education of Laz and other endangered languages
- A systematic review of research on educational practices regarding other endangered languages around the world to reach implications for the local context
- Studies on the experiences of learners with a Lazuri background in mainstream educational contexts

It is, as a result, worth ending this book with a quotation by Penfield and Tucker (2011, p. 291): 'We call for more applied linguistic training and research focused on endangered languages, more attention to endangered languages within second language pedagogy programmes and a heightened awareness of the need for teamwork across all stakeholders in endangered language contexts.'

References

Anderson, G. D. S. (2011). Language Hotspots: what (applied) linguistics and education should do about language endangerment in the twenty-first century. *Language and Education, 25(4), 273–289*.doi:10.1080/09500782.2011.577218.

East, M. (2020). Task-based language teaching as a tool for the revitalisation of te reo Māori: One beginning teacher's perspective. *The Language Learning Journal, 48*(3), 272-284.

Erdem, F. H., & Öngüç, B. (2021). Süryanice anadilinde eğitim hakkı: sorunlar ve çözüm önerileri. *Dicle Üniversitesi Hukuk Fakültesi Dergisi, 26*(44), 3-35.

Hammine, M. (2020). Educated not to speak our language: Language attitudes and newspeakerness in the Yaeyaman language. *Journal of Language, Identity & Education*, 1-15.

Hinton, L. (2017). Learning and teaching endangered indigenous languages. In Van Deusen-Scholl, N. & May, S. (Eds.) *Second and foreign language education. Encyclopedia of language and education.* (pp. 213-223). Springer, Cham. https://doi.org/10.1007/978-3-319-02246-8_18

Hinton, L. (2011). *Language revitalization and language pedagogy: new teaching and learning strategies. Language and Education, 25(4), 307–318*.doi:10.1080/09500782.2011.57722

Ilgaz, H. (2018). Bireysel farklılıklar kapsamında çevrimiçi öğrenme araştırmalarına ilişkin sistematik bir derleme. *Journal of Theoretical Educational Science, 11*(4), 1003-1018.

Khan, K. S., Kunz, R., Kleijnen, J., & Antes, G. (2003). Five steps to conducting a systematic review. *Journal of the royal society of medicine, 96*(3), 118-121.

Lawson, T., Çakmak, M., Gündüz, M., & Busher, H. (2015). Research on teaching practicum-a systematic review. *European journal of teacher education, 38*(3), 392-407.

Öztürk, B., & Eren, Ö. (2021). Pazar Laz as a weak verb-framed language. *Linguistic Variation, 21*(1), 247-279.

Penfield, S. D., & Tucker, B. V. (2011). From documenting to revitalizing an endangered language: where do applied linguists fit? *Language and Education, 25(4), 291–305*.doi:10.1080/09500782.2011.577219

Rymes, B. (2014). Communicative repertoire. In C. Leung & B. V. Street (Eds.), *The Routledge companion to English studies*, (pp. 287-301). Routledge Handsbook Online.

Tarsoly, E., & Valijärvi, R. L. (2020). Endangered and minority language pedagogy. *The Language Learning Journal, 48*(3), 253-258.

Turan, Z., & Akdag-Cimen, B. (2020). Flipped classroom in English language teaching: a systematic review. *Computer Assisted Language Learning, 33*(5-6), 590-606

Warner, N., Luna, Q., & Butler, L. (2007). Ethics and revitalization of dormant languages: The Mutsun language. *Language Documentation & Conservation, 1*(1), 58-76.

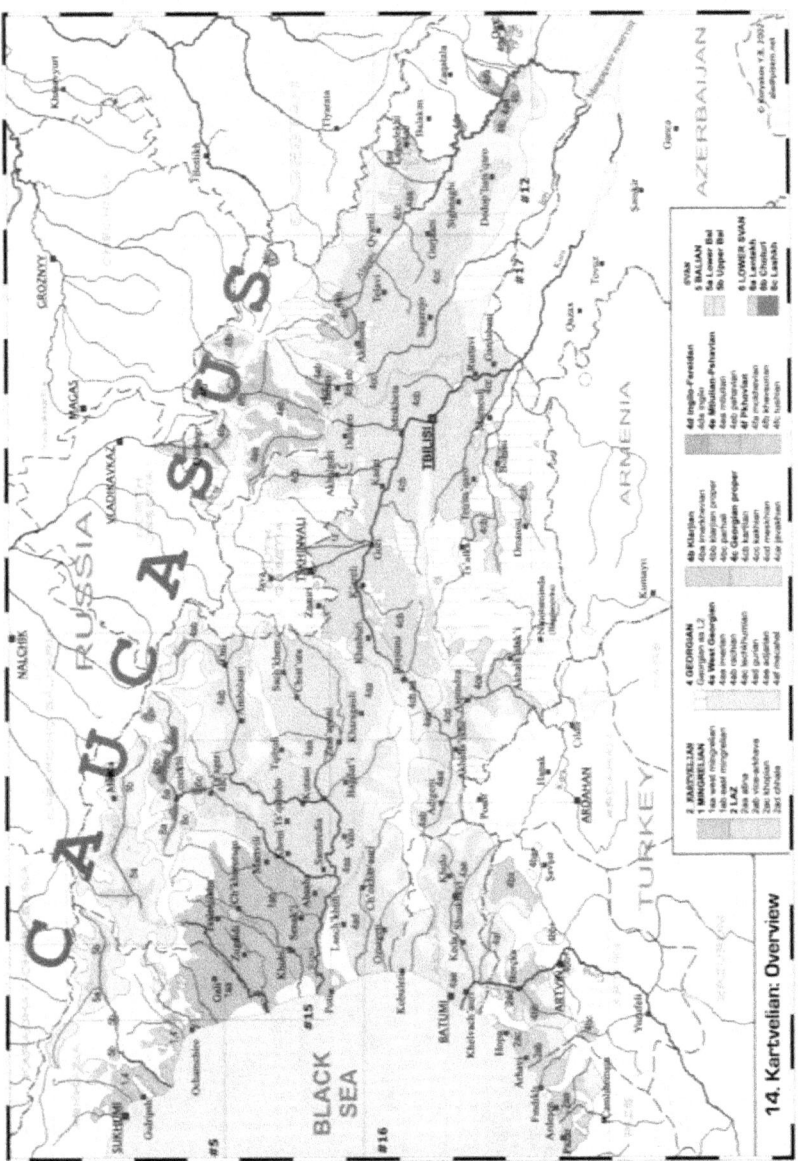

Figure 8.1 - Kuryakov, Y. (2002). Kartvelian: Overview [Map]. In Y. Kuryakov, *Atlas of the Caucasian Languages with Language Guide*. Moscow: Institute of Linguistics.

An Applied Linguistics Perspective on the Preservation of the Laz Language   215

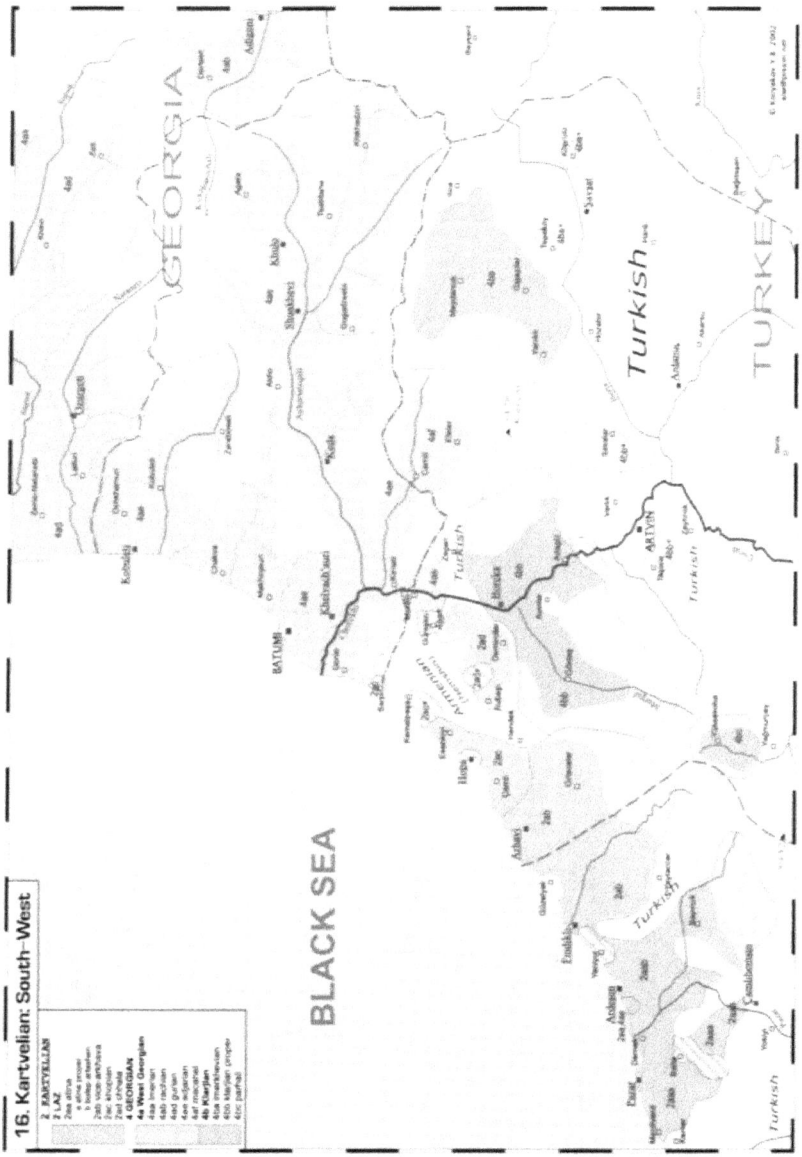

Figure 8.2 - Kuryakov, Y. (2002). Kartvelian: South-West [Map]. In Y. Kuryakov, *Atlas of the Caucasian Languages with Language Guide*. Moscow: Institute of Linguistics.

Figure 8.3 - Kuryakov, Y. (2002). Caucasian Languages in Turkey [Map]. In Y. Kuryakov, *Atlas of the Caucasian Languages with Language Guide*. Moscow: Institute of Linguistics.

Index

A

Abkhazia, 119, 120
Abkhazian, 63, 64, 69, 84, 141
accusative, 35, 36, 101, 102
Acedo Matellán, xlii, 54, 56
active-ergative, xxxvii, 35, 36, 37
Adjarian, 80, 81, 84, 120, 139
adpositions, 50, 59
affixal, 56, 58, 99
affixation, 87, 96, 97, 99
affricates, 78, 82
agreement calculus, 34, 44, 45
allative case, 53, 55, 57
alphabet, 114, 115, 119, 120, 121, 122, 128, 129, 131, 132, 133, 137, 203
ambiguity, 105, 106, 107, 191
ancestral language, 114, 116, 138, 141, 142
applied linguistics, 201, 204, 209, 210, 211
Ardeşen, xiv, 7, 116, 123, 126, 127, 128, 131, 132, 133, 134, 135, 136, 137, 141, 144, 150, 181
Arhavi, 1, 2, 7, 83, 116, 123, 127, 133, 135, 144, 150, 181
Armenian, 82, 88, 119
Artvin, 7, 82, 115, 116, 119, 127, 144, 177, 181
Asia Polyglotta, 65
Asian Journal of London, 80
Asiliskender, 89, 109
Atina, 7, 65, 116, 123, 127, 128, 144, 150

Atlas of the World Languages in Danger, 87
attitudes, 4, 16, 115, 177, 196

B

Batumi, 3, 63, 66, 67, 123, 144
Bengal Asiatic Society, 68, 81
bilingual, xiii, xiv, xvii
bilingual speech community, 4
bilingualism literature, 17
biodiversity, 114
biological diversity, 6
biotic communities, 115
Black Sea, 11, 13, 23, 25, 28, 29, 30, 31, 115, 118, 136, 139, 199
blue-collar participants, 9
Boğaziçi University, xiii, xvii, 1, 59, 111, 115, 175
Borçka, 7, 116, 123, 127, 144, 150
bound form, 98

C

Çamlıhemşin, 7, 144
case system, 34, 35, 36, 37, 86, 87, 101, 102, 103, 111
Caspian Sea, 118
Caucasian, xvii, 3, 63, 67, 68, 79, 81, 83, 84, 97, 113, 114, 115, 118, 119, 138, 141, 202
Caucasus, 20, 60, 67, 68, 79, 83, 84, 111, 115, 140, 141, 174
child-directed speech, 12, 14, 16
classical world literature, 130
cognitive, xviii, 61, 103, 107, 138

competence in Laz, 2, 6, 8, 14, 17
constructive discourse, 178
contact outcomes, 90
contact situations, 90, 95
contact-induced speech community, 139
continental European languages, 92
corpus usage, xxvi, 145
COVID-19, 96
creoles, 90, 96, 109
critically endangered, 5
cultural heritage, 114, 146
current status of Laz, 3, 90, 93, 201, 202
Çxala dialect, 127, 134

D

Dagestanian, 119
DAT, 38, 39
data selection and collection, 145
database planning, 145
dative, 38, 45
DCT, 36, 37, 38, 39
decline in Laz, 12
de-dentalized allophone, 79
deixis, 50
Dependent Case Theory, 36
derived intransitives, 45
derived transitives, 45
Devlet İstatistik Enstitüsü, 116, 140
dialect alteration, 128
dialectal diversity, 65
dialectal morpho-syntactic, 86
dialectal variation, 85, 86, 87, 108, 202
dialects of Laz, 85
dictionary writing, 115, 162

differentially marked, 35
directional and locative meanings, 51
document type definition, 145
domain analysis, 87
dual residence, 8
Düzce, 7

E

Eastern Anatolia, 6
Eastern Black Sea, 3
ecological approach, 86, 88, 89, 97, 107
ecosystem, 114, 178
ejective, 78, 82
English headwords, 63, 64, 69, 77
English-Megrelian, 81
ergative case, xxxvii, 34, 35, 36, 37, 58, 59
Ergative-Absolutive system, 86
ethnolects, 92
ethnolinguistic vitality, 5
Étude Sur La Langue Laze, 120
Evliya Çelebi, 64, 82, 83
expletive, 99

F

fairy tales, 113, 129, 130, 137
familial interactions, 86, 87
fiction, 130, 135
Figure, 53, 56
Fındıklı, 7, 116, 123, 127, 144, 181
first-generation migrants, 2
form complexity, 107
formal education, 2
free form, 98

G

gene pool, 97
geographical area, 88, 90, 168
Georgia, xvii, xviii, 3, 66, 84, 86, 113, 118, 119, 120, 123, 136, 137, 140
Georgian, xvii, 3, 60, 63, 64, 67, 69, 79, 81, 83, 84, 101, 119, 120, 121, 140, 141, 144, 174
Germanic and Slavic, 56
GIDS, 5, 115, 117
glossonym, 65, 69
glottalised, 78, 82
Graded Intergenerational Disruption Scale, 5, 115, 117
Ground referent, 52, 57

H

headwords, 69, 147
Hemshin, 88
heritage speakers, 2
heritage vernacular', 88
history, 63, 64, 84, 114, 138
Hopa, 2, 7, 116, 123, 127, 136, 137, 144, 181

I

Iberian, 84, 113, 115
identity, 20, 65, 111, 113, 121, 122, 133, 138, 168, 187, 194, 198, 203, 206
ideologies, xvi, 138, 177, 179, 180, 183, 184, 185, 194, 197, 198, 199, 206
idiolectal variation, 107
idiosyncratic, 45, 49, 165, 172
imperfective, xvii, 45, 46, 47

indigenous, 20, 113, 114, 115, 118, 119, 131, 134, 135, 138, 141
Indo-European, 118
industrial revolution, 114
industrialization, 6, 89, 90, 92, 96
inflection classes, 45, 49, 163
inflectional morphology, 85, 102, 103, 106
informal personal contexts, xxxvi, 16
Instructions of Compiling Vocabularies and Sentences, 68
intellectual wealth, 114, 115, 139
intergenerational transmission, 1, 3, 4, 16, 18, 116, 117, 144
interlocutors, 11, 12, 184
intransitive verbs, 37, 46
inventory complexity, 106, 107
Ireland, 92
Irish, 92, 94, 199
Istanbul, xiii, xvii, 1, 6, 115, 175, 177, 181, 199

J

Journal of the Royal Asiatic Society of Great Britain and Ireland, 63, 66, 84, 141

K

Kartvelian, xvi, xviii, 20, 60, 65, 101, 110, 119, 120, 121, 141, 202

L

language contact, xvii, 4, 17, 100, 109, 111, 183, 193, 194, 195
language endangerment, 3, 58, 86, 89, 94, 177, 179, 199, 212

language extinction, 114, 178
language fluency, 113, 203
language loss, xiii, 16, 20, 110, 114, 117, 141, 177, 179, 182, 183, 184, 199
language maintenance, xiii, 19, 114, 115, 138
language policy, xvi, 139, 141
language preservation, xxxvi, 5
language proficiency, 10, 17, 122, 128, 129, 182, 183, 184, 191
language shift, 3, 4, 5, 15, 16, 19, 21, 86, 87, 88, 89, 90, 92, 93, 110, 140, 177, 179
language transmission, 5
language valorisation, 138
Language Vitality and Endangerment, 5
Latin, xlii, 56, 58, 115, 119, 120, 122, 128
Latinized Lazuri alphabet, 113
Laz, xiii, xvii, xxxv, xxxviii, xlii, 1, 2, 3, 6, 8, 9, 10, 11, 12, 13, 14, 15, 16, 17, 18, 19, 20, 22, 23, 24, 25, 26, 27, 28, 29, 30, 31, 33, 34, 35, 36, 37, 38, 39, 40, 41, 42, 43, 44, 45, 49, 50, 51, 52, 53, 55, 56, 57, 58, 59, 60, 63, 64, 65, 69, 75, 77, 79, 80, 81, 82, 83, 85, 86, 87, 88, 89, 90, 91, 92, 93, 94, 95, 96, 97, 98, 99, 100, 101, 105, 108, 110, 111, 113, 115, 116, 119, 120, 121, 122, 123, 127, 129, 131, 132, 133, 134, 135, 136, 137, 138, 139, 141, 142, 144, 145, 146, 149, 150, 154, 156, 157, 158, 160, 161, 162, 163, 164, 165, 166, 173, 174, 175, 181, 194, 199, 201, 202, 203, 204, 205, 206, 208, 211
Laz Cultural institute, 13

Laz language, 201
Lazian, xliii, 63, 64, 66, 67, 69, 75, 79, 81, 82, 84, 141, 202
Lazistan, 80, 84, 120
Lazona, xxxvi, 115, 127, 138
Laz-Turkish, 8, 9
Lazuri, xvi, xxxv, xxxix, xlii, xliii, 96, 113, 114, 115, 116, 118, 119, 120, 121, 122, 123, 126, 127, 128, 129, 130, 131, 132, 133, 134, 135, 136, 137, 138, 139, 141, 154, 157, 158, 160, 174, 175, 177, 179, 181, 182, 183, 184, 185, 186, 187, 188, 189, 190, 191,192, 193, 194, 195, 196, 197, 203, 206
Lazuri Alboni, xliii, 113, 115, 121, 138, 139, 203
lazuri nena, 119
Leibnizian sampling preferences, 69
lemma, 147, 164, 170, 173
Lesga Langauge, 119
Lesser Caucasus, 115
lexical, 54, 55, 56, 57, 61, 63, 64, 65, 77, 83, 120, 123, 146, 147, 151, 152, 153, 159, 161, 162, 164, 165, 166, 167, 169, 170, 171, 172, 173
lexicographer, 63, 65, 151, 166
lexicography, xviii, 81, 82, 83, 145, 146, 150, 160
lexicon, xiii, 60, 147, 150, 151, 152, 153, 154, 164, 165, 166, 167, 168, 169, 173, 190
lexico-semantic groups, 63, 69
lexis, 64, 75, 82
Lezgian language, 65
Li, 16, 17, 20, 74
lingua franca, 114, 193
Lingua Lasga, 65
Lingua Lesga, 65, 119, 140

linguicide, 114
linguistic complexity, 85, 86, 87, 88, 95, 99, 109, 111
linguistic diversity, xxxvi, 5, 18, 114
linguistic variation, 201
List of English Words and Sentences, 68
literacy, xiii, xvii, 5, 9, 10, 11, 15, 16, 18, 19, 114, 122, 138
literary books, xxxvi, 113, 115, 122, 128, 138
Living Laz project, 3
loanwords, 128, 189, 190, 191, 194
local ethnic language, 116
Luǩa Lazuri, 129
lušnu nin, 119

M

macrostructure, 147, 148, 150, 153, 165
margaluri nina, 119
markers, xiii, xvii, 34, 58, 97, 99, 100, 101, 104, 106, 107
Marmara, 3, 6, 9, 11, 12, 14, 15, 16, 18, 23, 25, 28, 29, 30, 31, 144
MAXQDA, 181
megastructure, 147, 153, 154
Megrelian, xvii, 3, 63, 64, 69, 81, 83, 119, 174
memoir, 130, 136
mesostructure, 147, 152, 153
metadata, 145, 147, 151, 154, 164, 165, 166, 167
microstructure, 147, 151, 153, 160, 165, 169
millet, 88, 109
Mingrelian, 63, 67, 69, 80, 83, 84, 119, 120, 137, 141, 144

Ministry of Education, 13, 18, 89
minoritised language, 179, 180, 181, 196
monolingual, xiii, xiv, 87, 148, 172, 180, 188, 191, 192, 194
mother tongue, 2, 5, 8, 15, 18, 116, 133, 136, 138, 179
Motion Event, 55
motion verbs, 50, 56, 57, 58
mountain of tongues, 118
multilingual, 1, 17, 20, 65, 82, 89, 109, 118, 138, 145, 162, 163, 164, 167, 168

N

narratives, 178, 179, 182, 183
nation, 88, 92, 194, 198
national language, 88, 93, 94, 158, 185
nationalism, 89, 114
nationalistic policy, 89
native dialects, xxxvi, 138
native Lazuri speakers, 116, 136
natural languages, 34, 45
neologies, 128, 129, 137
New World, 92, 94
North Caucasian, 118, 119
North Central Caucasian, 119
Northeast Caucasian, 118, 119
Northeastern Black Sea, 113
Northeastern Turkey, 90, 91
Northwest Caucasian, 118, 119

O

Occupation, 12, 22, 24, 27, 29, 30, 31
OE, 88, 89, 94, 95
official status, 5, 13

Only Laz, 8, 11
oral contexts, 11, 16
orthography, 115, 120, 138, 139, 147, 155, 170
Ottoman, 88, 90, 93, 96, 109, 110, 113, 116, 120, 144

P

Partial paradigm of Comparative Case Forms, 101
particles, 50, 59, 61
path-based typology, 50, 55, 56
Pazar, xiii, xvii, 1, 2, 6, 34, 59, 60, 65, 85, 111, 116, 123, 127, 144, 150, 181, 206
pedagogy of endangered languages, 208
Persian, 113, 115, 189, 194
phonemic system of Laz, 78, 82
poesy, 130, 132, 133
poetry, 113, 129, 130, 131, 132, 134
Political Fiction, 130, 133
Pomak, 88, 93
pragmatics, 105, 106
prefix, 37, 38, 39, 40, 51, 52, 53, 54, 55, 97
pre-root vowel, 43, 45, 47

R

receptive bilingualism, 17, 196
reflexive constructions, 85, 87, 96, 202
reflexive marker, 96, 99
reflexive pronoun, 96, 97
reflexivity, 85, 99
reflexivization, 37, 85, 97, 98, 99
residential segregation, 92

revitalization, 20, 115, 117, 140, 144, 146, 160, 162, 198, 211, 212
Rize, 6, 115, 116, 119, 123, 127, 144, 177, 181
Romance, 56
Royal Asiatic Society, 63, 66, 80, 81, 84, 141
rural areas, 6, 10, 11, 86, 87, 91, 94, 116
Russia, 66, 67
Russian, 20, 83, 84, 113, 116, 120, 144

S

Sarpi, 3, 119, 136
satellite-framed languages, 56, 57, 58
semantic relation, 35, 37
semantics, xvii, 46, 47, 54, 59, 61, 99, 147, 158
semasiological, 147, 148, 150
sense of cultural identity and consciousness, 113, 203
Seyahâtnâme, 64
short stories, 113, 130, 134, 135
socialization, 15, 116, 141
South Caucasian, xiii, xliii, 3, 59, 87, 97, 113, 118, 119, 144, 203
southeastern Abkhazia, 119
Southwest Caucasian language, 113, 114
spatial prefixes, 49, 52, 53, 54, 55, 56, 57, 58
specimina, 64, 65, 79, 81
speech community, 115, 139
stops, 78, 82
strong satellite-framed languages, 56, 58
structural complexity, 94, 96

Suanetian, 79
suffixes, xiii, 107, 151
Svan, 3, 63, 64, 69, 79, 81, 119, 144, 174
Svanetian, 67, 81, 84, 141
Svenonius, 50, 51, 54, 61
Swanetian, 63, 69, 84
symbolic, 13, 198
syntactic hierarchy, 34, 41, 42, 43, 44, 58
syntax, xiii, xvii, 59, 60, 95, 99, 102, 103, 104, 110
system complexity, 85, 94, 99

T

the Ottoman Empire, 88, 109, 120
theoretical research, xlii, 33, 34, 38, 44, 45, 49, 58, 202
thesauri, 148, 150, 164
thesaurus, 145, 147, 148, 158
transitive, 36, 38, 39, 47, 48, 59
translation, 63, 82, 83, 120, 123, 129, 133, 134, 157, 168, 182, 186
transliteration, 63, 68, 77, 78, 79, 82
Turkey, xiii, xiv, xvi, xvii, xxxvi, xlii, 1, 3, 6, 15, 16, 17, 18, 19, 20, 82, 86, 87, 88, 89, 90, 91, 92, 93, 95, 110, 111, 113, 115, 116, 118, 119, 121, 122, 123, 127, 129, 130, 131, 136, 138, 139, 140, 141, 144, 194, 195, 198, 199, 203, 206
Turkic, xvii, 20, 110, 118, 141, 199
Turkish, xiii, xiv, xvi, 2, 8, 9, 10, 11, 12, 13, 14, 15, 16, 17, 21, 22, 27, 28, 29, 36, 39, 41, 79, 82, 86, 87, 88, 89, 90, 93, 94, 96, 97, 98, 101, 116, 117, 121, 128, 131, 132, 133, 134, 135, 136, 137, 148, 150, 156, 166, 177, 181, 182, 186, 188, 189, 190, 191, 192, 193, 194, 195, 196, 199, 203

U

unergatives, 37, 38, 39, 40, 47, 49, 57, 98
UNESCO, 1, 3, 5, 15, 17, 20, 21, 87, 114, 140, 141, 179, 199
UNESCO's classification, 1, 15, 17
urban areas, 3, 6, 10, 11, 92, 93, 94

V

verb classification system, xiii, 34, 45, 49, 202
verbal agreement system, 34, 40
verbal reflexive, 96, 97
verbal spatial-marking system, 34, 202
verb-framed languages, 56, 58
Viçe dialect, 127, 128, 130, 134

W

weak satellite-framed languages, 56, 58
weddings, xxxvi, 8, 13, 16
white-collar jobs, 9, 11, 13
Wisdom Literature, 130, 133
WordNet, 148, 150, 153
World War I, 89, 135
written script, 114, 115
written transmission, 139

X

Xopa dialect, 127, 131, 132, 133

Y

younger generations, 1, 8, 15, 16, 86, 87, 88, 96, 98, 183, 184, 185, 197

www.ingramcontent.com/pod-product-compliance
Lightning Source LLC
Chambersburg PA
CBHW071349290426
44108CB00014B/1480